Creating Culture Change:
The Key to Successful Total Quality Management

Philip E Atkinson

IFS Ltd, UK

British Library Cataloguing in Publication Data

Atkinson, Philip E.
  Creating culture change.
  1. Industries. Quality control. Role of personnel
  I. Title
  658.562

ISBN 1-85423-071-9 IFS Publications

© **1990 IFS Ltd,** Wolseley Road, Wolseley Business Park, Kempston, Bedford MK42 7PW, UK

Phototypeset by InterGraphics (Luton) Ltd.
Printed by Short Run Press Ltd., Exeter

To Ann, Sarah and Jonathan

ACKNOWLEDGEMENTS

IFS Publications wishes to thank the following Publishers for special permission to reproduce figures/diagrams/tables:

Consulting Psychologists Press, Inc., Palo Alto, CA 94306, USA, from "Myers-Briggs Type Indicator" by Isabel Briggs Myers and Katharine C. Briggs. Copyright © 1977 and 1988. Further reproduction is prohibited without the Publisher's consent.

Heinemann Professional Publishing Ltd, Oxford OX2 8EJ, UK, from "Management Teams" by R.B. Belbin. Copyright © 1981. Further reproduction is prohibited without the Publisher's consent.

Jossey-Bass, Inc., San Francisco, CA 94104, USA, from "The Leadership Challenge" by James M. Kouzes and Barry Z. Posner. Copyright © 1988. Further reproduction is prohibited without the Publisher's consent.

Kepner Tregoe, Princeton, NJ 08542, USA, from the "New Rational Manager" by Kepner Tregoe. Copyright © XXXX. Further reproduction is prohibited without the Publisher's consent.

McGraw-Hill, Inc., New York, NY 10020, USA, from "Business Week", August 14, 1989 issue. Copyright © 1989. Further reproduction is prohibited without the Publisher's consent.

Penguin Books, New York, NY, USA, from "Understanding Organizations" by Charles Handy. Copyright © 1980 and 1986. Further reproduction is prohibited without the Publisher's consent.

Prentice-Hall, Inc., Englewood Cliffs, NJ, USA, from "Organizational Psychology: An Experimental Approach to Organization Behavior" 4th Edition by David A. Kolb. Copyright © 1984. Further reproduction is prohibited without Publisher's consent.

CONTENTS

SECTION 1:
THE STRATEGIC ISSUES

1 PURSUING EXCELLENCE

"We estimate it will take you 20 years to be where we are now, and by that time we will have progressed further. We have moved from quality philosophy to measuring defects on an acceptable quality level basis to reducing our defect rate to below 5 to 6 parts per billion. Our last product recall was 1969 when we first started introducing what you know as Total Quality Management."

We had just completed a 2 hour tour of the Tokyo plant in Toyoda City, Japan. We had been sitting with the senior management team and asking questions about Total Quality Management (TQM). At first our hosts were bemused. To them, TQM was no more than business as usual!

Japanese companies seeking innovation

In 1950 Toyota developed 'Statistical Quality Control', nothing new to Western Industry. In 1951 they introduced their first 'Suggestion Scheme' and in 1961 'Total Quality Control' (TQC). 1962 saw the advent of 'Quality Circles' which in 1963 became a company-wide programme. In 1965, Toyota improved quality to such a standard that they received the coveted Deming Prize. They went on to further success in 1966 when they introduced a company-wide 'Quality

Assurance System' (many companies in Europe still do not have such a system). 1970 saw the development of a programme to improve managerial ability. 1983 saw the beginning of the 'Improving Office Campaign' which in 1985 was extended to a 'More Spontaneous Office Activities' programme. Since then, the company has been working on general 'Quality Improvement'.

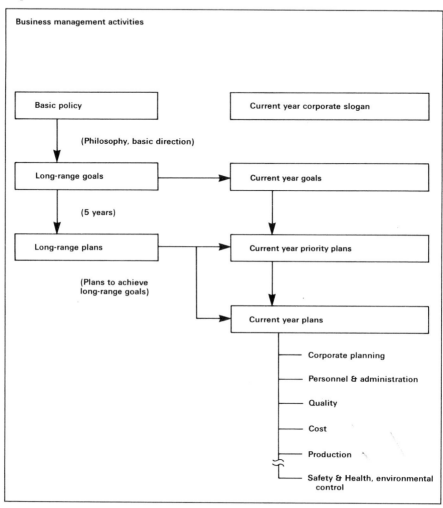

Fig. 1 Basic TQC activities at Toyota

Companies like Nippon Denso ran similar changes in culture starting with 'Quality Control' in 1956, receiving the Deming Prize in 1961. In 1964 'Quality Circles' were introduced, deploying resources to promote '100% Reliable Products and Services.' In 1983 these resources also helped promote the campaign which was to herald Nippon Denso as producing the world's no. 1 products and the world's best Corporate System – reflected in their approach "Nippon Denso of the World, TQC by everybody."

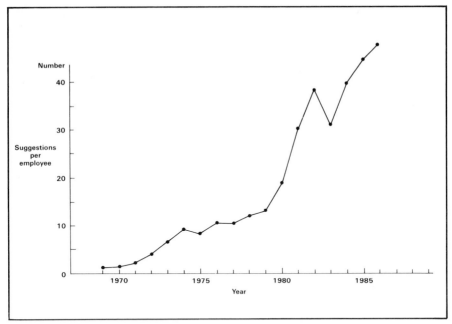

Fig. 2 Employee suggestions at Toyota

Comparison of companies in the East and in the West in terms of quality

If we look at a comparison of quality products from the 1950s to today, we see a big difference in the commitment to quality in the West and in Japan. We can note that quality improvement has increased much faster in Japan from year to year than in Europe and the USA.

Dr Joseph Juran recognised and published this fact many years ago, but companies in the West took little interest. Thirty years ago, the Japanese were noted for poor quality products and this was evident in the cheap toys and textiles they exported. Today, the Japanese and other Pacific Basin countries have greatly improved their quality and have overtaken us in international markets.

Much of Japanese TQM expertise is a direct result of the Korean and Vietnamese Wars. The US invested heavily in Japan to ensure that equipment and technology could be repaired quickly and sent back to the front lines. The experience of working with quality systems gained during these two major conflicts has had a significant influence on the Japanese approach to quality.

The Japanese tend to target a market and go for it and to this end have now captured many European markets. The interesting thing is they don't keep this a secret from us Westerners. Recently, it was acknowledged that Japanese companies have targeted the pharmaceutical industry and the financial services sector. The Japanese are huge users of 'prescribed drugs' and feel that there is an opportunity to move into a new manufacturing area.

Consider the damage and the loss of market share to the automotive, motor-cycle, electrical household components including TV, audio equipment, video, watches, shipbuilding, electronics, cameras and photocopier markets, etc. in recent years. Manufacturers of these items were aware of the competition but they did not take it seriously. Ten years ago, the Japanese had little part to play in world banking and finance. Today nine out of the top ten banks in the world are Japanese.

The increase in financial services in recent years is a sufficient incentive to move into Europe. Their banking sector can service new initiatives in this area. Many of the major manufacturers in pharmaceuticals including Johnson & Johnson, Dow Merrill, etc, have developed TQ Drives to improve their perfor-mance — but what of the financial services-sector? The tradition of banking and insurance has not moved sufficiently. Although some concern is being wit-nessed by the promotion of customer service campaigns in this sector, a com-mitment to TQM is not yet in evidence.

The Japanese have no special advantage over us, they simply examine the process of doing a job and try to improve upon it. To quote the Chairman of Toyota, Mr Ohno. "QUALITY is both thinking why something is done, and why it is done that way; then thinking differently to improve it."

We will drive them back into the Pacific

The Americans felt they had to respond to the influx of Japanese cars in 1978 and suggested that the automotive industry should invest a great deal of money in new technology, robotics, etc. This initiative was orientated to improve quality, protect market share and give the American product a com-

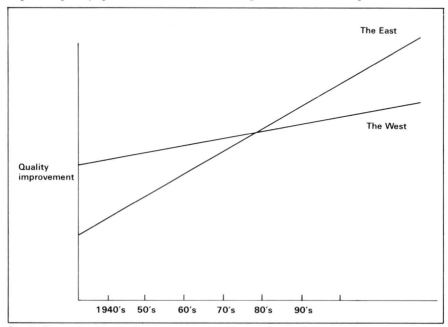

Fig. 3 Comparison on Quality improvement of companies in the East and the West

petitive advantage. The US car industry believed that throwing money at a problem would solve it. In particular, a major automotive manufacturer stated that they would invest $40 bn in the next 10 years and send the Japanese back into the Pacific. They were wrong, they invested over $68 bn in that decade and still lost market share. However, their share prices rose in 1988 when they sold off spare capacity and admitted that they were trying to hold on to a realistic percentage of the market.

Quality is about attitude. Spending money does not promote quality, although it may provide the tools. Throwing money at problems does not make them go away. Investing in technology and robotics is not a route to TQM. You may invest in the wrong technology or implement it badly. Quality is something which is engineered through effective human relations.

Reject stereotyped beliefs

The sooner we in the West move away from the old stereotypes about unfair competition, dumping cheaper unit price items on European and American soil, cheaper wage costs etc., the sooner we can start our drive to be the best in the world. It is not too late, it will be in 5 years. For companies to establish superior manufacturing practice and provide superlative service, the race to catch up must start now. It is no good in 1995 complaining about the advantage our competitors have over us — without putting some of their ideas into practice now.

If their practice was 'culturally biased' we would expect that Eastern companies based in Europe and the UK would not have developed as well as they have done. We are constantly surprised to find that the particularly Japanese approach to the management of quality has worked in Japanese companies such as Nissan, Hitachi, JVC, National Panasonic etc, in the UK with British workers. There is nothing magical about their culture — they just apply the principles. Companies such as Jaguar, British Airways, Mars, Corning Glass, Dow Chemicals and many others have succeeded not just by looking and admiring the Japanese but by applying ideas on improving the quality of what they do.

Tough words: you won't do it!

For the reader, this is all pretty depressing in a book orientated towards promoting TQM in Europe and the USA. However writing platitudes and confirming prejudices does not and will not create the needed change. Don't expect to find them in this book.

Honest, plain speaking is required. Overall, we produce lousy products and services. There are too many managers in industry who think that change is not necessary — thinking we can return to mid-1974 before things started to get tough! It is not going to happen. Senior officers in companies have to be able to learn to be responsive, to anticipate and plan for change. They have to be able to turn their companies around and anticipate the competition becoming better in every way they cannot stay the same.

Having the answer — but doing nothing

What bothers me most is that when we have the means of resolving problems we studiously ignore them. The more difficult the implementation and change —the more we ignore it, or say it won't work. Then later, when the inevitable happens and we lose market share, we whinge about unfair competition, customers transferring loyalty and lack of government protection.

Purpose of the book

This book could be a valuable aid to a management team intending to promote TQM. To the 80% of companies who are going to fail when promoting TQM, because they are not really committed to it — I strongly suggest you give the book to someone else.

To those of you committed to being the best and to managing the transistion to TQM — this book is for you.

Summary and bullet points

- Don't under estimate the time and effort required to achieve the real benefits of TQM. It is a gradual process and is built upon a commitment to constant innovation.
- It is time that we in the West were honest about our losses in market share. 15 to 20 years ago people could predict the loss of market share in motor cycles, cars, TV's, shipping because of inattention to the quality of product and service. We did nothing about it.
- If, by 1995 companies have failed to become committed to TQM there is serious doubt that they will have any market share at all. A pessimistic note to reinforce this belief is that too few UK companies are switched on to 1992 so why should we assume they are switched on to TQM!
- Deming and Juran exported 'Quality Assurance' and the related tools to Japan with ease. Why is it so difficult to import these back into our own culture?
- The great fear is that we can be exposed to the secrets of TQM, have the answer to improving performance, but still find 10 reasons why we should not do it!
- Don't get wrapped up in moaning about unfair competition. Reject stereotyped beliefs about Japanese culture. TQM can work here. It is not culturally biased in their favour.

2 TOTAL QUALITY

Total quality is a strategic approach to producing the best product and service possible — through constant innovation. It is a recognition that concentrating **not** only upon the production side but also on the service side of a business, is tantamount to success. Of course, this perception exists because tangible improvements in quality can be seen but other areas in the business have at least as important a part to play.

Many companies can produce zero defect products but the company's quality still isn't right. There are other functions and departments which can let the company down. The right product delivered at the wrong time can have catastrophic impact upon both buyer and seller. A research report conducted in 1984 found that 95% of companies deliver their products late. This later delivery can have just as much impact upon future buying decisions as can increasing the price of the product by 5%!

Invoicing can create problems. Delivering the right product but invoicing incorrectly can delay payment to the supplier for as much as 3 months or longer. Salesmen promising the earth in back-up can leave the disappointed customer cold and indifferent to further trading with the company. Quality is the responsibility of everybody.

TQM directed towards maintaining the competitive edge and security

Without doubt, the drive towards TQM comes about for a number of reasons but generally there are push and pull factors in operation.

Many senior officers of companies pursue TQ because they fear the future. They know the environment is constantly changing and that they are constantly being reviewed by their customers. Some customers, such as Ford, Jaguar, Marks and Spencer, IBM and many Japanese companies, refuse to do business with vendors unless they can prove that the quality of service and product they provide meets their exacting standards. Witness the number of companies recognising that BS 5750 is only the foundation for full accreditation as a vendor by Ford. The only way companies can do this is by being rated on a sliding scale of the Ford Q101 system, which requires a real drive for detail.

Senior staff in organisations understand that to continue to do business with customers will require dedication to get things right, first time, every time. Some company officers decide to pursue TQM as an act of faith. They know it is the right thing to do. A major American chemical company pursued TQM in a year of record profits. Nothing was wrong with performance. The product range was of good quality: but the over-riding motive behind the initiative was 'while the sun is shining let's get out and fix the roof'. Years later they are glad they did — because the Japanese focused upon their markets.

The manager responsible for the European TQM drive within this company was flying out to Switzerland and started up a conversation with a fellow passenger. He discussed TQM with this new acquaintance — and then stated that, although there was no threat in the ABS plastics market, the officers of the company thought it would be a good idea to promote TQM. The man produced his business card and handed it to the manager. He was the plant manager of a chemical plant producing ABS plastics. When asked to turn the card over, the manager found that the reverse of the card was in Japanese — as was the origin of the company.

Competitors in the West		Competitors in the East	
Arco	Hoechst	Mitsui	Nanya
Montedison	Enichem	Toyasoda	Samsung
Union Carbide	Monsato	Cheing Mei	Hannam
Dow Chemicals	ICI	PT Polychem	Ext Resin
Shell Chemicals	BP	Lucky Gold Star	Idemitsu
Borg Warner	BASF	Asahi	Taita
Bayer	Du Pont	Grand Pacific	
Rohm & Haas	General Electric	Mitsubishi	

Fig. 1 Competition in the plastics industry for the 1990s. Who will survive?

This prompted an investigation into companies producing plastics in the West and the East (see Fig. 1). Resulting data reinforced the belief that the company had to improve quality in order to maintain its edge. It was established that 50% of the ABS companies in the East had been set up over the past year — and of that total, 50% were exporting plastics to Europe.

It was found that what might have been known in one area of the company, a small section in marketing, was not common knowledge throughout the structure. Acknowledging that continual improvement is the only factor that keeps you ahead of the competition must be communicated to everybody. The resulting TQM drive helped people share the perception that their company had to be 'vigilent' and constantly needed to appraise its competitive position if it was to grow and succeed.

An organisation wide commitment to Quality

TQM is an organisation wide commitment to getting things right. Our experience suggests that the initiative can come solely from the production people. Recently, at a TQM presentation for a Multinational Engineering Company, it was noticeable that the marketing, sales and financial directors were absent. The sales director said he was busy with buyers from Italy. The financial director stated that he had to see the company secretary and the marketing director that he had an appointment with a public relations agency. The TQM message had been well 'sold' previously, but some were not listening, evidenced by the non-attendees still refusing to believe that quality was not a priority and had nothing to do with them.

Recognition that TQM problems originate in areas other than manufacturing

Many problems can arise in departments which service manufacturing units:

- The enthusiasm, but inattention to detail, of the salesman who will agree to any modification with customers, not understanding the chaos created on the shopfloor.
- The designer who feels that he knows best and does not need to talk with the operative making the component he designs.
- The purchasing manager who fails to appraise suppliers because he doesn't have time.
- The accountant who experiences cash flow problems extends the 30 to 60 day payment period to suppliers and then wonders why components are not delivered on time.

These are all classic examples of problems which arise in non-manufacturing areas — but they are not treated as quality problems.

These decisions in service units can have a horrifying effect on quality on the shop floor. That is why we talk of 'Total' quality.

Founded upon quality control, inspection and statistical process control

TQM is founded upon these areas of quality management. It is always desirable for a company to have developed some level of Quality Control (QC), Quality Assurance Systems (QAS) and Statistical Process Control (SPC) prior to TQM — but it is not essential. Now, this might sound strange — but it is not. TQM is concerned with turning a company around in terms of improving overall performance by focusing upon quality. TQM starts at the top. If these and other initiatives have been going for some time, TQM is a guiding influence which can bring them all together in one drive.

Tailoring TQM drives to the organisation

TQM drives are designed and tailored to the needs and maturity of the company. Philip Crosby's *Maturity Index* is of use in understanding where a company is now in terms of quality — before deciding where it is going to be in 3 years. For instance, British Telecom engaged upon a major TQ drive some time ago. This is now becoming part of their culture and recognisable signs of success are evident. However because of the sheer size of the company, the full impact of the drive may take up to 15–20 years to realise. This does not mean that TQM has been unsuccessful but that the initiative has to follow certain stages before the full benefits can be realised. Likewise, if British Rail engaged on a TQM drive it would adopt a different approach to that of other companies.

For instance, having worked with three different chemical companies over the last 3 years, all American owned, the TQM initiative in all three companies has been very different. Although the three companies did produce similar products, their cultural bases, the quality methods they employed and their 'management styles' were all different. Consequently, what worked for one company wouldn't work for others.

Organisations employ differing technology, have different histories and backgrounds, serve different markets with different products and employ people from different cultures — so the drive to improve quality has to be managed differently.

Driven by top management A major theme which runs through this book is commitment. If senior officers in organisations fail to drive TQM it will fail.

Getting the drive started is not where the responsibility for change finishes. Long-term 'Ownership' is the role that senior management take on. They have to lead others by example. They will have to demonstrate new ways of working and, through actions, reject the old ways.

Dependent upon the actions of everyone The great danger of talking about 'Senior Management Commitment' is that others within the structure assume that all the effort must come from the top. Wherever people fit within the hierarchy they have a part to play. Quality initiatives need to be generated and driven by everyone within the company. Of course, we can't expect this to start from day 1 of the TQ drive but, over time, everybody should have a responsibility.

A never ending process Total quality is a process which goes on forever. There will never be a time when quality is 100% right. There will always be new ways of doing things in product and service areas. Again, there is often too much emphasis placed on the manufacturing side. Although here we can see the greatest changes in terms of concrete and tangible examples, often the greatest waste is identified in non-manufacturing areas. Deming, Juran and other quality gurus claim that 80% of quality costs originate in areas other than manufacturing. It is possible to improve procedures and systems to reduce time-consuming, low value activities. It is just a matter of educating people in these functions to understand that they do have a significant role to play.

TQM is more than QAS. The quest for quality is not over when a company receives its accreditation to a quality standard, although some companies feel that the drive is over as soon the certificate goes up on the wall in the reception area.

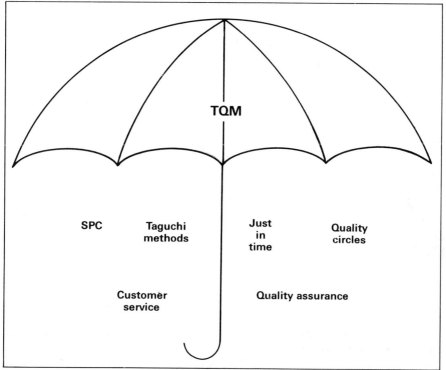

Fig. 2 TQM and relationship to other Quality initiatives

TQM is based on 'right first time' and prevention

TQM is a preventative strategy replacing rework, fire-fighting and crisis management with planning, co-ordination and control. This means company officers orientating themselves to generating the long term resolution of the really important problems which impact upon the organisation. In order to do this, we have to spend less time putting things right after they were done wrong.

TQM is the umbrella under which a great number of quality initiatives can be managed, including SPC, Taguchi methodology and Just in Time. It is not the purpose of this book to detail the growth of these approaches to Company Wide Improvement (CWI), although they are briefly explained.

Bear in mind that the use of these techniques or approach to CWI is no alternative to TQM. In fact, it is difficult to establish these practices without a TQM culture. Let us explore some of the developments in recent years.

Quality circles

For too long many managers have confused the growth of Quality Circles (QC) with TQM. QC are groups of people, often structured on normal work groups, who meet on a voluntary basis, together with their direct supervisor, to discuss 'improvements'. They may discuss productivity improvement or suggest new and better ways of doing things. The important point to note is that they are voluntary in nature. They meet because they want to. They can be based in manufacturing or service areas — although most have been established in production-type environments.

QC members will have had some training in problem solving. They will work on a project and present to management their proposals for change. Basically it is a 'bottom-up' change strategy. Commitment is given from the top of the organisation and managers throughout the structure should help facilitate change. There have been many successful QC activities but, in all honesty a great number of initiatives have failed. They fail for all sorts of reasons but the most obvious are lack of visible support from senior management, blockages to implementation of improvements by line management and lack of momentum and direction.

QC help to create the environment for change but often fail. TQM as a structured approach does not rely on volunteers; it is a structured company wide strategy for change.

Customer service

Many service companies use this approach to improve the quality of service to their customers. It can be a great boon and often works. The most notable examples in recent years have been the British Airways campaign and the radical turnaround of SAS with the leadership of Jan Carlson who created the

'Moments of Truth' concept. Each customer can make up his mind about a company in a 15 second interaction. There are literally millions of opportunities each day to demonstrate to the customer that he or she made the right decision. Carlson saw to it that his staff, at all levels, were trained to be totally customer orientated.

Well-designed customer care programmes can work remarkably well. However, there can be a fundamental conflict in understanding effective customer service. There is little point spending a great deal of time on PR activities in preference to 'educational activities'. Effective customer service is based upon changing the attitudes of 'boundary personnel', the people who come into contact with the customer. It is not to be confused with PR telling the customer how great the company is by using advertising.

A company in the financial services sector spent a great deal on a TV campaign focusing upon their speedy response to the customer. Eight thousand disgruntled viewers wrote to complain that their experiences did not match this. The company recognised that it had a major problem and that it had to improve the service through action not advertising.

The second problem with CS is that managers focus upon processes which take place between the customer and the organisation —thinking that this interface is critical. It is fairly important — but if the company has developed excellent relationships with the customer — while the service provided between internal customers and suppliers is poor — the overall quality provided to the customer is still poor — except they may be shielded from it by a facade.

Total quality service or total customer care can be incredibly powerful. Emphasis should always be on the internal dynamics of the organisation, recognising that meeting the requirements of the internal customer is as important as meeting the needs of the external customer. British Airways saw the good sense of adopting both approaches — using TQM inside the company and customer care with its passengers.

Quality control and assurance

Traditionally these functions are concerned with checking for errors during and after the process of manufacture, controlling, at its most basic, can take place at final assembly. Here everything is checked to see if it works. If it does not it is rejected and either reworked or scrapped. If there is a major problem with a product, or the company is becoming more quality conscious — knowing that too many errors are being shipped to the customer, they can develop a Quality Control System (QCS) which is very useful and helps identify where errors arise.

The big problem with traditional QC activities is that there is a heavy requirement to depend on the activities of inspectors. When companies experience a quality problem there is a natural inclination to inspect, inspect, inspect! This creates an increase in errors spotted, but does not prevent them arising in the first place.

The problem with this approach is that people try to inspect quality into the product. Quality can only be designed and manufactured in at every stage — not inspected in. TQM is not inspection orientated but will work well if founded upon a healthy QC Culture.

From QC we have the growth of Quality Assurance Systems (QAS). These are designed in order to verify that all attempts are made to reduce non-conformance with the product specification. QAS enable us to check for progress identify and isolate where a product is in the production process and QA is founded upon the inspection approach — but is strongly preventative in nature. Although the majority of people in a QA section may be inspectors, the QA manager spends an increasing part of his time developing sophisticated systems to ensure there is not a breakdown in quality in the company.

TQM is partly founded and reliant upon QA techniques. TQM does not contradict QA but goes far beyond it by relating to all functions in all areas. It is a behavioural intervention requiring attitude change, although it is founded upon measurement and control.

Statistical process control

SPC is widely accepted in industry as a method of regulating conformance to requirements for a product — in other words it gives you the tools and techniques to measure the performance of an operation. From measurement you will be able to assess whether things are running smoothly or whether there are requirements for adjustments.

Simple charting is an extremely useful technique of SPC. Operators may test every twentieth item, or randomly, and record it on a chart which allows comparisons to be made. Most products will have specifications and it is to these that the measurements relate. Measurements that fall outside agreed tolerances indicate a potential problem. This could be as simple as a machine requiring to be reset or inferior material being used. Whatever the cause, SPC allows us to measure conformance to specifications. It provides the data upon which we create corrective action.

TQM requires SPC. It is a valuable tool and must be taken seriously. Too often it is not. Two instances, perhaps extreme, will illustrate the point. The cases are based on a discussion with operators on the use of SPC.

An employee working a CNC machine fails to plot any data on the graph in front of him. In discussion he is asked why. His honest reply was, "Today is Tuesday, the man from . . . . . . (the customer) doesn't come until Friday. The charts will be marked up then." It is clear that charts in this case are used for impression management purposes. They have little intrinsic value to the organisation, although creating a sham for the customer. Worse still, the commitment to their use from management is poor and is indirectly telling the operator that SPC and quality are not important.

The second case involves an operator refusing to complete the charts. When he was asked why, he said, "They are a waste of time. I have been filling in charts for the last 3 months. There are plenty of times when there have been problems and these are recorded. But nobody takes any corrective action. Why should I waste my time?"

SPC is an extremely powerful technique if used properly. Many companies use the technique to the best advantage but there are too many who abuse it and try to benefit from it use for the wrong reason.

SPC works marvellously — even in service areas. To be successful it requires total commitment and someone who can explain the use of statistics simply.

Taguchi methodology

Dr Genichi Taguchi is famous for his methods for improving quality engineering at low cost. This approach to problem solving helps quantify the loss due to lack of quality of a performance characteristic and directly relating it to its deviation from the target performance. Taguchi methodology demonstrates the efficient use of analytical and experimental techniques to identify the real cause of a problem. It concentrates on the design of products, reducing variations of performance characteristics and parameter design.

A colleague, who originally helped instigate the Scottish Taguchi Forum, spent 3 days with Dr Taguchi. From his discussions and tours around companies practising Taguchi methodology, he learned that most companies in Japan, and increasingly in the USA, are using this methodology in system, parameter and tolerance design. The American Supplier Institute are foremost in promoting Taguchi, but this approach and tool of TQM is not widely understood in the UK and Europe. The rigorous application of Taguchi methods, although not a subject of this book, is gathering ground in industry and it is suggested that it should become a vital interest to European engineering and manufacturing managers. However Taguchi methods are unlikely to be applied successfully in a culture which is not heavily committed to TQM.

Just in time

Just In Time (JIT) principles are concerned with improving productive efficiency and reducing waste. Most perceive this to be a means of strictly regulating the flow of materials into the company which is restricted in its outlook. At first sight JIT is used as a technique for minimising storage of excessive inventory through planning and meeting the exact requirements of the customer. JIT also requires the use of fairly analytical techniques for correcting problems in the manufacturing process.

Preventative maintenance, foolproofing and set up time reduction are some of the outputs of this approach. It is impossible to create JIT without the TQM culture. It is possible to reduce inventory in the short term but, if there has been a failure to remove the problems underpinning excessive inventory, the problems will be intensified.

Barriers to TQM in recent years

Clearly there are many initiatives which fall under the TQM umbrella, but require the TQ culture to make things happen. It is for this reason that many innovative programmes fail. Management perceives a technique as being useful and apply it in an environment and culture which is hostile and where it cannot grow and prosper.

Too many companies fail to give TQM a chance. TQM will not produce results in the short term (see chapter 3 on costing quality). Overall, there is an expectation that the cost of rework and wasteful practice will drop considerably. This will only happen when there is a major investment in preventative type activities, which will only happen in the long term.

If TQM or a related activity, ie JIT, MRP or QC does not live up to the short-term expectations of senior staff — new projects are not given an opportunity. Just as projects are starting to gather ground, senior officers introduce a new management 'fad'.

The frequency with which we are told by workshop participants that TQM is no more than briefing groups, quality circles, participative management, MBO is incredible. We are also reminded that many of these approaches failed in their companies in the past — so why should TQM work?

Ten reasons to make it fail Attitude and resistance to change are major problems in British industry today. Good ideas for quality improvement can be rejected by the group who are intent on making ideas fail. Sometimes they portray the 'Not Invented Here' approach. "It's okay for the production people — where all the problems arise —but no good for the service side."

Digging up the past and making it reality Too many people in organisations live in the past. They remember the problems created between units and functions and the personalities involved. They generate stereotyped images of people and 'Win-Lose' attitudes towards work are created at every opportunity. There is a chance that the past will relive itself. We should spend more of our energy thinking and planning for the future — rather than reliving old battles.

The National Quality Campaign and professional bodies

The National Quality Campaign by the (DTI) in the UK has focused on systems and helped over 9,000 companies gain BS 5750 status.

However this success has often created a failure to promote TQM in the same companies.

Early in the campaign there was so much emphasis given to BS 5750 that many chief executives and senior officers became confused, believing that the secret of TQM lay in application of systems. Unfortunately, it was perceived that the quality manager within the company now had responsibility for company wide quality improvement. This misconception was the bias towards Manufacturing Management.

The publicity and videos, incorporated in the DTI packages, reinforced this belief and were all geared to the promotion of systems — implying that this was what quality was all about.

There is still a great deal of confusion today and this even extends to TQM conferences. At at least two venues in 1989, at which I was present, there were speakers talking about systems and BS 5750 — although their sessions were described as 'Implementing Total Quality'.

Recent DTI initiatives have been 'broader' but they are still not focusing on the key issues. In a similar fashion, the British Quality Association (BQA) and the Institute of Quality Assurance (IQA), although providing excellent services to their members and advancing the body of knowledge, have done little to promote the broader idea of TQM. They still persistently cling to their beliefs that overall company wide quality is the responsibility of the quality assurance manager. The longer this is evident the longer it will take TQM to get off the ground.

Summary and bullet points

● TQM is orientated towards maintaining the competitive edge of the company. It is not a short-term programme, a cost-cutting exercise or a new productivity prescription.
● Total quality impacts upon everybody everywhere in the organisation. It is as much the responsibility of the QA manager as it is the financial accountant, purchasing manager, designer, salesmen, personnel specialist.
● Understand and reinforce the belief that 80% of quality problems originate in areas other than manufacturing.
● TQM is based on the systematic use and application of QA, SPC and QC.
● TQM is the umbrella which covers all improvement activities including SPC, QC, Customer Care, JIT, Taguchi methods etc.
● TQM drives must be tailored to the special needs of the organisation.
● TQM must be driven and be the responsibility of the senior management, ownership must reside at the top.
● TQM is a never ending process. It does not end when a certificate is attached to a reception wall.

3 COSTING QUALITY

The majority of senior managers are unaware of the true costs of how much it costs them to 'get things wrong'. Most financial directors have little idea of how much 'Non-Quality' costs them each year for the simple reason that the 'Cost of Quality' (COQ) never shows up on a balance sheet. In many cases, they have never been asked to measure the price of 'Non-Quality' and would not know where to start.

The term COQ is really a misnomer — it is more accurately described as the cost on non-quality, a measurement which indicates how much it costs per year to provide quality in everything the company does, whether product or service related. There are other terms which refer to the same measurement and they include the cost of non-conformance and the price of quality. The different terms relate to the same concept.

Unbelievable figures: COQ

When companies start COQ exercises they cannot believe the figures generated. In Europe it is estimated that the average manufacturing company is operating with a COQ of about 15–25% of turnover. In the service sector this can be as high as 40–50% of turnover! In some parts of the public sector these costs could be even higher!

When these high figures are quoted at first it appears unbelievable. People wonder how their company actually makes a profit. The proof of such figures has to be explained with examples — but it is real and it is tangible! It is possible to monitor COQ in all activities — manufacturing and service alike. Companies like IBM, Corning Glass, Unisys, Jaguar and British Telecom originally experienced COQ as high as 40% of turnover. Many senior officers openly proclaim this figure, which is not unusual. Most companies without a rigorous approach to quality may well be operating in excess of this figure. If you doubt this, one or two days data collection can produce horrifying results.

Costing quality (CQ) is an extremely important activity. It has driven many companies to promote TQM in order to reduce COQ in the long term, which is achievable and possible.

However, it can be a healthy sign if companies pursue the TQM route for its own sake — believing that the current devotion to quality is poor, and wanting to change things for the better. Organisations which portray this 'act of faith' will gain more benefits than those which perceive TQM as no more than a long-term, cost-reduction exercise. However, having said this, it is important for companies to have a yardstick by which to assess progress and disclose wasteful activities. COQ measurement helps here.

CQ is an exercise which organisations have to pursue if they wish to improve their competitive edges. Assessing the COQ creates the thrust needed. Many companies openly proclaimed that their COQ is 40%. In the service sector, where COQ is 'non measurable' and intangible, the COQ far exceeds the figures quoted. To get a better idea of the costs associated with non-conformance, we need to ask, what is the COQ, and how can it be measured?

Measuring everything and understanding nothing

When asked to assess costs one of the greatest problems is that we tend to isolate those things which can be measured from those which are intangible or non-quantifiable. The first mistake is to measure only tangible items, eg direct labour for rework, scrap wastage or materials. Many organisations make this mistake and come to the conclusion that the cost of rework is low. We wish this were true. If this formula is used as a measure it will not reflect the true costs. While working on a quality assignment with a US multi-national telecommunications company we were surprised to find that the COQ was calculated using this simple tangible method.

The costs of manufacturing rework were low — 3–5% of manufacturing costs — but the rework in the service area was never calculated. We know this was extremely high because installation teams often had to return to customers in Eastern and Northern Europe, South America, Canada and the USSR, to fix or recallibrate the product. The costs incurred, including salary, bonus payments, accommodation, air travel and entertainment, were never included in the 'cost' for that project. Although a team of five men could be away from the plant for 10 days, working with a customer with a defective component, the costs incurred were never transferred to a particular product or project.

The COQ was widely inaccurate. No one seemed to mind too much until a customer requested a reduction of 10% off his invoice. When questioned the customer said he refused to pay the 'rework' costs of the company. The company spokesman denied that they were being charged for rework activities. The customer agreed that this might be true at the surface level but someone was indirectly funding all this unnecessary rework and it was probably him!

First assess the COQ in non-manufacturing

The major costs associated with getting things wrong rests in the non-manufacturing sector. Deming claims that 85% of quality problems are created by people who never touch the product. It is common practice for companies to start collecting data which relates to manufacturing first and in too many cases managers responsible for service departments are less than willing to share such information. They claim that it is difficult to measure 'waste' and 'non-quality' in a service area. This is nonsense. All company functions and departments have goals and objectives and these should be able to be translated into responsibilities handled through various grades and levels of management. Tasks are allocated to managers, to reflect the goals and objectives, and resources are distributed to ensure that work is completed on time. If service people state that their efforts and output is intangible it is time to revise department goals. This is referred to in chapter 13 when we discuss departmental purpose analysis.

Over the years we have amassed a great deal of evidence from companies that many of the problems are created 'unintentionally' through those in the service area. For example, consider an organisation producing a standard technological product for the telecommunications industry.

Those running the company are keen to promote the growth in market share of their product over competitors. Salesmen are the 'real' company men. They spend a great deal of time with interested customers and are keen to agree to their special requirements. Sales staff, in this example, agree to modifications to their standardised product. This works out fine for the company —but they should be careful that these modifications do not become too excessive and time consuming for those in manufacturing to produce.

Soon the company managers recognise that customers are keen to have 'specials' manufactured. The company starts to get a great name for becoming 'customer rather than product led'. Meanwhile, new sales are pouring into the company which, in turn, creates problems further down the line. It creates further problems for designers and draughtsmen, for inventory control officers who have to order non-standard components, for the shop floor which has to develop different approaches to production and assembly. In one case, this degenerated into the company moving from 'selling what it made' to 'making what it sold'.

Although orders flooded into the company, the back-up service for the salesmen was not as good as it needed to be. Salesmen needed engineers to agree to the feasibility of technical detail or modifications. In many cases, sales people, because of their ignorance of the complexity of 'modifications', omitted to define customers' requirements in sufficiently specific terms to develop accurate design drawings from which to manufacture. Part numbers of components were guessed and ordered. Materials management problems arose and the company wondered why its stock of inventory was so high. New materials and components were being bought in while existing standard items, no longer required, sat dormant in the materials control section. The impact this had on the rest of the company was predictable. Its competitive edge was harmed almost permanently.

Management had failed to recognise that the market was changing. The few agreed modifications had turned the large batch production line into a jobbing shop. As the change had been gradual, no one had noticed. Many senior managers had failed to grasp the fact that a company's back-up system must be 'spot on' if the sales staff promoting 'customised' products to customers. We would strongly support a 'customer driven' rather than a 'product led' strategy for companies to pursue — but they must have the right culture to support this approach, all the way through the company. The quoted company failed to understand that companies can still go out of business with full order books — if they fail to promote the internal dynamics to support an external push for customised sales.

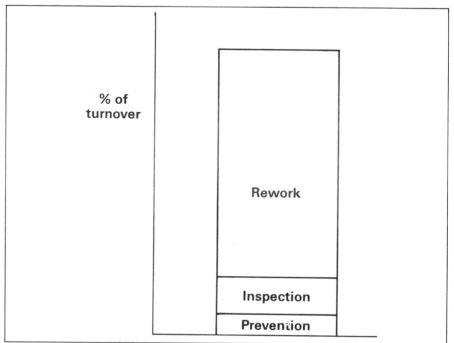

Fig. 1 Cost of quality

How do we assess the cost of quality?

COQ is composed of three key elements. The largest proportion contributing to the COQ is the 'Cost of Errors'. In other words, the action that has to be taken to finish a job. Often referred to as 'Rework', this cost is very high. Traditionally, we measure only the tangible aspects of the manufacturing process; materials, scrap, and direct labour — but neglect to measure other costs. What about measuring the cost of indirect labour? Some examples have already been highlighted but many people in service functions fail to recognise that this cost is very high.

A typical example includes the costs associated with sales staff visiting clients to put right what was wrong. A company sales manager responsible for Northern Europe, calculated that each week he spends 2 days away (40% of his available time) discussing quality problems with clients. Not all the problems were associated with poor quality manufacture, 50% of the time was spent apologising for late delivery, inaccurate invoicing and poor after sales service, etc. The major concern to him was that he wasted so much time. He calculated that it was costing the company a fortune, although it would never show up on a balance sheet.

The cost of his 2 days each week was at least 40% of his direct salary in addition to expenses, including travelling and accommodation, etc, and the 'opportunity cost', which couldn't be calculated, or what he could have done in the 2 days if he had not needed to get involved in 'rework'. The cost was very high — but it appears bearable! The sales manager was busy and the customer was satisfied at the end of the day but he had not added any real value to what he did —selling the product. He spent an inordinate amount of time fixing the mistakes which others had created for him. He 'reworked' the errors of others.

In another company the finance section had just employed two well-qualified members of staff. It was surprising to find what they were to spend their time doing. The purchase order system in the company appeared too complicated. Line managers were confused and often incorrectly quoted the codes of purchase orders, especially when dealing with suppliers. Consequently, suppliers were invoicing the company with inaccurate purchase order numbers. Payment was delayed and it created a large number of problems with 'internal control'. The two new employees were employed, not to develop a new system or make the old one work, but to 'rework' all purchase orders to check and ensure that resources were deducted from the correct departmental budget.

How many people in companies spend all their time 'reworking' the errors of others? Does it not make sense to prevent problems arising and to get it right first time? However, some companies have whole departments engaged in 'rework'.

Customer service departments and rework

Some companies boast that they have the largest customer service departments in the industry. They may also claim that they provide a warranty which is second to none. This is not something of which to be proud. This means that the company is committed to 'getting it right second time'. The cost can be tremendous. At one company, the customer service unit was visited to find that the size of the unit had grown and new staff were now sighted in a new office complex. What impact had the new office area on the COQ for the company? No one seemed to think about doing things right first time and prevent errors arising.

Order re-entry, retyping, unnecessary travel and use of the telephone, conflict and fighting between departments are just some examples of waste which contribute to the COQ. These are all assessed as leading to the cost of 'doing things again'. To get into further detail, there can be two types of 'reworks' which relate to internal or external failure. If the product fails in the field the costs can be attributed towards external failure. If failure is in-house it is internal failure! It is interesting to examine ratios between different companies in the same industry. These two areas can be further subdivided into 'necessary' and 'unnecessary' rework.

'Necessary rework' would be associated with redrafting a document or redesign. It is unlikely and, some would argue, undesirable to hinge on getting creative pieces of work absolutely right first time. However there comes a point when 'rework' becomes unnecessary. It is to these areas that we would turn first to reduce waste. The interesting point about 'rework' is that very few of us create 'rework' for ourselves. Our supervisors and managers would comment and our inefficiency would stand out.

'Rework' is usually created for others — probably the person who is next in line. So 'rework' is created for you by people down the line who feed you information, decisions, materials and resources. You in turn can be a major source of 'rework' for those in the company who depend on you. If you don't do your job right first time — they have to fix it.

The cost of inspection

The secondary element of the COQ is 'Inspection Costs'. Typical examples include the costs associated with maintaining QC, the cost of calibration, the cost of tooling and the cost associated with policing a system, etc. The cost of inspection is high, particularly in administrative areas. People spend a great deal of time checking. Some of this inspection is necessary and some is unnecessary. It is the latter element that needs to be eliminated.

Inspection activities are pursued by companies who have major problems with product and service quality. If things are not right — inspect, inspect, inspect. Inspection does not build quality into the product — so is wasteful. Is it so unusual that many large companies have very strong quality control and assurance sections? One thing we must remember — that no amount of inspection will increase quality. Prevention is the key.

There are 38 f's in Fig 2. Very few people get the number right first time. We

The necessity of training farm hands for first class farms in the fatherly handling of first class farm livestock is foremost in the minds of farm owners. Since the forefathers of the farm owners trained the farm hands for first class farms in the fatherly handling of farm livestock, the farm owners feel they should carry on with the family tradition of fundamental training of farm hands of first class farms in the fatherly handling of farm livestock because they believe it is the basis of good fundamental farm management.

Fig. 2 Count the total number of f's in the paragraph below

also find there are many differences in standards between people. This is down to perceptual differences and illustrates the general quality point that we all have different abilities and standards and no amount of inspection can identify all the problems. Prevention is the only alternative.

The cost of prevention

The third component of COQ is 'Prevention'. The activities normally associated with 'Prevention' include training, planning, forecasting, meetings and QA, etc. The best way to remember the role of prevention is: "One hour of planning saves ten hours of chaos."

Rework — or doing the same job twice
Retyping
Redesign and replanning
Recalls and expenses
Retraining
Reprogramming
Scrap
Excess inventory
Shortages
Reinspection . . . extra testing
Handling complaints
Forecast errors
Incorrect debit and delivery notes
Invoices matching with purchase orders
Lack of training in operational and supervisory areas
Failure to turn up for training courses
Failure to organise for absence while attending courses
Sample programmes not met
Poor communication
Downtime maintenance
No planned maintenance
Misinformation
Maintenance delay — cost of slow response
Morale
Housekeeping
Material handling damage
Failing to plan ahead
Not buying good quality material or good quality spares etc
Misunderstanding in verbal communication
Incorrect labelling
Changes not communicated
Material availability
Failing to follow agreed action
Material movements not documented
Purchasing failing to appraise supplier
Wrong interpretation of correct information by designers
Time management
Inadequate specification of requirements
Orientation to short term rather than long-term goals
Failure to react to causes of problems
Not maximising production rates
Non-effective monitoring of performance of people or plans
Not shutting down to maintain equipment
Lack of information flow
Accepting too many conflicting priorities

No identifiable mission
Time wasting in all forms
Not learning from previous experiences
Poor quality equipment/materials
'Make it cheap'
Verbal communications — reliance on memory
Delays from suppliers trying to identify our needs
Not enough clear communication — up, down and across
Suppliers not meeting requirements
Design FMEA not effectively carried out
Late delivery of material means job has to be interrupted
Lateness attending meetings — repeating or waiting
Customer schedule changes
Material variation — no agreed specification
Inaccurate fowarded information due to time demands
Defective parts manufactured and included in finished product
Part no's and quantities do not match advice notes
Late deliveries — holding up production
Over deliveries clogging up goods in stores
Inadequate or missing process capability studies
Component production not synchronised
Raw materials not available at right time
Tool failures
Missing drawings
Progress chasing
Parts right but wrong quantity
Parts wrong but right quantity
Parts wrong and wrong quantity
Parts and quantity right — wrong destination
Uneconomic use of raw materials
Excessive number of parts lost in set-ups
Non feasible design
Lack of consultation between R&D and manufacturing
SPC charts not completed
SPC guesstimates
Failing to act on SPC information
Data from capability studies not fed to designers
FMEA's not completed at appropriate time
AQP's not performed or used effectively
Few real design standards
Agreeing impossible requirements with customers
Drawing specifications
Lack of adherence to Quality System
Cost estimating
Computer database not maintained

Fig. 3 Activities associated with the cost of errors or rework

It is sad to see that so little time, effort, energy and resources are devoted to prevention in today's organisations. The way of life in many companies is 'crisis management' orientated. Fire-fighting becomes a way of life. Managers and staff get used to the culture and some actually start to enjoy it. Their time could be spent more effectively creating opportunities for the future and anticipating problems, rather than trying to solve yesterday's mistake.

Practical implications of rework, inspection and prevention

How much of your time do you spend on work which could be classed as 'rework' or 'doing work over'? Believe me, you spend more than you think!

How much time do you spend each week correcting errors? The errors could have been created by you but also could arise elsewhere! How often do you have to go through a report and rewrite it for a second time? How often do you say to yourself, "that will do"? As you put the report away, you know you will have to do it again, but you think you might just get away with it this time.

How often do you write a letter, send it to the typing pool and know that there are still some serious inaccuracies which need to be corrected?

Technology and lazy managers

Managers can become very lazy when new technology is introduced into a company. Time has been spent researching the human aspects of new technology. Work was carried out in a sample of organisations which had just introduced word processors (WP's). What had led to the decision to invest in WP's. The answers were all productivity based. Research suggested that there was no marked increase in productivity and in some areas, the generation of documents above one page in length, productivity had fallen.

Prior to WP's, managers spent time ensuring that the written communications were right first time, before sending them to the typing pool. They realised the problems that they would create with carbons, masters and copies, etc. Even lengthy documents, like detailed reports, were only typed 2 or 3 times. 'Rework' was evident — but was necessary. What was found when we looked at productivity after the introduction of WP's was that the number of drafts had increased.

Since the introduction of WP's, the number of average drafts for lengthy reports had increased from 3 or 4 to 7 or 8. The material and content of letters and reports has stayed constant, but the ability to change documents easily has created a great deal of flexibility and, with it, 'rework'. Managers had not realised that they had created problems for their secretaries and the typing pool. Their interpretation of flexibility had led them to be less structured when writing text — believing they could change it at a later date. The constraints under which they had previously worked had been removed and the impact upon performance had been negative.

Managers believed this flexibility would improve the quality of what they did but it also created 'rework' for others. Knowing how easy it is to change a document created a casual attitude among managers. Secretarial staff were spending more of their time reworking the mistakes of others, rather than becoming more productive. Although the aim of 'Office Automation' was to increase productivity, in many cases it has not had the desired effect. Instead of the output of documents increasing, more drafts are being processed for each document.

Case study: the personnel department

A company had a number of quality problems. As part of the quality pro-gramme, the personnel department were taken through a series of manage-ment development activities. Time management had been reached. Seven members of the department turned up for the training session, each with time logs which they had been keeping for some time.

Each staff member was asked to talk through the major activities in which they had been involved and they were requested to classify the items under three headings, ERROR, INSPECTION & PREVENTION.

On analysis, it was found that, on average, the department spent 54% of time **Reworking** errors and doing work again, 41% of time involved in **Inspection** activities, and 5% on **Preventative** action.

No wonder they hardly achieved anything. No wonder they came into work at 8 am and stayed late. Little wonder their morale was low!

The most surprising thing about the department was that they knew they spent too much time in meetings and involved in routine paperwork, but they had never looked at the focus of the work using these 3 criteria before. The cause of the problem had to be found!

Line managers creating rework for service departments Whatever personnel managers say, it is extremely difficult for personnel to become more proactive rather than a reactive service department. These departments exist to meet the needs of others in the organisation. In this case, the department was working continuously with and reacting to line managers.

Personnel provided the usual recruitment and selection services as well as induction and appraisal. The personnel manager was bright and had sought to introduce many new initiatives into the company. She had tried on many occasions to train line managers to understand the problems with recruitment and selection, and get them to appreciate the huge costs associated with either appointing the wrong person or attracting and shortlisting the wrong group from whom to select.

Right second time On many occasions, posts had been re-advertised and interviews held time and time again. It transpired that line managers were not spending any time at all preparing documentation for personnel. They were using job descriptions which were years old and did not reflect the changing nature of some of the engineering posts. They were not taking care and being selective in using the material. The consequence of this behaviour was rework for others!

Some line managers were guilty of not training their supervisors in the use of the disciplinary code. Consequently, some staff were unfairly dismissed and this created costly administrative rework and other costs to the company.

Generally, because the relationship between the line and staff function (personnel) was poor, the personnel department was suffering. The only way to remedy the situation, and reduce the chances of spending all their time in the future reworking line management's errors, was to invest time in developing the right sort of relationship with the other managers. This could be defined as 'Preventative Action'.

Originally a target was set to double the time the personnel people spent on prevention type activities, and it was known that in the end this would reduce errors, rework and inspection. Getting closer to the managers and spending time explaining the problems the department faced, the quality of the service they could provide if given detailed and accurate information, looking at company priorities and forgetting department differences and negative stereotypes, were all factors which helped reduce the amount of time they spent on correcting rather than preventing errors.

Everyone involved in the exercise was asked to think before they started a task:

"What is the best use of my time right now, and how can I ensure I spend time preventing errors arising in the future?"

This type of analysis helps many managers focus upon their key result areas in a different way. Thinking through your work in this way should help you spend less time fire-fighting and more time planning and preventing problems occurring.

The impact of total quality

How much of your time do you spend on work which could be classed as rework or 'doing work over'. Believe me, you spend more time than you think!

Making the Quality Manager redundant The often quoted statement, "The role of TQM is to make the QA department redundant" is a myth but, nevertheless, the major TQ thrust is to have the QA department spend more time preventing rather than inspecting or correcting errors. The impact of this action on the COQ is to reduce the overall costs of 'non-quality'. Resources can then be deployed from fire-fighting to prevention. The organisational culture should gradually change to reflect the 'error free work' culture. This is the major shift in the 'Quality Cost Formula'.

Moving from rework to prevention Spending time preventing problems to bring down rework is not easy. Don't expect this to be a straight swap, especially if the culture of the company is strongly orientated to fire-fighting.

In Fig. 4 the reduction in rework and inspection through an injection looks marvellous, but it is not that simple. When people are used to working in a set way — it is not easy to get them to spend more time on planning and prevention. In reality we have to put in a great deal of prevention to start turning things round. At first we need 10 hours of prevention to stop 1 hour of rework. Uneconomical it may appear — but it is realistic.

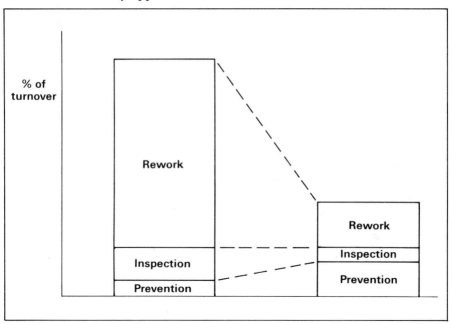

Fig. 4 Quality costs before and after TQM

A major concentration of prevention will change things more quickly than a more modest dose. Don't assume that 1 or 2 training days for all employees, identified as prevention, will turn a company round. After training, teams have to be formed and special efforts made so that they can develop planning, forecasting, meeting, diagnosing, solving and preventing problems happening. Never think it a straight swap. It can be after 6 months of a TQM drive, but not to start with. The real commitment to TQM becomes evident through the resources devoted to prevention at the commencement of a drive.

TQM is not cost cutting There is no short cut to reducing COQ. It can only be achieved through preventative measures. This means that the ideas for improvement must come from those with the knowledge and experience, TQM is user driven and cannot be imposed. TQM is not a cost reduction or a productivity improvement exercise. It is a major goal to get everybody to understand the COQ and its components prior to and after TQM. When the workforce recognises that the high COQ is creating an uncompetitive situation for the company, it will be committed to making TQM happen.

Strategic goals and total quality

Reducing the COQ must be the organisation's priority but it must not be a cost reduction exercise. There must be plenty of evidence to suggest that there is a major investment in prevention.

Overall, companies will be aiming to create a low COQ. It means that the company is in a better competitive situation. Typically, the COQ associated with many companies in the UK is in the region of 20–40%. Reducing this cost can have a tremendous impact on the 'bottom line'.

For those of you not convinced, look at this simple example. A small company with a turnover of £1m per year makes an after tax profit of 10%. Its COQ is a 'meagre' 20%. In other words, the profit in year one is £100,000 and the COQ is £200,000. If the company used its latent energy and resources and adopted a TQM approach, it could reduce its COQ significantly. Due to its size, it is able, in the first year of TQM, to reduce its COQ by 50%, a saving of £100,000. This has the same impact on the bottom line as would increasing turnover by 100%. Normally, companies would have to borrow large sums and deploy vast resources to increase the 'bottom line' by such a figure, but, because this company adopted TQM, it cut costs, trimmed its slack and began doing things 'right first time'. The competitive edge is strengthened and its growth in the market place is assured.

Identifying COQ measures

COQ measures are important within all areas of the organisation. People in the service sector tend to suggest that 'measures' are inappropriate and more suitable for manufacturing. This is not the case.

Every departmental manager or functional head must work with his team to identify key COQ measures which reflect a disproportionate amount of rework experienced within the section.

These should not be wildly sophisticated at first and should remain simple. Manufacturing never has problems with identifying measures, so let us address ourselves to the service sector.

Some examples may help to illustrate the measures. A training manager had problems relating to measurement, claiming his work was difficult to measure. We suggested that he record the number of trainee days per month completed.

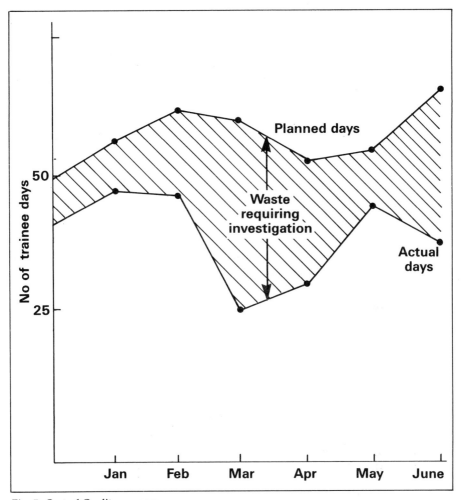

Fig. 5 Cost of Quality measure

Training on health and safety, time management and first aid were all to be recorded. We wanted the manager to keep fairly simple figures on 2 areas — planned and actual trainee days. As can be seen from Fig. 5, the larger the discrepancy between the two the bigger the problem. Although everybody was aware of this problem — no one had any data which demonstrated the severity of the problem. This data acted as a major push to work closer with line management. Through 'Pareto Charting' the training manager was able to identify the major causes of the problem and take action.

In a similar fashion, an accountant kept a simple record of expenses claims which were completed incorrectly. He also drew up a 'Pareto Chart' identifying the mistakes most commonly made. He took corrective action, produced documentation on the most difficult sections and recirculated it to all managers. In time, this reduced the rework he experienced.

The sales staff were concerned that customers were not receiving the product on time. An analysis was carried out identifying the problem in production. It was not the fault of manufacturing. Careful analysis identified the major holdup being the research and development area. It was found that 'missing' technical drawings in all areas were creating problems — 'missing' was later described as uncompleted. These were essential for tool design, inventory and purchasing and production. This was further complicated. If the most recent drawing was not available, people worked from the previous generation of drawings, creating many timely delays and major errors.

Our data helped to correct the problems with delivery. The most obvious reasons were related to computer time and CAD/CAM — there were insufficient screens for the workload required. This was a relatively minor problem which could be fixed with preventative resources, £28,000 (investing in additional screens), but which had created rework problems for all departments and cost 10 times more.

Overall, COQ measures can help enormously in promoting TQM — but measures must be established and kept up to date.

Workshop on waste and the cost of quality

Every employee takes part in activities which may be grouped under the following headings:

1. Rework: This means doing a job again — this may be because you were not provided with the resources, the correct information etc or perhaps you or others did not have enough time to do the work right first time.

2. Inspection: This activity is basically about rechecking, spotting and inspecting errors in a process or product. You may have to do this before you provide the good or service to other units.

3. Prevention: Identifying problems, finding the cause of the problems, and putting them right once and for all.

ACTIVITY 1

Now, consider what percentage of the day is taken up with each of these three activities.

a. Rework

b. Inspection

c. Prevention

ACTIVITY 2

Think of the activities associated with the following terms and list them under each heading.

a. Rework

b. Inspection

c. Prevention

Fig. 6 Complete the exercise. It should give an interesting view of waste within your organisation

COQ publicity

Collecting data and keeping it to oneself is not a good approach to TQM. The purpose behind using COQ measures is, first, to assess progress and, second, to publicise this to all your people. They must be aware of progress and be kept informed.

Graphical representation should be a predominant feature of any COQ campaign. Computers print out data on A4 and/or A3 paper, and as they look neat, managers pin up these graphs for publicity — but no one can see them. All areas should display COQ progress, monitoring at least 5–7 measures per function. These should be placed in areas where people gather. The data should be understandable and readable at four metres. Keep the graphs up to date and move them every 10 days otherwise people will get used to and ignore them. Most of all, recognise that people who are involved in TQM want to monitor progress — if the news is good they can celebrate. If it is bad they may want to take corrective action of their own choosing.

Monitoring and displaying progress is central to a successful COQ campaign.

COQ pitfalls

Although we have concentrated on why companies go TQ there are a number of pitfalls to avoid.

Don't focus on number crunching Managers must ensure that they don't become obsessed with finding a definitive figure for the COQ. This obsession can become a 'number crunching exercise', which can end in disaster. Collecting figures to prove a point is not always constructive because the method of calculation may be based on false assumptions.

Commitment to TQM is very much a matter of faith, although COQ is important. Being preoccupied with figures and trends coming down will do little to promote the co-operation required. Remember, TQ is chiefly concerned with changing the attitudes and skills of employees to 'right first time'. It is concerned with engendering a culture where prevention is the norm. Spending too much time on statistics can kill enthusiasm. However do remember that these figures are important for focusing on specific progress.

COQ and sales turnover If you compare COQ with turnover and turnover increases because of a new and unexpected project, does this mean that COQ diminishes? In fact it may increase. COQ measures identify problems within a company. If the problems are not solved why should COQ fall?

Many problems can be created when we equate COQ with sales and turnover. It might be appropriate to assess how much time each week you and your colleagues spend on work which can be categorised in terms of error and rework, inspection and prevention. Relate this to a financial measure later.

Trivialising COQ Don't trivialise COQ. When a document needs retyping don't assess its rework value. You are probably concentrating on the 80% of activities which contributes to the 20% of things which add to COQ. What we should be doing is working on key result areas, the 20% of activities which contribute to 80% of COQ. Develop the 'Pareto Principle' to rework and waste.

Competing against others Managers may use COQ in a competitive manner. They develop their own departmental COQ and then start competing with other departments. This is useless and self defeating. Most problems in organisations which contribute to a high COQ are problems shared between departments. As problems are so large, managers are loath to take responsibility. Who wants the responsibility of solving a problem which impacts on other departments? Managers are busy enough anyway. COQ is a company responsibility co-operation rather than competition is the key to reducing COQ.

Measuring like with like When you measure progress over time, be sure you measure like with like. It is probable that your first assessment of COQ is not as accurate as your second, which could be developed after you have become involved in a TQM drive. When you measure progress, compare like with like, otherwise the COQ may appear to increase over time.

Set realistic measures in all areas Finally, when you set goals, ensure that they are achievable and measurable. Develop yardsticks with which others agree. Don't impose your targets. Managers and staff are more committed to working towards their own goals than those picked for them TQM must be user driven.

Ciba Corning Diagnostics world leaders in the manufacture of high quality Diagnostic equipment for measuring body chemistry, recognised a decline in demand for their product in the late 70's. The reason for this was customers were sending back equipment for repair. The cost of getting things wrong was getting out of hand and impacting upon the competitive edge of Corning. Customers were turning to other sources of manufacture, namely the Japanese, who could provide products with zero defects.

Corning estimated that their Cost of Quality cost them 34% of turnover. Considering Corning were making $1.2 bn dollars a year, 'non quality' was costing a staggering $400 m.

Their Quality Drive over recent years has brought their COQ down to single figures while their turnover has gone through the roof. This has improved their competitive edge and consolidated market share.

Fig. 7 TQM success

Summary and bullet points

- Many organisations are unaware of how much it costs them to produce non-quality.
- Cost of quality does not show up on balance sheets, profit and loss accounts or operating statements.
- It could be costing a company as much as 40–50% of sales turnover to get things right.
- TQM has nothing to do with cost reduction.
- Measure the 'intangibles' in the service areas first. This is where the real waste is evident.
- 80–85% of quality problems originate in non-manufacturing areas.
- Cost of quality is greater when there is a great deal of interaction between departments.
- Cost of quality is composed of the costs of errors and rework, the cost of inspection and the cost of prevention.
- Rework and inspection costs can be reduced through an increase in activities and resources devoted to prevention.
- Rework can become the organisational norm characterised by fire-fighting and crisis management. Changing this culture requires a significant increase in preventative-type measures. The investment can decline as the drive for TQM intensifies but the investment at the start should not be minimised.
- We seldom create rework for ourselves. We create it for our internal customers — those next in line who are dependent on the quality of service which we provide. Likewise, our internal suppliers create rework for us. Managing this interaction between departments is what reduces company-wide COQ.
- Reducing rework can create a significant improvement in competitive position, but this will only occur in the long term and will only happen through expenditure of effort.
- All functions should identify COQ measures and keep up to date information on these.
- COQ measures should be displayed to promote quality improvement. Graphs should be accessible to all, and large enough to merit more than a passing interest.
- COQ measurement should not focus on number crunching and exclude meaning.
- TQM is very much a matter of faith and COQ measures should be used initially to communicate progress and maintain enthusiasm.
- If sales turnover increases so will COQ. Unless the underlying problems are resolved between departments, COQ will continue to rise.
- A win-lose mentality should not be created when displaying COQ. Some departments and functions will be more dependent upon the help and support of others to bring their COQ down. For some it will be easy to reduce COQ. Never develop a COQ league table — it will kill the enthusiasm of those who have a harder job to do.
- Try to measure like with like. Over time, the measure of COQ may tend to

rise when everyone thought things were getting better. The COQ measurement may become more thorough and precise and the trend may indicate problems, when in fact all it indicates is the quality of the measure becoming more accurate.

● Set realistic targets.

SECTION 2:
MANAGING THE TRANSITION
TO TQM

4 TQM IS BEHAVIOURAL CHANGE

Certainly, when managers are first confronted with the whole concept of TQM some tend to perceive it as another 'system' which can be grafted onto an organisation. When they are first exposed to BS 5750 and ISO 9000, etc, they tend to relate the quality business to a 'system'. Many soon learn that this is not the case — but others persist in the belief that achieving set standards is what TQM is all about.

When the DTI first launched the Quality Programme in the UK in 1983 there was a great deal of emphasis given to the application of systems. Most of the case studies in glossy brochures and on video tape were based on accreditation to BSI standards. It was not a surprise when standards and systems had been given such hype that people actually started to believe that TQM was simply about standards.

This misconception still persists today. A presentation was given to a group represented by a professional body. The 1 day conference was entitled 'Total Quality Management'. It was a shock to find that 2 out of 4 speakers were asked to speak on achieving BS 5750!

This doesn't mean that standards are not important. Of course they are — they are the framework for many quality systems. 9,000 companies presently hold accreditation in the UK and we know this gives many of their 'customers' confidence to either continue or start doing business with them. Accreditation may well help to improve their competitive edge — but it is only one step on the road to total quality.

Many TQM practitioners think that this 'approach' has created a great number of the problems that we have with commitment. Because BS 5750 was given such prominence, the attention of CEOs was focused on a 'system' for doing things and, as everybody knows, quality problems reside with the QA department. Consequently, there was a general lack of understanding when the reaction of CEOs was to make quality professionals totally responsible for TQ drives. There was a great deal of inconsistency because the National Quality Campaign put so much emphasis on QA — meanwhile the quality gurus, such as Deming, Juran and Crosby, were rejecting this in favour of TQ. The QA manager is the last person who should be made responsible for the new quality initiative. The argument continues and creates the myth that company-wide TQ can be developed through the 'systems' approach and, to some extent, this is the view projected by the Institute of Quality Assurance and the British Quality Association!

The quest for quality is over when you have achieved a 'system'

The trouble is, with some companies, achieving BS5750 can create a belief that the quest for quality is over. Too many documents and certificates adorn reception areas testifying to 'standards' but unfortunately these standards are not always maintained on the shop floor. Critics will immediately reject this claim, but there are companies where accreditation for standards is not always reflected in actual work behaviour.

The 'systems' only argument is one which has raged since the advent of TQM in this country in the mid 70s, and still has not been resolved. However, for a holistic approach it is important to consider the seven S's approach. Athos and Pascale[1] and Peters and Waterman[2] were perhaps the first to use this analysis in describing this approach to organisational change.

The seven S's approach

Strategy, senior officers in organisations can have a good idea of where they want to be in terms of quality in the next 3–5 years but find this difficult to articulate on paper. Consequently, a murky image or vision of what the company is going to achieve in 'Quality' appears but this is never transmitted to paper, discussed and communicated with others. Of course, an option to a

(1) Richard Tanner Pascale and Anthony G. Athos, The Art of Japanese Management, Penguin Business Library, 1986.
(2) T.J. Peters and Robert H. Waterman, In Search of Excellence: Lessons from America's Best Run Companies. New York, Haper & Row, 1982.

company wanting to look at quality at a strategic level is to provide training. Attending courses and defining a strategy is fine, but it needs to be operationalised. Let's assume this is done well — what else do companies tend to do?

Structures, if quality isn't too good we can always restructure and change the responsibility of the QA manager. We can retitle 'Quality Control' as 'Quality Assurance'. We can even change responsibilities. In large organisations we can decentralise the function to plants and locations or centralise in headquarters. Whatever happens, restructuring is a good thing. At least restructuring is doing something, it will create change and companies in Europe and the USA are pretty good at it too! Unfortunately change in structure and responsibility does not always create effective change.

Systems, if things aren't going too well we can develop new systems — apply for new standards and, if all else fails, buy software and hardware which guarantee JIT manufacture.

Much of what has been said is tongue in cheek, but the way companies react to quality problems tends to focus upon the hard S's approach. It is probably the most common reaction in the West to improving quality. This is the same the way we improve technological innovation, manufacturing output, people performance, etc. Generally speaking, until recently, most organisations have tended to focus upon the hard S's, strategy, structure and systems for doing things. It is a good start — but not enough!

Organisations which are truly excellent and strive to improve quality in everything they do include IBM, Motorola, Corning Glass, 3M, Dow Chemical, Toyota, Matsushita, Mitsubishi, Hitachi, ICL, Pedigree Pet Foods, Hewlett Packard, etc. They all use the hard S's approach — but they complement it with the soft S's.

These companies recognised that the hard S's are highly structured and tend to reflect our strengths as managers. We can all analyse, conceptualise, plan, develop systems and critical paths for making things happen. The soft S's approach relates to people and their actions and the roles they play, etc. Improvement does not come from strategy, structure and systems, it comes from the hard S's per se. Improvements in quality, movement in flexibility and creative ideas come from people.

Let's look at the soft S's and see how we can use them to create a TQM culture.

Staff, people are a company's most valuable resource — or so we say! The reality is that all too often we fail to consider just how much we can get from people. To be brutally honest, we don't usually treat them well enough to command 100% commitment from them. If we treated employees well, gave them opportunities to develop and be trained to their full capabilities and gave them control, then we would marvel at their performances. There is sufficient research, for instance, Argyris, Trist and Bamforth, Perrow etc, examining the impact of organisation structure on technology, organisational performance, job satisfaction, alienation and labour turnover, to fill a library. Why is it that we have failed to take account of the 'people' side of the business?

Skills, providing our people with the training in attitude, skills and knowledge is critical if we expect our workforce to be as lively, innovative and knowledgeable as our major competitors — the Japanese. In all honesty we need to improve significantly the training experiences of staff at all levels, provide more resources (see chapter 12 for a detailed review of training implications for TQM) and give people the opportunity to 'get on with it' — rather than stand in their way.

Style, This is probably the most critical of all the soft S's. Here we are suggesting that the management or leadership style of those driving TQM through the organisation will determine the rate at which TQ is accepted. Chapter 6 deals with style and leadership issues.

Shared values, overall, the purpose is to create a new organisational culture where quality of product and service is valued. This means we have to examine the culture, identify the predominant value system and replace it, if necessary, with a forward thinking, preventative culture which is geared to continuous improvement. (This is the focus of chapter 10.)

Organisations which take equal cognizance of the blending together of the hard and soft S's will stand a much greater chance of making TQ a dominant force within the culture. Those companies who rely more on the hard S's will have tremendous difficulty in establishing success in the long term. They will also find it a difficult task to get the workforce to take it seriously, for the simple reason that the senior officers will be using a mechanistic solution to solving a human problem.

Being self critical

The key to TQ rests within each of us. Quality does not happen because of applying a particular technique. Utilising 'Failure Mode Effect Analysis' or Taguchi methodology will not create TQ. What each of us does with the technique and how we involve others determines success.

In order to succeed, we all need to be self critical. If we fail to question our assumptions and the values we hold we will probably fail. Too much attention can be spent looking for the fault — or what causes non-quality — and after the solution has been found we spend an inordinate amount of time allocating blame.

The allocating blame culture

If we spend time allocating blame how can we expect people to be self critical and talk about possible improvement? In chapter 12 the focus is on members of staff being open and trusting in training workshops, picking up on a problem in their immediate area of work where progress can be made and doing something about it.

They are encouraged to take corrective action — to stop non-quality — or take preventative action so that the problem never arises again. It is extremely unlikely that staff will be open and trusting in a fear-driven culture, where admission of working in a non-TQM manner is an almost certain guarantee of replacement and/or an extremely bad time from direct supervisors.

Perhaps this attitude is most prevalent at meetings, where managers and supervisors are present, not just to transact business, but to 'cover the backs' of their departments. Loyalty is often not a corporate ideal, but departmentalised. People have to feel 'loyalty' to their function and this is encouraged by the presence of strong norms. Anyone going against these strongly held values, norms and behaviours is classed as disloyal — even if their actions are in the best interests of the company in the long term. Killing this culture is imperative. Failing to do so — patting each other on the back so that nobody is critical of himself — creates a culture which discourages change.

People are boss watchers!

Everyone watches everybody else and, in particular, most people are 'boss watchers'. They watch to see what the boss does or says. If he fails to be self critical and will not admit to being able to do better, improve performance and stop doing things which hurt the company and other departments, then there is little chance that others will be sold on the idea of TQ.

Even before we get started, some effort should be made to unfreeze the old culture. Chairing a table of senior officers who all nod at the right time is not what commitment to change is all about. Commitment to change — whether it be a commitment to lose weight, to quit smoking, to get 'fitter', to lead a stress-free life — is only actualised when a person is open about the way he or she is currently living. In other words, they verbalise a need to change the way they do things.

People can only change when they are ready to reject their present behaviour as being undesirable or harmful. If they feel their behaviour is not creating harm to themselves or others, there is little incentive to change the way they do things. For instance, the successful treatment of alcoholics only starts when the alcoholic admits that he is dependent upon alcohol. People only give up smoking when they realise the high health risks and dangers of failing to do so.

Creating a TQ company requires the same commitment. We all know how difficult it is to give up smoking, cut back on eating or reduce our consumption of alcohol, etc. It is not easy — although in simple terms all we need to do is stop putting food in our mouths, refrain from opening that bottle of wine, or tie up the running shoes, open the front door and put one foot in front of the other, and so forth. However, changing these little things is not easy. Once we have acquired a habit it is difficult to break.

If these 'personal things' are difficult to change, how easy is it for us to change the really difficult things like the way we manage, the way we talk to people, the way we prioritise and the way we solve problems, etc.? It's extremely difficult. This is perhaps the biggest reason why TQM initiatives don't provide the results for which we hope. We need to look realistically at changes which are necessary.

Words and workshops change nobody

Running training sessions and projecting the TQ ideal is interesting and satisfying, but never easy. When we talk of the features and the need for TQ it is with relative ease. When we look at implementation, we often find that there can be disagreement about the likelihood of certain actions happening. Some people, but not all, are pessimistic in outlook, look back at company behaviour throughout their employment and come to a quick conclusion that change is never going to happen.

Some pessimistic souls take us back in time to the '60s and the '70s and paint pictures of MBO, quality circles, participative management and team briefings being good initiatives which were introduced in the organisation but failed for a host of reasons. Genuinely, if people express this problem in workshops you cannot sweep it under the carpet. You have to debate it and other issues openly.

It is believed that each of us has to influence, discuss and reason with people — you can't run a successful training programme without answering objections. You can't run the programme over them. We should use the challenge to persuade, discuss and debate the key issues. Airing feelings and anxieties and discussing them is the only way to introduce TQ. Sometimes admission of past mistakes will give the workforce the confidence to give TQM a good try.

In a 'Blame Driven Culture' it is not unusual to spend 75% of the time managing change in discussion and debate with participants. Failing to do this creates a belief that the 'trainer' is there to present a case and do little else. This reinforces the old culture: things being done 'to you' rather than 'with you'.

Now the point which is important is how much change do we create? In all honesty some training sessions produce little in terms of tangible results, (reasons explained in chapter 12) apart from a commitment to think about things and to improve 'something' within the immediate work environment.

How can we expect the 7–8 hours of a training day to create the 'inspired action-man' who will reject the 'old behaviour' and become TQ orientated overnight? This is certainly unrealistic.

Fig. 1 shows a strong relationship between the difficulty of changing those things about ourselves and the time taken to make the change. The more difficult the change the longer it takes!

For instance, it is relatively easy to get people to 'feel' good about change and, in particular, TQ. TQ makes good sense and is not founded upon ivory tower conceptualisation. TQM trainers should be able to make people feel good about the concept. They can then go away from the training session with a warm glow and an inner commitment to the words and arguments — but unfortunately this doesn't mean that change will take place. Change happens when people do things differently. Taking people beyond the 'feeling' stage requires some form of self direction to do something, to get and to see results. Getting people to do 'one thing' differently is not so easy. Agreeing to apply a concept in an area and to report back later on progress should not be difficult in theory too but, believe me, it can be difficult in practice.

Getting people to do not just one thing right, but to adopt the new behaviour as a consistent way of working, takes a long time. If managers and staff have a 'role model' upon whom they can model their own behaviour — someone who leads by example and reinforces good behaviour — then the chance of success is high. The absence of a 'role model', adverse or critical comments from senior managers or supervisors will quickly be leapt upon by those who 'want TQM to fail'.

Overall, we need to remember that people are 'boss watchers'. If the boss says one thing and does another — there is ambiguity in words and deeds. Be sure, too, this information will be fed back to others and will spread like wild fire! Information which confirms the prejudice about change, and reinforces the belief in the 'old culture', will make TQM a 90-day wonder.

Consistent behaviour is one thing, but changing management style, attitude and values is something else. It takes time. People do not change as quickly as

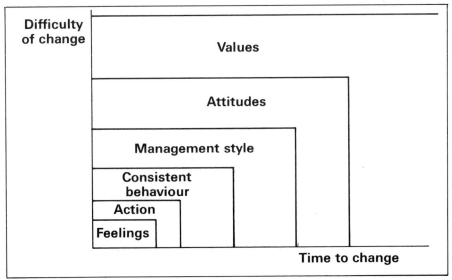

Fig. 1 Case: Fear of being open

we would like them to. So, we need to develop conditions to promote change. This is easier said than done, but a failure to create a readiness for change will delay the benefits of TQM from taking hold.

In order to facilitate the transition to TQ, we must examine why people resist change.

Members of a management team agreed they would develop 5-7 COQ measures each within their immediate work areas. They were all based in manufacturing areas and should have found it comparatively easy. They were provided with handouts of how to develop COQ measures. Six weeks later, only 40% reported back with the measures. Why was there a 60% failure rate? They found too many reasons/excuses not to provide the data! "Too busy", etc. In effect they did not want to do it. Why? It transpired several months later that they were concerned about what the data would be used for and who would see it at corporate headquarters.

Resistance to total quality

People resist change for a host of reasons — let's explore these and put forward tentative solutions.

Fear, the first thing which people do when they hear of change is personalise it and say, "How does it affect me?" Unsubstantiated rumours, which are not confirmed or rejected, add to a situation where the worst possible scenario is perceived. Simply by talking with people about the likely outcomes is sufficient to put them at ease. This means we have to think carefully before sending out messages. We need to communicate the same message without deviation and develop briefing sessions which 'dot the Is' and 'cross the Ts'.

Perceived loss of control, when change comes about there is a real loss of control. Prior to changes, people perceive they have some security in what they do. Change means doing things differently, creating new knowledge and information which has to be learned and applied. It is to be expected that people will be concerned. What we need to do is specify what changes will take place and how this will impact upon work. Even if we don't know the full extent of changes over time, we should be able to point to a few non-threatening examples which we can communicate to others.

Personal uncertainty, this is best summarised as, "Can I live up to the expectations of others? Am I competent to do the new things?" Here the anxiety is internalised. People have heard grand phrases — examples of Japanese and other organisations committed to TQ. We project continuous improvement statistics which are hard to believe. We hear talk of the work of 'Corrective Action Teams', etc. It should be no surprise that employees feel as they do and have some self doubts.

The solution here is to tell people how long the change will take, the likely consequences, the gap between present performance and future expectations, and the actions the organisation is taking to help staff at all levels rise up the learning curve. Above all, gradual change is an important factor which must be reinforced. People cannot change in a day — so why frighten them into believing that they need to?

It may mean more work! It most certainly will! Companies do not become world leaders and renowned for quality without a great deal of expenditure of effort from their most valuable and flexible resource — their people.

There will be times when TQ will appear to be backsliding. For every two steps forward — you may slide back two and a half. If TQ were so easy we would have done it years ago — so don't build up unrealistic expectations. We all know we have to pursue preventative type activities in order to get things right first time. Doing so reduces rework in the long term. There is not a straight substitution of preventative activities for rework.

In reality, we have to put 10 times more effort into the preventative activities to reduce rework, for the simple reason that rework has been in the culture for so long it is difficult to change. We do need to expend 10 times more energy, at least initially, to remove old practices. The old culture and its procedures, departmentalisation and demarcation lines will reject the collaborative preventative approach — so the 10:1 ratio is not so unrealistic.

Past resentments, how often have you heard the phrase, "I'm not working with the guys from personnel — they are too interested in scoring points"; or "The marketing people really let me down on the customer tour — I'm not exposing my customers to those prima donnas again. They did no preparation at all"; or the good old stereotype about manufacturing, "They work well on a day to day basis — but they really don't have an appreciation of the problems we have in our preventative maintenance programme."

My concern is that there is a lack of trust between units and departments — a concern that working with 'others', even within the same company, may inhibit our effectiveness.

What is most concerning is that this departmental/functional or location stereotyping is counter productive. It is hard to believe that the organisation exists to meet the needs of all — that a team effort will bring prosperity and security for everybody. If we could break down these false, destructive and negative barriers and practice more horizontal management, i.e. spending time working on cementing lateral relations, then we may be able to benefit from TQM. Failing to work with others, inventing and reinforcing negative stereotypes does nothing for TQM. Utilising the negative energy in a positive way is a sure method of making the change to TQM.

Flavour of the month, this is a very common attitude and difficult to defeat if an organisation has been known for its short-term commitment to a variety of programmes. What happens is that a new fad creeps into management circles and, without proper appraisal, assumptions are made, packages and videos are purchased and everyone is hit with the fad. Unfortunately, this does not last long. It may well have worked if it had been given a chance, more resources and time, but it failed. Using short-term criteria for measuring performance really killed it. Especially when managers said, "What impact did it have on bottom line results?" Luckily, it fails just in time to catch onto the next 'flavour'.

TQM dead by 1993, if sufficient people discredit TQM because they fail to give it a chance — they treat it as a current 'flavour' or give the idea little support and resources when required — by 1993 TQM will be no more than a 3-letter abbreviation from which companies will steer clear. Bad reputations for ineffective change strategies spread quickly and the major opportunity for improving the competitive edge of many companies will not have been given a chance.

The only way to avoid this is to plan, plan and plan again. Communicate these plans, the visions and the practicalities to all your people. Remember, if you promise something by a set time, you must deliver.

It may go away if I ignore it, suffice to say that this is a natural reaction from those subject to the 'flavour' approach. This phrase is destructive because the attitude of the person is so geared to failure. The only way to resolve this is to lead by example. Failing to do so will confirm the negative prejudices.

Unwilling to 'take ownership' and be committed, this is a very strong attitude sometimes experienced at supervisory levels. Supervisors and first line managers have been 'in between' for too long. They have to satisfy conflicting demands of management, "Produce it and ship it on time — but it has to be the right quality," while at the same time being in the unfortunate position of having their resources reduced through 'cost reduction programmes'. These conflicting goals, together with dealing with problems from the shop floor, can be an unbearable burden — especially when they know that their purpose is to 'absorb conflict' rather than pass it up the management hierarchy.

Supervisors can see it as just one more chore — knowing commitment is skin deep. The actions needed to clear this image are obvious and revolve round being the first to demonstrate real change.

Case study: total quality and cost reduction

Some time was spent talking with the total quality manager of a computer manufacturer. It was noticed that his department was adjacent to the cost reduction department.

Apparently, both departments would appear to use the same strategies for achieving aims which are inconsistent with each other. For instance, the cost reduction department will recommend that head count be reduced in a key manufacturing area. The person who goes does much cleaning up — keeping workstations fresh, tidy and free from clutter. Six months later, the same person is brought back as a 'preventative measure' to aid manufacturing, taking pressure off assembly workers.

Clearly, someone somewhere should be co-ordinating things — this should be settled once and for all. Nobody appears to be taking ownership!

It's your responsibility, the most common time to hear this is when those in control of service areas suddenly realise that TQ might have something to do with them. They quickly get hold of the QA manager and ask him to pay a visit. The visit is composed of 5 minutes listening to the QA manager and then passing the responsibility to others.

If there is no QA manager available, blame will be attached to the shop floor. Proof of this will be instamatic photographs of scrap bins, disorderly tool handling, damaged tools, dirty drawings, poor housekeeping, men standing waiting for setters to tool up, men waiting for urgent supplies of components, and lorries bringing back reject goods from customers, etc. Little attempt will be made to be self critical and appraise quality in the service area.

Here it is obvious that not all the management team have got the message. Those in charge of non-manufacturing areas project, non-verbally, the difficulty of identifying waste and the subsequent measures required for monitoring progress. Hands are thrown up in horror. Faces wrinkle. Heads shake with disbelief that waste can occur in areas other than manufacturing. This can be particularly pronounced in accounts, marketing, data processing, and research and development.

The answer lies in collecting data at the audit stage to convince leaders of service functions that they have a part to play in promoting TQ.

"First you change, then I will", this is a variant of "You put your hand in the fire ... then I will" and is sure to lead to non-activity. It is founded on the belief that if someone is strong enough to oppose the action required this will create the stimulus for total inactivity. Just to be safe — to avoid being branded a 'Luddite' — different members of the management team take it in turn to reject proposals and be identified as the instigator.

If allowed to continue, people fail to turn up for meetings, physically withdrawing; others turn up half heartedly, psychologically withdrawing from the commitment; others turn up with half the promised information, suggesting that data collection was too difficult and besides, "We have to spend our time on real work ... not discounting the 'tremendous business pressures' with which we have to work on a day to day basis." These are all fine excuses for doing nothing!

A simple solution — the CEO fires the first person who fails to do what he has promised. A bit extreme you may say — but what else would move such a comfortable culture?

"They will find out that what I have been doing over the years is wrong. I could be penalised", very rarely is this verbalised, but it is evident. Moving from a strong culture based on 'Cover Your Ass' (CYA), where blame is the norm and punitive measures are a day by day occurrence, is not easy. Moving from a culture where people are fired for doing wrong things, i.e. sending out defective equipment but knowing if they had quarantined it they would have been given hell anyway! — to a climate where problem identification is encouraged is alien to many supervisors. Who can blame them for their concerns? This behaviour and treatment is real to them. In times when redundancy is not uncommon, when older managers and supervisors are let go, it is not surprising that few managerial staff are willing to orchestrate their own 'end' by admitting to generating non-quality actions.

Trust is the only way of resolving this problem. This takes time. Knowing that resistance is evident, and indeed is normal, is important for both internal and external change agent.

Change is not easy — but at least an appreciation of why people resist change gives us all scope to erode these 'resisters' before TQ is introduced.

Assessing the readiness for TQM through organisational values and culture

We have made some effort to project the importance of the soft side of the organisation and indeed, change will not take place until actions have been taken to recognise this. This leads us to the terms 'Organisational Values and Culture' which may mean little to many people. They seem to conjure up the image of woolliness and intangibility. People speak a great deal about 'managerial values' and 'organisational culture' but find them hard to define. Select any 10 people within an organisation and ask them to write down statements or phrases which reflect the managerial values and the culture of the organisation. In many cases you will get 10 disjointed views.

What does this tell us? That those who manage the organisation do not see it fitting, or of value to promote, a common view of how its managers and employees should do things. It also tells us that by some magical process the spirit of co-operation is created throughout the company and somehow comes together at the right time. Companies today need to consider organisational culture and values as being the real issue for change in the 1990s.

Summary and bullet points

- TQ is not something which can be created by a system or an accreditation system.
- Quality systems can be a route which companies take to implement TQ but form only 1 step of the process.
- TQ is a philosophy of getting things right first time, every time. It has to be owned by everybody within the organisation — whether departments are service or manufacturing based.
- The seven S's form a good approach to implementing TQ.
- Don't rely too much on the hard S's to the exclusion of the soft.
- Strategy, structure and systems will give the basis for a TQ approach —but they are just the framework upon which to build.
- TQ comes from people. Creativity, flexibility, teamwork, participation, continuous improvement and leadership are critical. Without staff, skills, style and shared values, TQ will never give the benefits it could.
- Turning a company round and rejecting the culture which allocates blame, rather than working together to put things right, is the right path to follow.
- People are 'boss watchers'. They recognise that deeds and actions reflect 'Total Commitment'.
- Change is not easy — it's difficult enough giving up personally damaging habits. Asking people to change the way they do things at work is more difficult and takes time.
- Be patient. Necessary change never came easy.
- Be aware that resistance to change is natural. This does not mean it is desirable — but accept it. Diagnose the reasons for it and do something positive to break it down.
- It's a reality of life that people fear change. Prove them wrong and communicate your intentions.
- Change will mean a temporary loss of control — especially for people in supervisory and managerial positions. Take them with you. Communicate and inform frequently. Learn to listen attentively to their concerns and address these.
- Living up to TQ is not easy. Examine the concerns and the training needs of staff at all levels and address them now.
- Whoever tells you TQ will not mean more work, at least in the short term, is not being realistic. Nothing good ever came by chance — certainly not the cultural transition we are talking about. Additional time and resources must be found to make things work.
- Bury old resentments between functions and personalities. TQ is not about reliving the past and reinforcing old stereotypes. It is about developing a more secure future — for us all.
- TQ should be here to stay. In some cases it may appear to be 'flavour of the month' but, overall, 99% perspiration and 1% inspiration will improve your performance.
- Once a company is committed to TQ, it will not go away. It's there to stay. Remember what it can do for you and your people, and progress it every

day — even by only a small percentage.

- At first everyone has doubts about the role he/she can play. But persevere —don't ignore your contribution, however small. Seize TQ as an opportunity to make things happen — all the things you would want to do if you were the chief executive.

- Remember, everybody has a responsibility to create change. It does not matter where you are in the structure — you can do something to make your company more competitive and become a better place in which to work.

- Reject the old idea of "You change before I do." It is negative and self defeating.

- Every day try to find one reason to make TQ work. You may be surrounded by some who find 10 ways to make it fail!

- Do what you can in your own way to reward people for their successes. Avoid the negative attitude of finding fault.

- Project the belief that TQM is not about penalising the wrong doer but is about putting things right. Celebrate the achievements which people make.

- Assess the culture and values of the organisation. Do your best to build on the good positive parts of the culture and work on destroying the negative parts.

5 MANAGING CULTURAL CHANGE

What is organisational culture and why is it important in promoting TQ? Culture sums up the 'way organisations function'. It has been defined as "The way we get things done around here." If we want to promote TQM we have to go some way towards promoting a culture where people feel free to contribute their ideas, where involvement in problem solving and decision making is the norm. Culture is the set of values, behaviours and norms which make an organisation tick.

We can all tell a good culture from a bad one. Most of us have walked into organisations and quickly come to conclusions about how things are achieved. We create an instant picture of what we see and feel. Perhaps the biggest indicator of culture, at least at a fairly superficial level, is when people attend for a job interview. Most get a good idea whether it is the sort of place they can work or not. It is somehow like a 'sixth sense'. Culture is difficult to pinpoint — but it does stand out. People do tend to trust intuition and feelings to make decisions — they don't tend to base their judgements just on objective senses.

Culture and artifacts, signs and symbols

Organisational artifacts are those things which stand out and indicate certain ways of working — these are signs or symbols which the organisation displays either consciously or not. If some companies recognised the impact of some of their 'symbols' of culture to outsiders, they would certainly consider a cultural audit!

Artifacts, symbols and company culture can be summed up in terms of office design, display of messages, architecture, posters, messages to employees, allocation and proximity of car parking spaces, office decor and open door policy, etc.

To examine culture and its impact upon people, consider how people are dealt with at the reception area of a company. How friendly do employees appear to be? Do receptionists use titles frequently or less often? Do they project the informal first name approach? These tell us much about company culture.

When phoning a company, the response of people answering the phone, the concern for taking messages, the promptness of a response all say something about their concern for you. Their behaviour also tells you a little bit about how they are treated as well. Other symbols of culture and concern for people are the cleanliness of staff eating areas, up-to-date noticeboards, safety reporting and posters, etc. — they all portray a picture of what is important and encouraged and what is not. The interesting point is that we can all pick up the cultural vibes. Many senior officers in companies are not aware that many of the 'vibes' are not deliberate — they may be negative in nature but the company is not aware of the intensity. Given a choice, in many cases, companies would surpress the poor cultural image they portray.

Changing the symbols to create cultural change

When a new plant manager started at a US-owned UK plant the first thing he did was to create change. He said that everybody was waiting for him to do something — it did not matter what it was, just an indication of how things were going to be from this time on. He changed the car parking allocations.

Subsequently all the customer and visitor spaces were to be adjacent to the reception — not a quarter of a mile away from the entrance. "This," he said, "is to ensure that our customers recognise themselves as being important." The second thing he did was revolutionary! He located all the senior officers of the company at the far end of the car park, approximately a 4 minute walk to the reception area. There were to be no exceptions; these were the allocated spaces.

When asked why he did this, he replied, "There is a good chance that the officers may bump into some of their people on the way in and out everyday — it will give them the opportunity to talk. They have never seemed to have the time before."

It is possible to create significant change in an environment by influencing just one or two things.

The culture breaker: kick the sherry habit

The newly appointed training manager in a financial services company decided that enough was enough in terms of organisational culture. He had recently taken responsibility for creating change to promote team development in what had been a very stable and traditional business with little change in the 1960s and '70s. There had been plenty of indication that the culture suited a bygone age. The old culture was strongly autocratic with a heavy dose of departmentalism. He and others were in charge or turning this into a thriving, breathing, entrepreneurial environment — where teamwork and motivation were key values. He looked at the culture and one sign seemed to say it all. 'Sherry at lunch time'.

Now this guy was not a killjoy but he asked himself why managers drank sherry at lunch-time. It was a sign of the old culture, part of the organisational heritage — which is fine for a Christmas party but not to be encouraged in a business which was experiencing severe competition. Should managers drink at lunch-time? The training manager was clearly of the opinion that replacing sherry with soft drinks was reasonable behaviour — and one way to tell managers that things were changing.

The soft drinks were provided. This small change created so much movement in management circles that he is still renowned as the guy who killed an 80-year-old tradition. This one action won him the nickname of 'Rambo'. It was only a small start but people became aware that he meant business and that the company was being serious about changing to a new approach to 'doing things'.

Disorganised factory floor

Consider going onto a factory floor where we find that 'housekeeping' is less than perfect, where everybody is running round in a mad frenzy and where the great majority of staff is involved in chaotic fire-fighting. This tells us about how the organisation is run and what is important in the enterprise.

First impressions tell us a great deal and are usually a good impression upon which we can make judgements. These are only the superficial, outward signs of what is important but they tell us a great deal about how we manage.

A social example

Consider for one minute a social, not business, context. You are attending a restaurant in town with your spouse. Your first impressions as you walk through the door are that it is poorly lit, wallpaper and decor is past its best and rancid smells permeate the building. Those outward signs of the culture and atmosphere of the restaurant tell us much about the likely care and attention which the 'owner' will lavish upon us during our meal.

Now there are always exceptions to the general case — but how many people at a first visit would stay to sample the haute cuisine? Probably very few. This example is not very different from the organisational experience.

The culture indicates certain behaviours and suggests particular values which guide behaviour. These are the assumptions which we make about a company and they are the visible signs which employees pick up and live with.

Robert and the 'Coke' cans

Robert was in charge of TQ within an engineering company. It was noted on a trip to the factory floor that there were a great many 'Coke' cans in the work-in-progress bins. Robert took photographs of the locations and displayed them on the noticeboard with the message, "Coca Cola plant" — it seemed to do the trick.

Interestingly, whenever he wanted some of the manufacturing and quality control people to take an interest in the work they were doing, he would orchestrate a 'walkabout' past the scrap bins. Robert was tall and noticeable. His presence would create an interest which would then focus attention on waste and quality improvement.

Culture, management style and assumptions

Management style is driven very much by the 'assumptions' we make about how things should be done and the culture and values which underpin them.

We all know bad, negative or weak cultures when we experience them, but they are not always the same. A strong culture can be negative as well as positive — it is just that certain things stand out.

Cultural change is the secret to implementing TQM. First make some attempt to decide on changes which are required within the culture — what is it that you can change about those things which project a low interest in quality? Change to those things which convey the TQM message and reinforce your changes with 'leading by example'.

Creating a culture

Changing cultures is easier said than done. Most cultures have been around for a long time. Founders of companies create the original cultures. The beliefs of the founder and the senior management team are translated into rules and systems, norms, style of managing, etc. These are passed on to people who join the company — whether the values which underpin the culture are consciously driven or hidden.

Turnover and cultural loss

One problem which cultures suffer from is people leaving the company. The higher the turnover at certain levels, the more the culture needs to be reinforced. One nationwide sales organisation has a turnover of 25% for sales executives per year. Bearing in mind the 'demographic timebomb' (the shortage of good quality staff) and the difficulty of attracting good people into the south east of England, the company decided to do something about its culture. Realising that for people to stay in the company they needed to feel there was a place for them now and in the future, the company used assessment centres, succession planning and career development to formulate a development plan for each member of its staff. It rejected the idea of just 'throwing money' at the problem and offering higher salaries for jobs. Changing the culture to be caring and developing helped somewhat in retention of staff who may otherwise have been attracted elsewhere.

Knowing where turnover is highest in the company, the levels of people who tend to move on and the reasons for moving can help us isolate key areas for change. The purpose being to strengthen the company by changing personnel policy.

For instance, staff at the lower levels of a company hierarchy in a service area will need to have the culture reinforced on a day to day level. However, it is not unusual for the culture in sales and marketing to be quite high in comparison to other units. If there are problems in these two areas the overall problem is more serious.

While working with one service company, we witnessed an event in a training session which said much about company culture. Representatives of the credit control unit and marketing were present and it was evident that there was a lot of negative stereotyping between the units.

Credit control was very strict about how work was carried out. There were strict demarcations between jobs and work was very serious and not much fun. The marketing unit was noisy and always seemed to be partying. There was a mutual dislike between the units and the company had to do something about it. There was no commonality between the cultures. The units were housed in the same building on the same floor but there was little involvement between unit members. Clearly this was a case where unit heads had to take some responsibility for making things happen. They came up with a simple strategy — get each of their senior staff to make a point of meeting with someone different from the other unit each week. The meetings would take 15–20 minutes with the purpose of exchanging information about each other. These sessions grew and people started to meet informally and to view each other differently.

Traditional cultures

Many traditional companies portray the old culture which is not exactly geared up for TQM. Symptoms include poor layout and design of office and manufacturing areas, dirty and uncared for staff facilities and poor lighting and environmental conditions, etc.

This can be further reinforced by managerial behaviour. Behaviour is erratic and geared to achieving short-term results. Ends are more important than means and punitive measures are the major ways of getting things done. Tie this in with outmoded procedures — a commitment to repair instead of preventative maintenance and a 'that will do attitude' — and the story and the culture start to unfold. This is a pretty negative culture. You can bet that people won't hang around at the end of the day.

However, things are not always so obvious. For instance, a temporary secretary was not looking forward to working with a client. The word was that this company had a bad name for man management and that when secretaries were given assignments they felt that they had drawn the short straw. On the other hand, things did not seem so bad — there was another company which was even worse. Rose, the secretary, told a horrifying tale of being in a secretarial pool for five weeks during which time very few people talked to her, including managers. Her first contact with management was an interesting one too. She was approached at great speed by a balding grey-haired manager who thrust a typed document at her and said, "Are you RB?" (her initials) "Correct this and bring it to me straight away." Needless to say these stories spread and help create a culture which may not be too flattering.

Cultures are created by heroes and anti-heroes

Culture can be good and bad but its growth or continuation is dependent upon the stories which pass around about the people who propagate the culture. Deal and Kennedy describe these stories as 'legends'. Often these legends are stories about critical incidents which have taken place in a company. These 'legends' become part of the company. The more frequently they are told and retold the more credence the legend has. This reinforces company culture and the 'how we do things round here' phenomenon. The legends tell people in the company what is acceptable behaviour and what the culture will permit. Legends also feature people as the key movers in the stories. People and their actions demonstrate what is okay and what is not. Cultures can't exist without people doing things. Those who make stories alive can be described as heroes and heroines — but only if the stories are positive. If the stories are negative then we have an anti-hero — and we all know too many of them!

Stories originate and abound. For instance, "Did you hear about John and the way he closed the sale with Websters. It was textbook stuff. It got the company right off the hook and the commission was the highest anybody has been paid." These stories and legends abound. Even if the hero leaves, the story continues. Stories like this are legion in really positive companies. They are told and retold always with a positive message — but what about the other side of the coin?

We can all think of stories which reflect the company in good light but there are other stories which reinforce the belief that people are working in a negative culture — where nobody cares. These legends abound too. "Hey, did you hear about Bert? He tried to get all those drinks at lunch-time put on the food bill. Will that guy stop at nothing. He cheats the company all the time."

This story can always be bettered by others in the immediate vicinity who either reinforce the negative element of the story or introduce another 'legend' which puts Bert in a bad light.

Believing the worst!

This can be really dangerous for companies. People join all the time. Suppliers and customers are often treated to these revelations about managers and this creates a bad impression. In all honesty, if we are told about a person whom we have never met, and the stories we hear are negative, very few of us will be open and objective when we finally are introduced to this individual.

There will be a tendency to use 'selective perception' and look for data which confirm what we have been told.

It is imperative that companies examine the culture they project, because the culture and legends which support it are transmitted to others who make business decisions about the company.

The type of culture also gives us an indication of whether TQ will be successful or not and where it may fail.

Culture and the Japanese

Anyone who has taken a trip round a Japanese company committed to the TQM concept will immediately note an open and trusting climate, where teamwork and interdependence is encouraged. How else could it win the commitment of its people to generate literally thousands of new ideas for making things better?

On a trip round a Toyota plant in Japan, it was hard to believe how people could avoid getting involved in continuous improvement. A visit to Kawasaki Steel told a similar story. How was it that the environment was so clean, that newly drawn posters proclaiming 'quality improvement' were tidy and free from dust and that the area for coffee and lunch breaks was as pleasant as a modern office in any high-tec company?

The Japanese have no special advantage over us in their country. Many, however, continue to claim that it is impossible to create the TQM culture in Western companies. The culture, they say, is something unique to Japan.

Nonsense. Take a trip around any Mitsubishi, National Panasonic, Hitachi, Nissan plant in the West and you will find a culture propagated by Westerners.

MAKING JAPAN'S MAGIC WORK IN THE U.S.

In the early 1980s, when U.S. carmakers called for their Japanese counterparts to produce cars in the United States, they argued that it was only fair that the Japanese should build where they sold, just as General Motors and Ford did in Europe. But they had another motive as well: They assumed that the move would wipe out much of Japan's competitive edge. They were convinced that Japan's unique culture was responsible for its economic success. If Japanese auto makers had to leave behind their homogeneous, well-educated, compliant work force, and employ unruly, less dedicated, unionized Americans, the productivity of their workers and the quality of their cars would plummet. And so would their sales.

That's not quite the way it worked out. Instead, Japanese transplants have taken firm root in American soil and are expanding rapidly. Eight Japanese carmakers are now operating assembly plants in North America, either independently or with U.S. partners. Output at these plants is expected to hit 1.5 million cars this year and 2.1 million by 1991.

Japanese management, it turned out, was as exportable as its products. Its guiding principles — granting employees broad authority to organize their tasks and insisting on high quality from workers and suppliers — are now proving themselves in towns such as Marysville, Ohio, where Honda is building Civics and Accords with quality levels nearly equal to those from Japan. And in Fremont, Calif., Toyota managers in a joint venture with General Motors have turned a former GM plant with a history of labor strife and shoddy quality into a showplace of quality and productivity. Given an opportunity to contribute, the plant's American workers — about 50% black and Hispanic — have proved their worth in ways that flowed through to the bottom line.

Fortunately, there are signs that American auto makers are beginning to learn from the success of their Japanese rivals in the U.S. (page 30). Progress is slow, and much more has to be done in such fields as labor and supplier relations, technology management, and innovation. But the most important lesson has clearly been absorbed: Using American workers, it can happen here.

Fig. 1 International Business Week — August 14 1988

An article in *International Business Week* (see Fig. 1) reports that the workers of Nissan's Smyrna plant in Tennesee have formed anti-union groups which demonstrate to reject the idea of unionism within their own company. It would appear that the employee commitment to the culture is so strong that people are taking part of it home with them. They reject any form of organised opposition to their culture. There is also evidence to suggest that the values inherent in the culture are rapidly being adopted by employees as 'personal values'.

Organisational culture creating personal values

When Corning Glass (now Ciba Corning Diagnostics) were implementing its educational programme reflecting TQ, a story existed of a married couple who were working together in the same company. The husband worked in the manufacturing operation and the wife in an administrative role. The training really impacted upon this couple. The strength of the training and, in particular, the emphasis placed upon changing values became so powerful that the couple chose to re-evaluate their lives together.

The values inherent in TQ acted as a catalyst for the couple who had clearly never given much thought to their 'value systems' prior to that time. There were many more examples of how the TQ drive at Corning created change in the way people did things — not just in their work but in their total lives.

Values: the building blocks of culture

This takes us to the building blocks of culture, the value system which predominates within an organisation. Not many people give much thought to the key values but they are critical in helping to manage change — but only if people live up to them.

What are values? They are stable, long-term beliefs that are hard to change. Values cannot be proven or disproven — but they can be refuted or substantiated by the actions of key people in the organisation. They define what is 'right' or 'wrong', 'good' or 'bad' and 'correct' or 'incorrect'. Values are often hard to articulate in words but still have a great deal of influence in how we behave and how we run our organisation.

Organisational values constitute the 'culture' of the organisation — the set of beliefs that people share about what sort of behaviour is 'correct' and 'incorrect'.

A group of managers brainstormed the factors they thought important in indicating the predominant culture within a company. The results are listed below.

Atmosphere: Did it feel good? Was it a nice place to work?
Ethos: The way things were laid out
Spirit or teamwork
Warmth and friendship
Ideals: Company messages and how they were displayed
Management style: What people did, not what they said
How they talk to you: The tone and manner of communication
Listening to us: Is there evidence?
Attitudes to employees portrayed through noticeboards
Involvement: Did people incorporate the ideas of others?
Ambience: Was it a nice place to be?
Telephone response: Speed, nice or nasty
Promises not kept — especially between departments
Events: Was there evidence of a corporate get-together?
Criteria for selection/appraisal: Was it a pleasant experience?
Type of communication
Negative rumours and the failure to address them
Reception: Staff entrances and goods inwards and outwards
Stereotypes of departments: What is projected by opinion leaders?
Answering the phone: Was there a concern for helping?
Tidyness in all areas
Clutter in non-manufacturing areas
Participation: Did people participate?
Belonging: Did they feel at home?
Motivation: The process — was it carrot or stick?
Shared corporate values: Were they known by all and displayed?

Fig. 2 Indicators of corporate culture

When these organisational beliefs conflict with individual personal values, people are likely to distance themselves psychologically from the organisation. There is a fundamental rift between employee and employer. There is a failure to share the same beliefs and ways of doing things. The response by many is reflected in the symptoms of withdrawal. Here, the presence of the '9 to 5' attitude, the 'us and them' syndrome, the 'work to rule mentality', the 'not invented here' attitude, resistance to change, aggressiveness in labour disputes and sheer obstinacy are the most obvious examples!

If employees do perceive a conflict of values, they can usually accommodate this but fail to be committed to the goals and aspirations of the organisation in the long term. They will see the role they play in the company as a means to an end and at this stage their commitment will cease.

Culture and people

The observed behaviour of people can be deceptive. Although, on the surface, people may tend to project the '9 to 5' mentality, show little creativity in their work and fail to come up with suggestions, etc., it does not mean they are not capable of doing so. It means they choose not to. Many people who attend work are imaginative and display enthusiasm when working on projects they enjoy — probably outside work! They will throw themselves into activities which interest them and give them a level of satisfaction. On the whole, the vast majority of people are imaginative, keen to contribute, creative, flexible and enthusiastic. However, the important question is why, in many instances, are these behaviours more common outside the work environment than inside? What have we done to people to drive all their energies outside into other interests?

Values: you have to learn to value your people

A reason these behaviours may not be displayed when working in an organisation is that the 'culture' inhibits and counters the initiative which people want to project.

A culture opposed to development, a culture which treats people as a resource which needs to be controlled at all times or where reinforcement of behaviour is punitive, is an organisation which is on the slide downwards. Absence of vitality, trust and value for employees is tantamount to organisational suicide.

To promote the right value system which is sensitive to TQ, managers have to learn to do one thing. Learn to love their people as they do their own family and themselves. Learning to value people, looking at them as people, not staff or hourly paid or blue collar workers is a major step. Looking at your people from the neck up, not from the neck down, is a good starting point.

Values on growth and success

"The principal reason for the organisation's existence is to create added value for the company and provide staff with stable employment."

We can achieve this by:

- Anticipating and meeting the requirements of our customers.
- Maintaining a competitive position by utilising the talents and capabilities of staff.
- Rigorously adhering to standards and communicating these to our people.

Values on safety

"Our aim is a safe and hazard-free working environment."

We can achieve this by:

- Developing safety rules, procedures and education in advance of current legislation.
- Following rules on safety and prevent accidents arising.
- Thinking safety, to train and reinforce the 'safety first' mentality.
- Protecting our people, our customers and visitors and the environment in which we work.

Values on job content

"It is our objective to provide everybody with a satisfying job and the opportunity to improve skills and develop."

We will achieve this by:

- Promoting job satisfaction through the redesign of work.
- Consulting and involving our people in job changes and the introduction of new technology.

Values about corporate and community responsibility

"We will lead, act as an example to others and be a responsible member of the local community."

We will achieve this by:

- Participating in community affairs.
- Pursuing the interests of the community.
- Promoting confidence in our actions by communicating openly and actively with the local community.

Values of communication

"To provide accurate, reliable and valid information to our people and ensure that we listen to the opinions of others."

We will achieve this by:

- Ensuring that our managers' key responsibility is to promote effective communication horizontally within their responsibilities and across boundaries with other functions.
- Educating and informing everybody about our plans for the future and how we intend to achieve our objectives.
- Recognising, encouraging and valuing people who promote effective communication.
- Being honest and telling people what we think, rather than what we want them to hear.
- Understanding that there are many views on subjects and valuing different perspectives, opinions and viewpoints on subjects.
- Generating teamwork and working together.

Values about ethical standards of behaviour

"The methods by which we achieve results."

We will achieve this by:

● Promoting honesty.
● Ensuring that when there is a conflict between interests — personal and company —
all perspectives are examined.

Values on people development

"The person who fails to develop and go forward takes one step backwards."

We will achieve this by:

● Providing our managers with responsibility for the development of their people.
● Keeping our people up to date with changes in job design and the acquisition of job
skills and knowledge.
● Providing our people with the opportunity to develop through a staff development
programme.
● Recognising and rewarding people who take responsibility to develop new ways of
working.

Values on quality

*"It is the policy of the company to provide customers with defect-free goods and
services, on time every time, without defect, error or omission."*

We will achieve this by:

● Ensuring that all our people are trained in quality management.
● Promoting teamwork and taking preventative action.
● Developing a climate of involvement and joint problem solving with all staff from all
areas.

Fig. 3 Typical company values

Value statements

Value statements reflect our intentions. However, they do not create a change
in behaviour on their own. This can only be achieved through marrying
'managerial behaviours' to specific value statements — and this does not happen by accident.

We may need to spend time thinking through the values which are important to us as an organisation. Having these statements posted up in the reception area is not sufficient. Time and effort has to be expended to make these
'managerial behaviours' the norm by which all supervisors measure their
ability to manage people.

We should devote time to making these values explicit to ourselves and
others. Consistently coaching our managers in these values will provide us
with standards which are understood by all within the organisation.

Value statements can be of two varieties: values which are projected exter-
nally towards the community, our customers and suppliers; and those which
are projected inward and relate to the management of people. These internal
values are implicit in promoting quality of product and service throughout
the company.

In studying the performance of 80 companies, Deal and Kennedy found that the more successful companies were those which had strong cultures. The strong culture was categorised thus:

- Had a widely shared philosophy of management.
- Emphasised the importance of people to the success of the organisation.
- Encouraged rituals and ceremonies to celebrate company events.
- Had identified successful people and sung their praises.
- Maintained a network to communicate the culture.
- Had informal rules of behaviour.
- Had strong values.
- Set high standards for performance.
- Possessed a definitive corporate character.

Peters and Waterman in "In Search of Excellence" identified 8 organisational characteristics which tended to be a major feature in the excellent companies. 'Hands on — value driven' was the characteristic which most closely reflects the importance given to organisational culture as such. The 'hands on — value driven' culture is broken down into 10 'beliefs' which reflect that culture. These are:

- A belief in the importance of enjoying one's work.
- A belief in being the best.
- A belief that people should be innovators and take risks, without feeling that they will be punished if they fail.
- A belief in the importance of attending to details.
- A belief in the importance of people as individuals.
- A belief in superior quality and service.
- A belief in the importance of informality to improve the flow of communication.
- A belief in the importance of economic growth and profits.
- A belief in the importance of 'hands on' management; the notion that managers should be doers, not just planners and administrators.
- A belief in the importance of a recognised organisational philosophy developed and supported by those at the top.

Fig. 4 Organisational performance and strong cultures

Overall, it is necessary for the senior team to recognise that TQM really is a cultural change requiring significant alteration in behaviour reflected through our values — those things which we hold most dear. If the values are important to us we find that they guide our behaviour. In other words, "We value what we do and we do what we value." Can there be a better philosophy to work to?

The level of consistency between what we 'value' and what we 'do' will only come about through example. How can we possibly expect others, lower down in the organisation, to promote TQM if we have not done as much as we could to create the right climate and culture for change by exploring our values?

Charles Handy, in his books *Understanding Organisations* and *Gods of Management*, makes constant reference to organisational culture. He has developed a working definition which enables us to examine culture from a tangible perspective.

Organisational analysis

This analysis helps us stand back and assess the success and operation of our organisation and in particular the organisational culture. It is a useful exercise to take some time off to assess success, the organisation's strengths and weak-

DIAGNOSING ORGANIZATION IDEOLOGY
Roger Harrison

Organizations have patterns of behavior that operationalize an ideology — a commonly held set of doctrines, myths, and symbols. An organization's ideology has a profound impact on the effectiveness of the organization. It influences most important issues in organization life: how decisions are made, how human resources are used, and how people respond to the environment. Organization ideologies can be divided into four orientations: *Power* (a), *Role* (b), *Task* (c), and *Self* (d). The items below give the positions of the four orientations on a number of aspects of organization structure and functioning and on some attitudes and beliefs about human nature.

Instructions. Give a "1" to the statement that best represents the dominat view in your organization, a "2" to the one next closest to your organization's position, and so on through "3" and "4". Then go back and again rank the statements "1" through "4", this time according to *your* attitudes and beliefs.

Existing   Participant's
Organization   Preferred Organization
Ideology   Ideology

1. A good boss is:

___ ___ a. strong, decisive and firm, but fair. He is protective, generous, and indulgent to loyal subordinates.

___ ___ b. impersonal and correct, avoiding the exercise of his authority for his own advantage. He demands from subordinates only that which is required by the formal system.

___ ___ c. egalitarian and capable of being influenced in matters concerning the task. He uses his authority to obtain the resources needed to complete the job.

___ ___ d. concerned with and responsive to the personal needs and values of others. He uses his position to provide satisfying and growth-stimulating work opportunities for subordinates.

2. A good subordinate is:

___ ___ a. compliant, hard working, and loyal to the interests of his superior.

___ ___ b. responsible and reliable, meeting the duties and responsibilities of his job and avoiding actions that surprise or embarrass his superior.

___ ___ c. self-motivated to contribute his best to the task and is open with his ideas and suggestions. He is nevertheless willing to give the lead to others when they show greater expertise or ability.

___ ___ d. vitally interested in the development of his own potentialities and is open to learning and to receiving help. He also respects the needs and values of others and is willing to help and contribute to their development.

3. A good member of the organization gives first priority to the:

___ ___ a. personal demands of the boss.

___ ___ b. duties, responsibilities, and requirements of his own role and to the customary standards of personal behavior.

___ ___ c. requirements of the task for skill, ability, energy, and material resources.

___ ___ d. personal needs of the individuals involved.

4. People who do well in the organization are:

___ ___ a. shrewd and competitive, with a strong drive for power.

___ ___ b. conscientious and responsible, with a strong sense of loyalty to the organization.

___ ___ c. technically effective and competent, with a strong commitment to getting the job done.

___ ___ d. effective and competent in personal relationships, with a strong commitment to the growth and development of people.

Existing   Participant's
Organization   Preferred Organization
Ideology   Ideology

5. The organization treats the individual as:

____ ____ a. though his time and energy were at the disposal of persons higher in the hierarchy.
____ ____ b. though his time and energy were available through a contract with rights and responsibilities for both sides.
____ ____ c. a co-worker who has committed his skills and abilities to the common cause.
____ ____ d. an interesting and worthwhile person in his own right.

6. People are controlled and influenced by the:

____ ____ a. personal exercise of economic and political power (rewards and punishments).
____ ____ b. impersonal exercise of economic and political power to enforce procedures and standards of performance.
____ ____ c. communication and discussion of task requirements leading to appropriate action motivated by personal commitment to goal achievement.
____ ____ d. intrinsic interest and enjoyment to be found in their activities and/or by concern and caring for the needs of the other persons involved.

7. It is legitimate for one person to control another's activities if:

____ ____ a. he has more authority and power in the organization.
____ ____ b. his role prescribes that he is responsible for directing the other.
____ ____ c. he has more knowledge relevant to the task.
____ ____ d. the other accepts that the first person's help or instruction can contribute to his learning and growth.

8. The basis of task assignment is the:

____ ____ a. personal needs and judgment of those in authority.
____ ____ b. formal divisions of functions and responsibilities in the system.
____ ____ c. resource and expertise requirements of the job to be done.
____ ____ d. personal wishes and needs for learning and growth of individual organization members.

9. Work is performed out of:

____ ____ a. hope of reward, fear of punishment, or personal loyalty toward a powerful individual.
____ ____ b. respect for contractual obligations backed up by sanctions and loyalty toward the organization or system.
____ ____ c. satisfaction in excellence of work and achievement and/or personal commitment to the task or goal.
____ ____ d. enjoyment of the activity for its own sake and concern and respect for the needs and values of the other persons involved.

10. People work together when:

____ ____ a. they are required to by higher authority or when they believe they can use each other for personal advantage.
____ ____ b. coordination and exchange are specified by the formal system.
____ ____ c. their joint contribution is needed to perform the task.
____ ____ d. the collaboration is personally satisfying, stimulating, or challenging.

11. The purpose of competition is to:

____ ____ a. gain personal power and advantage.
____ ____ b. gain high-status positions in the formal system.
____ ____ c. increase the excellence of the contribution to the task.
____ ____ d. draw attention to one's own personal needs.

12. Conflict is:

____ ____ a. controlled by the intervention of higher authorities and often fostered by them to maintain their own power.
____ ____ b. suppressed by reference to rules, procedures, and definitions of responsibility.
____ ____ c. resolved through full discussion of the merits of the work issues involved.
____ ____ d. resolved by open and deep discussion of personal needs and values involved.

Existing   Participant's
Organization   Preferred Organization
Ideology   Ideology

13. Decisions are made by the:

—— —— a. person with the higher power and authority.
—— —— b. person whose job description carries the responsibility.
—— —— c. persons with the most knowledge and expertise about the problem.
—— —— d. persons most personally involved and affected by the outcome.

14. In an appropriate control and communication structure:

—— —— a. command flows from the top down in a simple pyramid so that anyone who is higher in the pyramid has authority over anyone who is lower. Information flows up through the chain of command.
—— —— b. directives flow from the top down and information flows upwards within functional pyramids which meet at the top. The authority and responsibility of a role is limited to the roles beneath it in its own pyramid. Cross-functional exchange is constricted.
—— —— c. information about task requirements and problems flows from the center of task activity upwards and outwards, with those closest to the task determining the resources and support needed from the rest of the organization. A coordinating function may set priorities and overall resource levels based on information from all task centers. The structure shifts with the nature and location of the tasks.
—— —— d. information and influence flow from person to person, based on voluntary relationships initiated for purposes of work, learning, mutual support and enjoyment, and shared values. A coordinating function may establish overall levels of contribution needed for the maintenance of the organization. These tasks are assigned by mutual agreement.

15. The environment is responded to as though it were:

—— —— a. a competitive jungle in which everyone is against everyone else, and those who do not exploit others are themselves exploited.
—— —— b. an orderly and rational system in which competition is limited by law, and there can be negotiation or compromise to resolve conflicts.
—— —— c. a complex of imperfect forms and systems which are to be reshaped and improved by the achievements of the organization.
—— —— d. a complex of potential threats and support. It is used and manipulated by the organization both as a means of self-nourishment and as a play-and-work space for the enjoyment and growth of organization members.

INDIVIDUAL AND GROUP PROFILES

Sums of Ranks

	a. Power Orientation	b. Role Orientation	c. Task Orientation	d. Self Orientation
Existing Organization Ideology				
Participant's Preferred Organization Ideology				

Tally of Lowest Scores of the Group Members

	a. Power Orientation	b. Role Orientation	c. Task Orientation	d. Self Orientation
Existing Organization Ideology				
Participant's Preferred Organization Ideology				

This instrument was developed by Roger Harrison, Vice-President for Overseas Operations, Development Research Associates, Homestead Farm, Mountain Bower, near Chippenham, Wiltshire, England, and 16 Ashton Avenue, Newton, Massachusetts 02159. The author would be interested in receiving normative data from readers.

Fig. 5 Diagnosing organisation ideology (Source: The 1975 Annual Handbook for Group Faciliators, 1975)

nesses, and take appropriate action. A useful diagnostic model to use is the questionnaire based on the work of Roger Harrison (see Fig. 5).

Handy suggests that we can classify organisations into a broad range of four cultures. The formation of 'culture' will depend upon a whole host of factors including company history, ownership, organisation structure, technology, critical business incidents and environment, etc.

The four cultures he discusses are 'Power', 'Role', 'Task' and 'People'. The purpose of the analysis is to assess the degree to which the predominant culture reflects the real needs and constraints of the organisation.

Handy uses diagrammatic representation to illustrate his ideas (see Fig. 6).

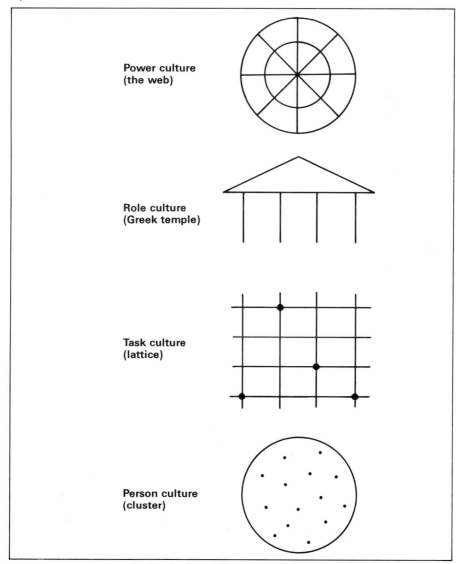

Fig. 6 Handy's four organisational cultures (Source: Understanding Organizations, 1980)

The power culture, Handy describes the power culture as a 'web'. He suggests that this reflects the concentration of power of a family-owned business, which can either be extremely large or small. The family operation with strict responsibilities going to family members — responsibility given to personalities rather than expertise – creates the power structure of the 'web'.

Examples to which Handy refers include the massive institutions in the USA, run as a small family business at the top and known as 'robber barons'. Power is concentrated in a small area, the centre of which is the wheel or the centre of the web. Power radiates out from the centre, usually a key personality, to others in the family who send information down to either departments, functions or units.

The important point to note is that, because power and decision-making is concentrated in so few hands, the strategists and key family members create situations which others have to implement. It is difficult for others outside the 'family network' to influence events. ('Dallas', the long running TV soap displays this culture with the Ewing family.)

The ability of the power culture to adapt to changes in the environment is very much determined by the perception and ability of those who occupy the positions of power within it. The power culture has more faith in individuals than committees and can either change very rapidly and adapt or 'fail to see the need for change' and die.

The role culture, has been typified as a Greek temple and has often been stereotyped as portraying bureaucracy in its purest form. The apex of the temple is where the decision making takes place, the pillars of the temple reflect the functional units of the organisation which have to implement the decisions from the apex. The strength of the culture lies in specialisation within its pillars. Interaction takes place between the functional specialism by job descriptions, procedures, rules and systems. This is very much an organisation culture run by a paper system. An authority is not based on personal initiative but is dictated by job descriptions.

Co-ordination is by a narrow band of senior staff. This is the only co-ordination required as the system provides the necessary integration.

Handy states that the job description is more important than the skills and abilities of those who people the culture. Performance beyond the role prescription is not required or encouraged.

The authority of position power is legitimate. Personal power is not. This reflects Weber's pure theory of bureaucracy. System effectiveness depends upon adherence to principles rather than personalities.

Handy suggests that this culture is appropriate in organisations which are not subject to constant change. The culture functions well in a steady-state environment, but is insecure in times of change. The role culture is typified in goverment departments, local authorities, public utilities and the public sector in general. This sort of culture finds it extremely difficult to change rapidly. The role culture is typified by rationality and size. You will have experienced this culture if you have ever worked with a large, state enterprise.

The task culture, is characteristic of organisations which are involved in extensive research and development activities — they are much more dynamic. They are constantly subject to change and have to create temporary task teams to meet their future needs. Information and expertise are the skills that are of value here. The culture is represented best by a net or lattice work. There is close liaison between departments, functions and specialities. Liaison, communication and integration are the means whereby the organisation can anticipate and adapt to change quickly.

Influence in this team culture is based upon expertise and up-to-date information where the culture is most in tune with results. The dangers for this culture exist when there is a restriction in resources causing it to become more 'power' or 'role' orientated.

The person culture, is characteristic of the consensus model of management, where the individuals within the structure determine collectively the path which the organisation pursues. If there is a formalised structure, it tends to service the needs of the individuals within the structure. Organisations which portray this culture reject formal hierarchies for 'getting things done' and exist solely to meet the needs of their members. The rejection of formal 'management control' and 'reporting relationships' suggests that this may be a suitable culture for a self-help group or a commune, etc., but it is not appropriate for business organisations.

Appropriate cultures

Handy's typologies of organisation structures suggest that we should try, whenever possible, to match the culture with the external demands and constraints on the organisation.

Different operating units require different cultures

One factor that must be borne in mind is that different operating units within the organisation require different structures. Some units or functions will be operating in a steady-state environment, where there are very few changes and the future is reasonably predictable, whereas others are subject to a great deal of change — not just in what they do but also in how they do it. Consequently, it is desirable to have different approaches to managing and different 'cultures' in different units. The characteristics which determine the culture of departments and functions total four in number and are undernoted (see also Fig. 7).

A *Crisis/breakdown* environment refers to decisions which have to be made

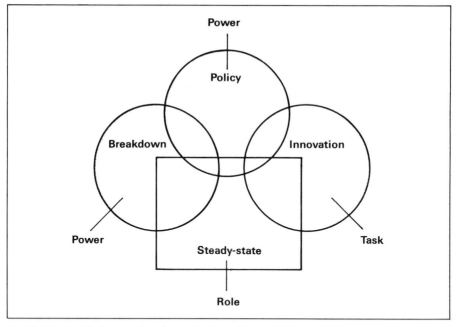

Fig. 7 Relationship between function and culture (Source: Understanding Organizations, 1980)

speedily and which impact upon the long-term effectiveness of the organisation. A culture to reflect the strategic side of things which requires constant
change, direction and re-evaluation must be 'power orientated'.

A **Research and development** environment is one currently requiring constant change. The process of creating innovation is also important. Experts have
to be taken from key areas and moulded together to reach a project objective.
The task culture is one geared for this activity.

The **Steady-state** environment typifies the repetitive duties in which all
organisations have to engage in order to remain efficient. This may include
accounting procedures, staff selection and recruitment, salary and wage
administration, inventory control and maintenance, etc. A culture based on the
predictability and procedural approach of the role culture would appear to
meet the needs of the function.

The **Policy making** environment refers to the creation of long-term plans for
the company. If policy making is perceived as an interactive process the task
culture seems the most fitting. Secrecy and security may tend to make this culture prone to the power orientation.

What Handy suggests is that different units which pursue different activities
should adopt a culture which reflects their needs. For instance, bookkeepers
working in a steady-state climate, where the certainty of the work they do is
predictable, will probably function best in a role culture. A task culture would
be inappropriate, because the systems and procedures which exist are sufficient for the purpose.

A research unit will need to project a task culture but would not work effectively with a power, role or person culture, and, likewise, policy making in a person culture is time consuming and divergent.

In other words, organisations should try to develop appropriate cultures for various aspects of the organisation.

In a large organisation, managing cultures is difficult, especially for those people who have to interact with other units having differing cultures. Imagine the likely problems of a QA manager, from a role culture, trying to get the chief accountant from a power culture to discuss the implementation of TQM in a task culture manner! Clearly we need to think about what sort of culture we need to operate in and the predominant culture in other areas.

Learning to manage horizontally!

Managers must understand the 'culture' concept and how it impacts upon their performance. It is critical that we learn to cope with people from different cultures. (The management of differences is pursued in chapter 11.)

We should be spending more time getting ourselves to understand different cultures. A quality initiative may well work in a steady-state environment like 'financial management' but the same initiative could die in a marketing or sales unit where cultures change rapidly. We need to concentrate resources on managing across boundaries rather than top down through functions. The real waste is always identified between boundary personnel — the internal customer-supplier link. Pursue this approach and TQM can be implemented very quickly.

Transition management and cultural change

Knowing what 'culture' is desirable, engendering the key 'values' — reflected by consistent managerial behaviour — will not, unfortunately, create the TQM change you want. You have still to manage the transition from one state to the other. Change takes time and, as we saw in chapter 2, can promote a great deal of resistance in people.

Understanding the changes which employees go through, their likely behaviours, their perceptions of situations and the support they need to manage and move on are complex.

Elizabeth Kubler Ross was interested in how people came to terms with change. Her research involved the investigation of the stages and behaviours displayed when coming to terms with terminal illness. Similarly, other researchers have spent time exploring how people come to terms with radical changes in their lives including divorce, alcoholism, bereavement and redundancy, etc. We have a great deal to learn from the research undertaken. Much of it is applicable to organisational change and, in particular, TQ.

Let us not minimise the effect of TQM on an organisational culture. It is a radical change strategy, which is geared to changing the culture in the long term. The fact that TQM is 'people driven' and requires a self critical approach with particular relevance to management style suggests that there will be a great deal of resistance. Although chapter 2 described the symptoms of resistance it is still necessary to examine the major stages which people go through when involved in significant organisational change.

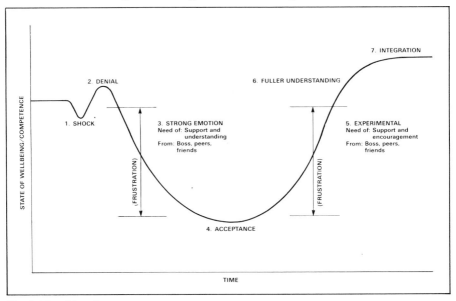

Fig. 8 Transition Curve

Steps in transition management

It is important to examine the sequence of steps and the major stages in any transition. With reference to the 'Transition Curve' in Fig. 8 it is clear that over time most people can come to terms with change. Time and support seem to be the deciding factors. On the vertical axis of the transition curve is 'Competence'. Let us call this the ability to master and manage the key activities of the job, coping with the unforeseen and managing people to get results.

Let's assume no change at all — or at least controllable change. Most people seem to prefer working in a stable environment. It is comfortable, most problems can be foreseen and stress can be controlled.

However, introduce change and what happens? With reference to the 'Transition Curve', managers experience shock (1). There is a downturn in their competence and comments include . . . . . .

"Why did the company decide to promote TQM now — we haven't even got over SPC yet."

"If you ask me, it will never happen. We have taken on too much. With new technology in the laboratory area we'll never find time for it."

"For sure it will mean more work — I just hope we have the resources to do the job well."

Typical characteristics of shock reverberate throughout the structure. Thankfully, man is a logical creature and he progresses to the next stage, that of denial (2). You will note that competence, the ability to do the job and cope with ambiguity increases, or so it appears. This false competence is fuelled by the belief that nothing is ever going to happen. People get together and reinforce this.

"TQM is too big — they would never introduce it into this company. Just to train the staff in this region would require at least 30 trainers. The company will never spend the money."

"Listen, TQM is just flavour of the month. Just keep your head down, say the right things . . . and we'll be into a new fad by next year."

This stage of false competence, reflected in the denial stage, does not last too long. When the messages of TQ cascade down the hierarchy, when COQ measures are identified and data collected, when training takes place and the senior officers go away to their workshops, there is a realisation that TQM is going to happen soon — and it will be involving everybody.

Next people experience strong emotion (3). On the one hand they are coming to terms with the reality of change and may be stressed. They certainly will be uncertain about the role they will play, how things will be in the future, how their job will change, what new skills they will require, what predominant values will be displayed and so forth. They need to unlearn the old ways and move to the new. However, this is not easy. There is a genuine fear. Failing to communicate the intention and the practice of TQ to all will further reinforce the negativity of change.

While uncertainty is the order of the day, there will also be frustration at doing things differently. Eventually, with support, help and realistic visions of the future, people go through the acceptance (4) stage. They have now stopped going downhill and start going uphill — through the experimental (5) stage. They are trying to learn the new ways. They have accepted that change has to take place but now they have different problems. They may not know how to change. Unless people have been shown 'how things are going to be' how can they practice these new behaviours? How do they get and interpret feedback?

It is all very well telling people that TQ is about getting things 'right first time' but leaving them with a slogan — with a passion — without a system and roadmaps is sheer lunacy. Expecting that people can make their own way, learn all they need to and practice behaviours is unrealistic. Here we can see that if managers fail to plan, communicate, involve and listen to their people, prior to the roll out of TQ, then a management team can create real problems for themselves.

From acceptance to the experimental stage is a natural progression. Organisations must provide the resources, the workshops, the training and counselling for staff who find it difficult to make the transition. Encouraging and adopting the right leadership behaviour (see chapter 6) is imperative to building a cohesive group of managers who are willing to tackle uncertainty.

During the experimental stage, managers will make mistakes but they should be encouraged to persist in their efforts. Behaviour will be similar on the shop floor. The company which takes time out to brief all its managers and ensures that this process is pursued 'throughout the structure' will benefit from real success. Companies which don't communicate will have a difficult time moving people along the 'Transition Curve'.

Eventually — through trial and error, support and leadership — the staff should progress to fuller understanding (6) and integration (7) stages.

Adjust your message — depending on where people are!

Knowing where people are on the 'Transition Curve' is important, but that is not the end of the story. Different people at different levels will have different perceptions of TQM. While the senior officers have progressed to the final stage, integration, others will be well back at shock, denial and strong emotion. If the Senior officers have little understanding of the dynamics of change they will not realise the impact their public announcements and assertions will have on others.

Working out where your audience is on the 'Transition Curve' — before sending messages about how marvellous TQ really is — is critical. People will see and experience only fear and frustration and will request a search for new ways of working. To address this imbalance your relative position on the 'Transition Curve' must be appraised in comparison with others — i.e. those whom you manage.

This concern for people and involvement is a reflection of the most caring behaviour exhibited by any senior team. This was demonstrated by many companies which took their TQM drives seriously; including Corning Glass (Ciba Corning), Dow Chemical Co. and Borg Warner Chemicals (UK) among others.

Taking account of the 'Transition Curve', where your people are, how they feel and their perceptions of the senior teams' performances, backed up by incidents and behaviours to confirm these or reject this are activities all companies should find time to pursue.

Summary and bullet points

- Don't underestimate the power of the organisational culture. It can take you up and it can take you down. Managers have control of what it says about your company. Ensure it says something that is strong and positive — not weak and flimsy.
- A culture is the set of values, behaviours and norms which tell people what to do, how to do it and what is acceptable.
- Artifacts, signs and symbols are the overt displays of culture. They can be conveyed consciously or unconsciously — but they are still received and understood by everybody.

- Consider changing things which lead to a negative view of the organisation. The change can be quite small — but its existence may say a great deal about your concern for doing things.
- You can never create TQM in an organisational culture which is negative and punitive.
- Choose your culture and create it through your example.
- The wrong culture creates people who are switched off, demotivated and want to get 'even' — can you blame them?
- Make your culture people orientated. Recognise that developing a culture in which people can thrive and grow is the route to quality improvement. Flexibility, creativity and continuous improvement come from a culture where people are treated as being more important than capital and technology.
- Challenge outmoded systems, procedures and ways of working which stop your people taking the initiative.
- Speeding up delivery and accuracy of information, reducing blockages and cutting across bureaucracy within units is what 'Horizontal Management' is all about.
- Developing relationships, delegating, team building and getting results through others are strategies which succeed.
- Cut out waste — rejecting the slow, bureaucratic process and culture for a quality and customer orientated approach.
- Cultures are created by the actions and deeds of 'Heroes' and 'Anti-heroes' — who are no more than people who work for you. The stories about these people and the incidents in which they played a part reflect the culture and are told and retold to your suppliers, customers, competitors and your people more often than you realise.
- Believe the worst of the stories which relate to your company. Do every thing you can to take actions which counter the negatives.
- Values are the 'Building Blocks' of culture. Reinforce them — practice them in your management behaviour and impress them on others.
- Culture is about 'People Management' and caring for your people. If you don't love them — you don't care.
- Assess the appropriateness of your culture. Consider what action you can take to reject the old fossilized culture and replace it with something dazzling and exciting.
- Recognise that change is not easy. We all go through transitions. Try to make it comfortable for those who will follow you through the curve.
- Do remember where you are on the curve. Where is everybody else? What action have you taken today to help others move through the transition curve?

6 TOTAL QUALITY LEADERSHIP: LEADING BY EXAMPLE

"Eighty percent of TQ initiatives in the UK will fail because they do not have the backing of the senior management team. The senior team in many cases does not realise that it has to change the way it manages, including its style. Many think that public exhortation of the TQM philosophy is their only responsibility. When TQM dies because of their failure to lead by example, they move onto the next 'managerial gimmick' hoping that it will give them the success they crave but have failed to work for."

Commitment is the foundation of an effective TQM initiative. Without it even the most carefully designed programme will never work. In some situations, management teams fail to understand the level of commitment required to make TQM a living, breathing reality.

This is understandable, especially when a management group is exposed to TQM for the first time. Many can get swept along on the wave of enthusiasm and forget about the hard work required over a fairly long period of time. The ideas and methodology of TQM are simple to understand and assumptions are made about the ease with which these ideas can be put into practice. In all honesty, if TQM was that simple, many companies would have done it years ago.

Leadership and commitment

Leadership is the key issue in promoting commitment. For example, the UK management team of a US-owned chemical company found that it wanted to follow the example of the parent company and pursue TQ. The initiative, developed in the US some years ago, was referred to as total quality leadership (TQL). Leadership is the foundation of TQ.

Leadership and commitment go hand in hand. If there is doubt about these issues, it is best to leave TQM until another day.

The team met (off site) for a two-day workshop. Some had already been exposed to the TQM concept but the operations director was keen to ensure that everybody was on the same part of the learning curve. The timetable is shown in Fig. 1 to illustrate the importance of the issues which were debated.

Day 1	
0900	Introduction and objectives
0910	The drive for total quality
0930	Costing quality workshop
1100	Preconditions for total quality
1300	Lunch
1400	Four principles of total quality
1410	Case study: Meeting customer requirements; XXXX Plastics: Appraising the internal customer
1515	Case study: XXXX Pharmaceuticals
1600	Preventative action
1800	Workshop closes
Day 2	
0900	Case study: XXXX Electronics: Creating total quality leadership and managing resistance to change
1100	Assessing readiness for total quality. Appraising organisation culture
1300	Lunch
1400	Action planning: Implementing total quality at XXXX
1800	Workshop closes

Fig. 1 Total quality leadership workshop

During the two day session the management team wanted to explore the key issues. In particular they wanted to examine: preconditions for TQM; creating TQM leadership behaviour; managing resistance to change; assessing the readiness for TQM through appraising organisational values and culture; and action planning. Although each of the workshops took some time to complete, some of the major points are outlined below.

Preconditions for TQM, few companies consider this and fail to grasp that TQM is a strategic issue. TQM must be the central strategic theme for the company for the years ahead. BSI registration, JIT and SPC are all subsets of the TQM process. We can introduce these aspects of quality separately but they will not work as well as if they had been introduced as part of a TQM strategy.

JIT will not work without a TQM organisation. SPC will not work if the company fails to take the right corrective action.

Case study: The death of SPC

A small engineering company had introduced SPC and some areas were implementing the recording process through charting. The QA manager demonstrated the commitment to SPC by careful recording, although there appeared to be little corrective action taken. SPC died in 3 months. The reason — the operatives could not see the point of filling in charts when no corrective or preventative action was being taken. The organisation culture was not committed to prevention and therefore stood little chance of creating effective change.

Case study: Failing to lead through communication

When working with a management team on a leadership initiative we agreed to set an action plan for change. The management team recognised that it had neglected supervisory team building over the years.

The managers would keep an up-to-date diary of their progress with supervisors. We wanted to appraise progress. Their task was simple. It was to programme the names of two, out of 20, supervisors into their diary each day for a month. Their specific role was to talk with each supervisor for 10 minutes per day — a total of 20 minutes. The purpose of the discussion was *not* to be related to day-to-day work but to highlight areas for long-term company improvement.

The results were poor. Most managers started off with good intentions but, as the weeks went by, the commitment to the task died. The reason given and agreed by the team was 'lack of time and fire-fighting'. Overall, the team was composed of a good group of managers but their failure to work through a simple 'management by numbers' exercise demonstrates the difficulty in trying to make a larger change initiative work.

Likewise, companies interested in, and apparently committed to, driving TQM through their organisations admit to having difficulty with other change initiatives. Examples include flexibility training and briefing groups. Responses included:

"Well of course TQM is different, all our managers are committed . . . although briefing did not work . . . the shop floor wanted that to fail."

Shop floor supervisors tell a different story . . .

"Briefing was never given a chance . . . it all started off well but after two months, the briefing notes were just pinned to notice boards and no one really wanted to hear what we had to say."

The major point which comes from this discussion is:

'If we can't introduce a briefing system based upon the simple elements of communication how are we going to introduce TQM, which is concerned with major changes in culture and management style?'

There are other issues which need to be considered including: organisational structure and redesign, communication effectiveness and TQM and strategic planning, etc.

'The route is simple. Don't run before you can walk. TQM is far more complex than some other change strategies and requires a great deal of commitment and planning.'

Creating TQM leadership behaviour, "leaders are born not made" is a statement which has little credibility with most managers. Provided that strengths and weaknesses are assessed objectively and is given the opportunity to develop most managers can learn to acquire new skills.

There is a general assumption in the UK that if you can do your job well enough you will eventually gain promotion to a managerial position. Some promotions to these dizzy heights can create problems for those who are ill prepared. We all know of engineers or technicians who were 110% effective at their jobs but, when promoted, made lousy managers. It must be about time that 'management' recognised that there is a serious problem and that managers have to be trained to manage and lead.

Professor Handy's research into 'Management Education' and the 'Management Charter Initiative' are geared towards recognising and meeting this major need to improve the managerial skills. It is a requirement that industry promotes this approach if we are serious about competing in the 1990s.

TQM cannot address the neglect of years

It is of concern that senior executives stated that, although TQM training was thorough and effective, their managers and supervisors attending the workshops still could not lead, manage a team, communicate with feeling or motivate a work group!

Years of neglecting to provide managers and supervisors with the necessary skills cannot be wiped out by sending them on a series of TQM workshops.

Clearly, any organisation using this approach needs to rethink its training strategy. It would pay the company to forget about TQM for a while, to institute a major 'Leadership Drive', and then pursue TQM when the leadership behaviour was in place. Sending unfocused, lost souls along to TQM workshops increases their tension and anxiety and creates even more ambiguity about TQM in the minds of others.

Case study: Afraid to attend workshops!

Some time ago maintenance supervisory staff from an engineering company attended a TQM seminar. Some members of the staff were fairly anxious — thinking they must have done something wrong to be on a training programme. They soon settled down when they realised that effective change and learning cannot take place in a climate of fear. However, one chap remained nervous throughout the session and took me on one side when I gave out case studies for analysis. He told me he had great difficulty in reading and would not be able to contribute to proceedings. This chap had been employed for fifteen years. His managers did not know of his 'affliction'.

How did he manage to conceal it from his colleagues and superiors? Perhaps a more pertinent question is . . . how was it that his direct manager had no knowledge of his condition?

If we can't train our staff in basics, how are we ever going to pursue a genuine competitive edge to our businesses?

What is leadership?

No one can disagree that 'Leadership' in any TQM initiative is imperative. However, what do we understand by 'Leadership' and does it mean the same thing to different people? Bennis in his book 'Leaders: The Strategies for Taking Charge' claims that "Academic analyses have given us over 350 definitions of leadership. Literally thousands of investigations over the last 75 years . . . have not created a clear understanding of . . . what distinguishes . . . effective leaders from ineffective ones . . ."

Much has been written on 'Leadership' and 'Management Style'. We can study the works of McGregor, Blake and Mouton, Reddin, Adair, Likert, and many others to examine their thoughts and theories.

As an example, McGregor suggested that the attitudes we hold towards others, and the level of perceived control they need/want to perform a task, will create a 'Leadership Style'. Two models of leadership style were developed which McGregor named 'Theory X' and 'Theory Y'. The 'X' manager was far more directive, had little trust in people and believed that strict control systems were needed to be in force in order to achieve results. Correspondingly, the 'Y' model was based more upon a democratic and participative approach — believing that people sought recognition and responsibility in their work (see Figs. 2).

The 'Theory Y' — or human relations — approach has gathered ground since then and Blake and Mouton and others have developed their own variants based on the premise that people are important and we need to utilise their talents in order to achieve results.

Commitment: Disturbing research evidence

There can be no doubt that people are our most valuable resource and managing them by utilising a style to involve them is critical — especially in a TQM

Assumptions about human nature which underpin McGregor's Theory Y

1. **Work is inherently distasteful to most people.**
2. **Most people have little interest in work, are not ambitious, have little desire for responsibility and prefer to be directed.**
3. **Most people have to be coerced, rewarded or punished to gain their commitment to organisational goals.**
4. **Most people have little interest in, or capability for, contributing towards the solution of organisational problems.**
5. **People are motivated only by reward or punishment.**
6. **Most people require constant control and are often threatened with sanctions to achieve organisational objectives.**

1. **Work is pleasant and is as natural as play, if the conditions are favourable.**
2. **Workers have discipline and self control to achieve organisational objectives.**
3. **Workers are motivated by things other than rewards (money) and punishment (sanctions).**
4. **The capability for contributing towards solving organisational problems is widely spread throughout the workforce.**
5. **People are motivated by things other than money. Motivation is a psychological process and involves recognition, esteem, social worth and group belongings etc.**
6. **It is natural for people to be self directed and creative at work, if the conditions allow.**

Assumptions about human nature which underpin McGregor's Theory X

Fig. 2 McGregor's Theory X/Theory Y model

drive. Bennis quotes important research findings which should give us all cause for concern — especially in the way we manage people. Research was carried out in the US with non-managerial workers.

It was claimed that:

- Fewer than 25% of all job holders say that they are currently working at full capacity.
- 50% said that they do not put effort into their job over and above that which is required to keep it.
- 75% said that they could be significantly more effective than they presently were.
- 60% believed that they do not work as hard as they used to.

There is no reason to doubt the authenticity of the research and there is no reason to doubt that similar results are in evidence in Europe. There is also no reason to doubt that this is characteristic of some managerial staff within Europe. What is most important is that TQM requires an additional contribution from people within the structure. TQM creates a climate of 'improvement' but can we create this with a workforce which is disillusioned.

What is concerning about the data above is why do people feel as they do? Are people alienated from work? Do they require a fresh direction? Is motivation something which is lacking from their jobs?

We do not know the answers to these questions but we can be sure that the way people are led determines the effort they expend on any particular job or task.

There are too many instances when a failure to lead is an everyday occurrence in too many organisations. Later we will be looking at the recent important contribution to 'Leadership' and 'Management Style' made by Kouzes and Posner, but now it is important to examine what 'Leadership' is really about.

We take the term 'Leadership' very much on face value and if we asked a group of people to define it we would probably generate a long list of desirable characteristics. Let's have a look at what the credible researchers say about leadership, examine their viewpoints and consider how we can generate real leadership behaviour in an organisation in the 1990s. Having a passion for TQM is no longer sufficient. We need to inculcate, at every level of management and supervision, a real desire to 'lead by example'.

Leaders and managers — what is the difference?

Warren Bennis and Burt Namus in their book 'Leaders: The Strategies for Taking Charge' suggest that empowerment — the ability to generate enthusiasm and vision and communicate this to people is critical in any leadership role. They start to draw the distinction between managing and leading: "Managers do things right. Leaders do the right thing."

This is an important distinction between managers and leaders. However, they were not the first in the field with this view. Wortman's research distinguishes between operating and strategic managers. His argument is that senior managers should think strategically in the long term whereas in reality managers are those who make things happen on a day to day basis. There may appear to be too many 'Operators' and too few 'Strategists'.

He suggests that too many managers are too concerned with day to day matters, something which concerns much of Goldratt's writing in 'The Goal'. Managers are too concerned with achieving short-term goals, i.e. maintaining productivity at any cost, keeping inventory at too high a level, reducing costs and agreeing short-term decisions which work against the long-term mission of the organisation, etc. This short-sightedness can cause a big problem when we consider the difficulty of creating a TQM culture which is completely at odds with the short term approach.

Leaders should be charismatic

Wortman contends that leaders should be charismatic, flexible and inspiring — especially with regard to those they manage. Leaders must be able to inspire others to create and manage change, to take responsibility and, above all, to take risks. Moreover this charismatic stance should not be like a bolt from the blue, a magical process. It can only be achieved through people. Involving, participating and actively listening to others is the only way we can create genuine improvement in everything we do. Wortman further contends that there is a fundamental difference in personal characteristics between the 'operator' and the 'strategist'.

Zalenznik, a researcher with similar views, argues that leaders and managers differ in many different ways and he draws this out by looking at four dimensions: attitudes towards goals, conceptions of work, building relationships with others and the sense of self.

Managers enjoy working with and relating to people. They achieve much of their esteem and recognition from such activities and work to maintain control, whereas leaders are visionary in outlook, risk lovers and independent.

Transformers and transactors

The important dichotomy is reinforced by Burns except that he calls leaders 'Transformational' and managers 'Transactional'.

Transformational leaders are independent, visionary and inspirational, driven by long-term goals, visions and objectives. They provide a mission for others to follow and they expect the same high standards from their people. They are real change makers! They have a clear view of what they want to achieve and are less concerned with detail than with getting what they want. They are interested in 'ends' rather than 'means'.

Transactional managers, on the other hand, are especially good at achieving short-term results, foster teamwork and work in a practical manner.

Clearly, transformational leaders and transactional managers need to work together. Teamwork is imperative. However, what is of concern is an organisation which fosters the growth of one type to the exclusion of the other.

Whether an organisation is peopled by leaders or managers will determine its success in implementing a major cultural change. Transformational leaders are especially good at creating new initiatives, stimulating action and loyalty and getting all to row in the same direction. Transactional managers are better at administering a system and making sure things happen on a day-to-day basis.

Leaders and managers develop different approaches to getting results but they both make things happen by managing others. They adopt different approaches but ostensibly focus upon the same 5 areas: giving direction, motivating, rewarding and recognising success, developing and meeting the needs of their people.

The important point to make is that, whether leaders or managers, what they do with their people will determine the success they achieve.

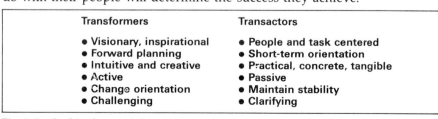

Transformers	Transactors
• Visionary, inspirational	• People and task centered
• Forward planning	• Short-term orientation
• Intuitive and creative	• Practical, concrete, tangible
• Active	• Passive
• Change orientation	• Maintain stability
• Challenging	• Clarifying

Fig. 3 Leadership characteristics

Developing balance between transformers and transactors

Whatever the behaviour of these leaders or managers, the outcome can be the same. However, a structured integrated outcome can only come from those in positions of power assimilating the talents of both sets of managers and leaders. For success in TQM both sets of individuals are important. Bearing this in mind, how much time do senior officers in corporations give to exploring the desirable leadership or management styles which they want their people to project?

Learning by copying the behaviour of others

In many cases, senior staff should consider developing a leadership pro-gramme prior to embarking upon TQM. In some cases people rising through the organisation adopt a style which is modelled wholly on the style of their manager. This stereotype is the only example upon which to model behaviour. If a key senior manager has risen to high rank using one style exclusively, very few middle or junior managers will adopt a style which is at variance with this, recognising that certain styles are associated with success.

Passion and systems

The conclusions we can generate from such important research have much relevance to leading a TQM initiative. To paraphrase Tom Peters there is a pro-blem with 'passion and systems'. An organisation composed almost com-pletely of transformational leaders may incite the 'passion' without the 'system' and organisations peopled by transactional managers will develop the 'system' without the 'passion'.

Where, however, does this leave us? What type of management style or leadership style do we encourage? In all honesty, there are too many organisations which adopt the transactional manager model. People are rewar-ded for achieving short-term perspectives. Progression to senior levels is determined by managers who 'do things' rather than those with vision. In too many cases rewards and recognition are bestowed on those who get the results we need today — not those who create opportunities for tomorrow.

Many organisations are now considering and applying human resource policies to inculcate the vision and creativity of their staff and the organisation, but these are too few and far between. We need senior people to create change and demonstrate the examples which others follow. At the same time we need people to follow through. Overall, we seem to have plenty of the latter but none of the former.

Achieving results through others

Leaders and managers have one thing in common, they achieve results

A large public-sector organisation decided that it would take its high flying graduates on a workshop to encourage innovation. Much of the training was of the outward bound variety and focus was on leadership and team building rather than the traditional administrative focus. At the end of the 2-week session participants were asked to generate a personal action plan for change. They were asked to 'bash' the bureaucracy, change things and make them happen — even if it did create chaos. They were told they had to be revolutionary, challenge the obvious and report back in 3 months.

One young man, Martin, went back to his job with lots of ideas and one day during the coffee break he looked out from his eighth floor office at the car park, which was adjacent to a railway station.

He noticed over a period of a week that there were at least 10 car parking spaces free. He went to his area manager and told him of his idea. As the location of the building was in a busy city centre, he might be able to rent the spaces to nearby offices. He was certain he could charge a fee of at least £500 per year per space. His idea was rejected.

Martin was not one to give in easily — so he went to see his divisional manager — who again rejected the idea without thought or discussion. Martin — still enthusiastic and knowing he had to report back on his action plan — decided to rent the plots. He wrote to a group of accountants, adjacent to his place of work, and received a cheque for £8000. He promptly set off for the accounts department and found to his horror that there was no mechanism for paying in the money!

He did not realise the organisational turmoil he would create. He left within 4 months to go to a lively US company who wanted people to challenge the obvious.

The moral of this tale is that there is little point developing the entrepreneurial vigour of staff if there is no concession to making good ideas work. Martin wanted to create change and build upon the foundations of the old culture. The old culture rejected his idea — and this was reinforced by the attitude and management style of the organisation.

Clearly this organisation fulfilled its own wishes. It is now peopled totally by managers to the exclusion of leaders.

George Bernard Shaw summed up the situation between the reasonable and unreasonable men thus . . . "The reasonable man adapts himself to the world: the unreasonable one persists in trying to adapt the world to himself. Therefore all progress depends upon the reasonable man."

Fig. 4 Why bother creating change!

through others. Kouzes and Posner have developed some original research work which has direct relevance to getting the most from and with people. Bearing in mind quality improvement, flexibility and involvement come from our people, then it is wise to start comparing our performances against what we 'could' do.

Kouzes and Posner were interested in studying the behaviour of the manager who achieved something quite extraordinary. They studied a large number of 'high achievers' and found that the stories of success which were told were seldom those found in textbooks. The research revealed a pattern of events leading to incredible success. What were the conclusions? They were that, 80% of the time, managers engage in activities which fall under 5 headings, discussed below. The incredible reality is that these factors are what differentiate the high flyer from the also ran! All these activities are connected with 'doing things with people'.

Challenging the process, leaders are pioneers — people who seek out new opportunities and are willing to change the status quo. They recognise that failing to change creates mediocrity. They innovate, experiment and explore ways to improve the organisation. Most importantly, they realise that not all good ideas come from themselves. They realise that others 'close to a problem' are probably more able to come up with a sensible solution. They recognise that listening is probably more important than talking. Leaders are also prepared to meet whatever challenges may confront them. This involves looking for new ways of doing things, experimenting and taking risks.

Leaders also recognise that the way they manage people is a testing and training ground for potential leaders. Risk taking is encouraged and mistakes are assessed as formalised 'learning experiences'.

Inspiring a shared vision, leaders look towards and beyond the horizon. They look to the future with a dream of what might be. They envisage the future with a positive and hopeful outlook. They believe that, if people work together, they can achieve the impossible. Leaders are expressive and attract followers through their genuineness and skilful communication. They do not deceive. They show others how common interests can be met through commitment to the overall goal. Leaders who project this approach look at the future, share and discuss it with their people and work towards their dreams.

Enabling others to act, leaders know that they are rewarded for getting others to achieve results. They can't do it alone. They need to infuse people with enthusiasm and commitment. They have to be persuasive. Leaders develop relationships based on mutual trust and they get people to work together — towards collaborative goals. They stress participation in decision making and problem solving and they actively involve others in planning, allowing them the discretion to make decisions — even if this means making mistakes. Risk taking is encouraged. Leaders ensure that people feel strong and able to do a job. This behaviour involves getting others to work with them and giving discretion to others.

Leaders 'empower' others to become leaders in their own way — not just to do as they are told. This requires an ability to manage ambiguity and take responsibility for others.

Modeling the way, leaders are clear about their business values and beliefs. They have standards which are understood by all. They stand up for what they believe in and they communicate this to their people. They keep people and projects on course by behaving consistently with these values and modelling how they expect others to act. Words and deeds are consistent.

Leaders make us believe that the impossible is within reach. They also plan and break down projects into achievable steps, creating opportunities for small wins. They make it easier for others to achieve goals by focusing on these steps and identifying key priorities. This means that they describe and 'model' how things should be. This often means setting examples and behaving in ways which reflect their values and beliefs.

Encouraging the heart, leaders encourage people to achieve difficult targets.

They persist in their efforts by relating recognition to achievements. They visibly recognise contributions to the overall purpose and give frequent feedback. Leaders let others know that their efforts are appreciated. They communicate the success of the team and celebrate small wins. Leaders nurture a team philosophy and go out of their way to say thank you for a job well done. They manage to sustain efforts and encourage others to put even more effort into what they do.

Overall these 5 basic behaviours differentiate an effective leader from his poorly performing counterpart.

Having a model to work with is extremely useful — but real progress with a management team comes from comparing performance with the model. An exercise based on this model is an extremely useful way of comparing performance and, to make it doubly powerful, it is possible to introduce the perception of others with regard to leadership behaviour (see Fig. 5).

Overall there is a belief that for a TQM initiative to work it has to be led from the top. The greater the commitment from leaders — the stronger the vision projected and reinforced through behaviour, actions and deeds, the faster TQM will become the dominant culture (see Fig. 6).

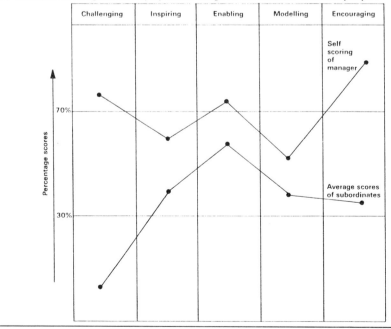

A senior management team agreed to undergo assessment of the 'leadership style' utilising a learning instrument based on the original work of Kouzes and Posner. All 11 managers completed a questionnaire based on self perception of 5 key areas. Six managers, working for each of the senior members of staff, also completed a similar questionnaire — this time based on their perception of their managers' capabilities in these 5 areas. The results were averaged and fed back. We found, in 30% of cases, there was an agreement with style — but in 70% of instances we found there was fundamental disagreement and this was narrowed down to two areas 'enabling others to act' and 'encouraging the heart'. The shock of examining the impact of leadership behaviour from the subordinates viewpoint was critical. The management team went away with specific things to do to project the image of the effective 'leadership style'.

Fig. 5 Learning to lead (Source: The Leadership Challenge, 1988)

1. Search for challenging opportunities to change, grow, innovate and improve.
2. Experiment, take risks and learn from the accompanying mistakes.
3. Envision an uplifting and ennobling future.
4. Enlist others in a common vision by appealing to their values, interests, hopes and dreams.
5. Foster collaboration by promoting co-operative goals and building trust.
6. Strengthen others by sharing information and power and increasing their discretion and visibility.
7. Set an example for others by behaving in ways that are consistent with your stated values.
8. Plan small wins that promote consistent progress and build commitment.
9. Recognise individual contributions to the success of every project.
10. Celebrate team accomplishments regularly.

Fig. 6 Ten commitments of leadership

Psychometric tests and TQM management style

The leadership issue is critical to a successful TQM drive and, for this reason, some pioneering companies have been adopting a number of approaches to assessing leadership among their staffs. With one company the management team and middle managers went through a series of psychometric tests (Myers Briggs and OPQ Concept 3, 5, and 4.2, 16PF, as well as Firo B) the purpose of which was to address managerial style inadequacies and deal with them positively.

The managers were keen to get involved. They drove the initiative and most benefitted from the experience. We were also able to assess resistance to change in some areas. This meant that we could take preventative action and ensure that new ideas were fully discussed with individuals who were most resistant and ensure that plans were monitored. This was also an important management development activity for the staff involved. The management team benefitted from the experience in particular with reference to its leadership behaviour, how the individuals work in teams (quality improvement teams or corrective action teams) and how they interact with others — motivate, organise and coach.

This is a similar approach to that used by a major finance house. It is pursuing TQM through cultural change. The 10 senior members of staff of this £1bn company have been through the process of self development through tests. They have taken this opportunity to assess style and to develop one more in keeping with the 1990s. The principal reason for this initiative is that 65 managers under their control also need to think through a style change in keeping with a 'team driven' environment and this, in turn, will impact upon their teams. This company recognises that people down the line will not change unless they see their superiors leading by example.

What is important is that managers can manage and lead. There appears to be plenty of managing but not much LEADING. Assessing personal strengths and weaknesses is critical to bringing change quickly (see Fig. 7).

In simple terms, organisations get the people and leaders they deserve. If they fail to invest in developing a coherent managerial style, understood by all, with rewards commensurate with actions, they cannot create a meaningful transition to TQM.

Managing resistance to change

Never minimise the resistance factor in organisational change. People at all levels can find 10 good reasons for making TQM fail, but not find one to make it work. Why is this?

It probably exists because some people crave stability and security. Once they have learned a job they don't want to have to relearn it and do things differently. Nowadays, most people are aware of the need to change to maintain present standards. Alvin Toffler, in 'Future Shock' and Charles Handy in 'The Age of Unreason' reflect the same message as Tom Peters in 'Thriving on Chaos', in that, as things are changing so rapidly, the only successful companies are those which challenge the process of doing things and make it happen. This is all very well but it creates problems when there may be people in the organisation (at whatever level) who resist (actively or passively) the process of change.

The TQM process is relatively easy. What organisations need to do is to address the factors which lead to resistance. Conquer these and a TQM culture will exist.

Managers who adopt a 'corporate change drive' through leadership behaviour will succeed while others are still listing reasons why they cannot change! Where there is ambiguity in the preferred management style, there is uncertainty in the minds of those leading us into the future.

Characteristic	Ranking	US managers (N = 2,615) Percentage of managers selecting
Honest	1	83
Competent	2	67
Forward-looking	3	62
Inspiring	4	58
Intelligent	5	43
Fair-minded	6	40
Broad-minded	7	37
Straightforward	8	34
Imaginative	9	34
Dependable	10	33
Supportive	11	32
Courageous	12	27
Caring	13	26
Co-operative	14	25
Mature	15	23
Ambitious	16	21
Determined	17	20
Self-controlled	18	13
Loyal	19	11
Independent	20	10

Kouzes and Posner, the Leadership Challenge, Jossey Bars 1988, p. 17.

Fig. 7 Characteristics of superior leaders (Source: The Leadership Challenge, 1988)

Leadership and action planning

This is the key. If the management team fails to come up with a structured approach to TQM it is unlikely that it will work.

It is not suggested that the team, without support and a framework, can generate its own TQM plan. It needs support and has to be guided through the key stages and the sequence of activities which lead to the creation of a TQM culture.

We develop a critical path outlining the sort of approach a company can take. During the diagnostic phase, we work closely with the senior team assessing progress. The areas which need clarification include:

- Choosing and recording COQ indicators
- Agreeing tangible milestones to assess progress
- Ensuring that all TQM objectives are achievable, measurable and compatible with company objectives
- Deciding upon the structure and commitment of action planning within the structure of supervision and management

There is a great danger at this level that the directors or senior managers running the TQM drive can 'pass the parcel' to others lower down the hierarchy. Being committed to doing as well as talking is paramount. If there is a failure to reflect words with actions others will feel, see and witness the failure to be committed.

If the senior team feels that it doesn't have the time or resources to devote to this stage, and pass it down to other levels, it is saying, in effect, "TQM is not my responsibility."

If the senior team really is committed, it should demonstrate this by doing what it tells others to do.

What is commitment?

Commitment is an essential element of a TQM drive. Commitment must exist at every level. It is a duty, an obligation and a responsibility to make TQM work. It is adherence to plans, principles and procedures. Beyond all these things it is a 'personal statement' — a guarantee, a pledge, a promise — and an undertaking not just to talk about but to promote TQM and act in a TQM manner at all times.

Commitment is . . .

'Doing what you say you will do."
"Ensuring that your behaviour and actions mirror your statements on TQM."
"Ensuring that others are involved in the process."

"Ensuring that staff is 'sold' rather than 'told' to get involved in TQM."
"Ensuring that TQM is not flavour of the month but a commitment to get things right first time — always."
"Leading by example."

Not being committed is reflected in . . .

"Talking not doing."
"Finding 10 excuses not to do something."
"Being cynical."
"Failing to seek involvement and rejecting personal responsibility."
"Blaming others."
"Assuming that others should do it first."
"Thinking that TQM affects others but not yourself."
"Failing to live up to promises or agreements."
"Doing nothing but that for which you are paid."
"Failing to be self critical."

Summary and bullet points

- The major thrust of any TQM initiative lies fairly and squarely with the management team. If it succeeds it does so by the teams efforts. If it fails, it does so because it has been allowed to fail by the team. Leadership in any company is critical to success, but, more than this, leaders should be CRITICAL of their own performances. They should look for feedback and take action to make things happen. They should not expect TQM to materialise through thin air, be created by a magical process or be the responsibility of somebody else down the line.
- 80% of TQM initiatives will fail because of a lack of commitment to lead by example. Ensure that your company is in the 20% success rate by developing strong leadership.
- Leadership and commitment are inseparable. If there is a major doubt about leadership — if commitment is failing — then stop TQM. You can't ever do TQM twice. No one believes you the second time.
- TQM is about creating cultural change — which means changing everything we do. This also means changing how people manage.
- 'Leaders are made not born.' Companies create the leaders they deserve. If little attention has been spent on developing a consistent style, take two steps back and correct it before you get involved in TQM.
- No amount of TQM training will undo the years of neglect and failing to train managers in the basics and how to manage.
- Leadership is about people — it is pure and simple. Leaders create a devotion for and from their teams. Leadership based on the hard 'bottom line results' model has its limitations — as does shouting at people. People are sophisticated — they need to be motivated and feel part of a team.
- Research suggests that people are unprepared to put as much into a job as they used to. Let's change this. People are unprepared to put effort into the

job if the conditions are not favourable. To create favourable conditions we need leaders who care, whose deeds and actions reflect their values and who are prepared to get into the heart of people management producing the conditions for change and empowering people to create change.

- Leaders should be charismatic. They should be liked. Although being liked is not a condition of leadership, if you are, you have a lot more power.
- Leaders should inspire others to manage change, confront the impossible and think the unthinkable.
- We should train our leaders to cope with ambiguity, stress and change.
- Encourage transformers. Organisations without leaders who fail to challenge the way they do things don't learn or grow. We need unreasonable men, innovators and mavericks to create the quantum leap to TQM.
- Ensure that the balance is correct between transformers and transactors.
- There is no recorded research indicating that too many transformers lead a company to failure. There is a plethora of research which tells us that unimaginative, safe, risk-averse management teams kill initiative, chase off their best managers and die a lingering death.
- Enjoy creating transformers. Challenge the way things are done. Success comes from challenging the old and producing something new.
- Clarify what is desirable management and leadership style now. Assume a bright young graduate asked you the question . . . "What do you need to do — to get on in this company?" Make damn sure you have the characteristics of a manager in your mind. If not, you don't know. There is no excuse for ignorance! If you don't have a picture or a vision of leadership talents — how do you create the vision in others for them to progress and achieve?
- You need passion for change and systems to make things happen. On the whole, we have enough systems — or at least they are easy to create. We need 'passion' for change and improvement.
- Create human resource policies to create real leaders. Make sure policy is seen in practice.
- Don't say "Create new ways; reject the old; make things happen" if the culture kills all initiatives.
- Lead and achieve through your most important resource — your people.
- Challenge the way things are done. The Japanese look for continuous improvement in everything. They leave no stone unturned. Ensure that this happens at every level in every function of your organisation.
- Inspire others and create a vision which is tangible and achievable for those who rely on you to make the future a reality.
- Enable others to do what you want. Give them resources, time and support.
- Model the way you want others to behave. Lead by example.
- Encourage people to achieve results. Find people doing one thing right and tell them why they did well. Reinforce behaviour in a positive fashion. Celebrate success, recognise achievement and share success.

- Assess the style of your management team. Look at its strengths, discuss weaknesses and take corrective action. Ask about the impact of your style on those you manage. Listen to what they say — even if you don't like what you hear. Change the way you do things.
- Learn to realise that most of us resist change. We like the stable and predictable. Learn and encourage others to love change and come to realise that this is what life is like in the 1990s.
- Decide what the management team wants to happen in terms of changing its leadership behaviour. Do it and monitor progress.
- Ensure that commitment is reflected in leadership behaviour.

7 PITFALLS — HOW TO AVOID THEM

This is the last chapter in this section dealing with the critical issues of 'Managing the Transition to TQM'. We have already established that TQM is a behavioural change which is concerned with assessing and preparing the way for 'cultural change'. This cultural transition can only be achieved through leadership, which is 'where management ends'.

We can now explore in a more general way the possible pitfalls and disasters which stand in the way of TQ. The issues for consideration fall within two areas — preparing the way for TQ and implementing it. Implementation is the focus of section 4. Preparing the ground is determined very much by the relationship which exists between those internal to the organisation who have to live with the problems of TQM, and the role of the external change agent or consultant. This is not to say that companies cannot implement TQ without the help of an outsider — but many companies opt for this because they want to tap the talents of experienced TQM practitioners from outside which should complement the enthusiasm and the skills of those within the company.

Attitudes: the role of the internal change agent

During a discussion with a company creating a TQM drive, one of the senior managers asked the likely qualifications of a TQM manager who was internal to the organisation. Before receiving an answer, another senior manager mentioned that one particular director, who was not renowned for his contribution, would be retiring in the next year and that this responsibility may suit him and the organisation.

Clearly, this sort of attitude never created significant change in the way organisations function. I prefer to think that this statement was naive rather than serious. However, the situation is real and does create some concern. We need to consider seriously the criteria used for the appointment of internal managers to champion TQM.

We know that the prerequisite of an effective TQM initiative is that the senior management team or board take full responsibility for the drive and 'lead by example'. So much is founded upon this important criterion that we can tend to forget the other factors which ensure that TQM is not just another 'quick fix'.

Management teams are fully aware that a TQ drive must fit the needs of the organisation and must be tailored to its special circumstances. Organisations can get so carried away with the inherent wisdom of TQM, together with the simplicity or 'good sense' of the concept, that they fail to take account of the important issues relating to implementation.

If TQM was so easy — we would have done it years ago

Implementing TQ is not easy. If it was we would have done it years ago. After all, we are asking managers to rethink the way they do things. We ask them to be critical and identify waste in their immediate areas of work. We encourage staff to be open and trusting and forget all about the 'history and politics' associated with the way organisations function. Can we all change so easily? I'm afraid it is not so.

If fire-fighting and reactive management are the normal ways of life, it is naive to believe that to change the culture and achieve the transition to TQ would not be difficult.

Leaders who change the culture

What is required are transformational leaders, who are not shy, who can create change and are, when necessary, capable, willing and prepared to be viewed as unpopular in order to force the key issues. Some would say that that is why we employ external consultants, but here lies an inherent danger. How can we be sure that when the consultancy team leaves the organisation, TQ will not leave with them? How can we ensure that TQ really is a breathing reality when the overhead projectors have been packed away and the dust has settled in the board room?

Clearly, there is only one answer — to ensure that 'champions' or 'heroes' exist within the structure who are keen and enthusiastic, who believe that TQM will give their company a competitive advantage and who ensure that the long-term benefits of TQM are not simply words written on paper. It is a major concern that managers should take responsibility for promoting TQM inside their companies and take over the role and responsibilities of the external consultant.

Responsibility for learning

Many consider this issue and take their responsibilities seriously. In other words, external consultants recognise that they owe clients a duty to create a team of facilitators who continue the message. The really successful initiatives are those where 'the internal TQM manager actively projects TQM within and outside the organisation.'

The TQM manager is the ambassador who creates confidence in staff, suppliers and customers

In one particular organisation, which manufactures components for the automotive industry, the TQM manager was active in promoting TQM with all the company's suppliers. After a comparatively short time, while managing training, development and other issues, he, in liaison with others, such as the purchasing manager, reduced the supplier base to a manageable number. They ran an external supplier development programme, told their suppliers what was expected and started working more closely with them.

Supplier development initiatives

There were many instances when suppliers were providing material for manufacture based on assumed specifications. This had created significant scrap but had existed for such a long time that everybody had assumed that nothing could be done to resolve the problem. It transpired that the manufacturing company had little idea of the specification of the material — because they had never questioned whether things could be improved.

There were many instances when supplier and customer came closer together. Hard as it may seem, suppliers visited the company, went through the manufacturing process appraising the reliability of raw materials and came up with alternative material which would be more appropriate for the use to which it was put.

Likewise, a QA manager at a US-owned company, manufacturing microwave antenna, organised a supplier development conference for 2 days. All suppliers were invited. Those who attended promised that they would make all attempts they could to resolve manufacturing problems. This conference generated other similar events when the QA manager would host sessions trying to reduce rework and build collaborative relationships with suppliers. This regular event has now become an acceptable part of the culture of the organisation and its suppliers.

Placement of supplier personnel with their customer

Suppliers now understand the quality of the service they provide. In some instances, suppliers are asked to locate members of staff at their customers so they can experience at first hand the quality of the material received. This short-term assignment gives instant feedback on what it is like to receive the 'product' and process complicated documentation.

Asking suppliers to do the impossible — then changing your mind!

This reversal of roles does much to enhance the service provided in all areas — it is not just product related. It is also interesting to see what sort of reputation 'customers' have with their suppliers. In one instance, the customer, a producer of original equipment to the motor industry, had made an emergency phone call to its supplier to set up special facilities to produce a large number of components (sub-assemblies) — to be delivered yesterday! These were to be assembled over a weekend and shipped to a major car manufacturer. The supplier set all the wheels in motion. It rearranged production schedules, and negotiated overtime and additional weekend and shift working with its employees. The supplier halted work in progress, stripped machines and set up new tooling and arranged for extra delivery of raw materials. There was to be a direct delivery from the supplier, 80 miles away, to the customer, and this would be processed and delivered to the car company. This emergency required a great deal of planning and preparation and called for the goodwill of companies and employees alike.

At the last minute, priorities were changed and the supplier was no longer under 'pressure' for the sub-assemblies. The result was an unhappy supplier, further down the chain, which had expended a great deal in financial terms to please its customer. The radical reorganisation had created 'ill will' with the supplier's staff — all for nothing. This 'accelerator' effect reinforced the image of a fire-fighting customer.

Helping suppliers develop their own systems

TQ managers with whom I have worked have also provided a support system to those suppliers which find difficulty in developing their systems to meet the requirements of their customers. The outcome of this is the finalisation of a separate 'Supplier Development Programme' and certification similar to the Ford Q101 system. Suppliers do find this of special value and find that they in turn can reduce their costs of rework — thus freeing resources to provide a cheaper and better quality product to their customers.

In some companies the 'Supplier Development Programme' has generated an initiative to create a 'New Products Implementation Programme' where suppliers are involved right from the start in the design of new products. This reduces unnecessary rework at all levels.

There are also instances when the 'cascade' approach has worked with regard to SPC and JIT. Suppliers seeking ways of improving their services have sought help from their bigger customers, looked at their systems and become committed to quality improvement. These efforts sometimes culminate in a major TQ drive.

Robbie the champion

Robbie Taylor, MD of a group of companies involved in diecastings and plastic injection moulding, has taken a brave step. He identified the bigger customers of each of his 4 plants in Scotland and decided to seek their views on his operations. A detailed questionnaire was circulated to the top 20 customers in terms of revenue and it was interesting to examine the results. There are always ways of improving what you do! He is a champion of quality and committed to improving quality of product and service. Robbie has now extended his research base to the 80% of customers who generate 20% of his company's revenue and he is sure that he may get a slightly different response. Now, what is important about his approach is that he is looking for things which are wrong. He wants to know what it is that 'turns the customer off'. Is it the product, or could it be documentation, delivery or consistent standards?

Robbie will find out how to improve because he canvasses his company's customers. How many other CEOs would risk the response from such an exercise?

Cascading TQM to suppliers

Many TQM initiatives started with the programmes described above and have created a TQ culture which has been cascaded down from customers to suppliers and so on. This is the chain reaction of TQ which is more prevalent in Japanese industry — with the resultant benefits.

Richard: The enthusiastic TQ manager

If we are not careful we can lose out on the impact of a TQ manager who is 100% committed to TQM. Richard Tinkler, a TQ manager for a very successful engineering company, was sold '100%' on TQM. He spent all his time talking to and converting people. Every time he talked with suppliers and customers alike, he sparked off enthusiasm. Every time he talked TQ, he added value to the reputation of his company. We all intend to develop this enthusiasm — it is a desirable trait in any TQ manager — but is it always present? It is questionable whether this is the norm. It is extremely important that the senior group thinks through the sort of TQ manager or co-ordinator it needs to do a good job (see Fig. 1). Too much attention is focused on technical expertise rather than on

---

Job description:
TQM manager

Objective
To ensure the success of the TQM drive

Responsibility
To managing director

Key job functions (specific)

● To co-ordinate the collection of data relating to COQ measures in all functions/locations. The TQM manager should be the recipient of information driven by line/functional management.
● Produce, collate and disseminate COQ information to the TQM co-ordinator.
● Collate, monitor and co-ordinate progress regarding action plans. Although, ostensibly, this is a line function — information must be collected at the centre to communicate progress.
● Collate functional/departmental plans for TQM progress. This requires collecting information and concentrating on milestones and methods for measuring progress.
● Ensure that all functions have developed their own CATs, and that each CAT has developed a short report/list of priorities from which to work.
● Ensure that CATs are formed on an inter-functional basis.
● Ensure that all staff/employees have attended TQM sessions.
● Ensure that publicity of TQM progress is promoted through the necessary media.
● To communicate with the quality improvement team (QIT) to assess progress.
● To ensure that functional areas take ownership of TQM.

Key functions (general)

● To be actively involved in setting up quality structures, meetings and other forums for TQ improvement.
● To promote the TQ concept and gain commitment from all employees.
● To arrange, as and when necessary, the setting up of training programmes for all employees in TQ concepts, processes and activities including training trainers and CAT problem solving, etc.
● To manage other trainers/facilitators as may be necessary. (It is anticipated that this would be a dotted line relationship because responsibility must lie ultimately with the functional head.)
● To maintain an effective marketing programme of TQM activities — this should include generating information for briefing meetings.
● To report progress to the QIT on a regular basis. Reports to include measurements.

Person specification (outline)

● Must be able to communicate effectively within the organisation. (He will need to be able to sell/reinforce the TQM concept at all levels.)
● Must be persuasive and influential. (A key function is to sell the concept.)
● Needs to be enthusiastic and persistent. (Someone will always need information/training.)
● Imagination is required — there is much scope for creativity, i.e. publicity and internal marketing.
● Organised. It is not envisaged that the post will carry a large staff back-up so it requires a logical systematic approach with the ability to keep ordered records of progress.
● It is not a prerequisite that the job holder needs specific experience in QA or TQM/SPC. Personality and enthusiasm are the key factors.

Fig. 1 TQM manager job description

the 'public relations' side of the exercise. There is little point in having a deeply analytical introvert as TQ manager when you have the choice of a self confident, assertive, charismatic individual without the same analytical powers. After all, the latter can always be equipped with the 'technical expertise' by teaming him up with 'analysts'. However, we do need an individual with influence and persuasion. Don't forget that there is not a trade off between analytical ability and ability to influence! So it is possible to gain the best of both worlds.

The pressure of TQM can create insularity

Too often, when a TQM initiative begins, TQ managers can be quite insular in their approaches. They have so much to think about that they stay within the confines of their specific responsibilities. Imposed targets and time constraints tend to reinforce this behaviour. It is just at this time that the TQ manager should stand back, avoid tunnel vision and ask himself whether similar companies have experienced similar problems. Finding out who is doing what and how with TQM will pay enormous dividends.

Spending time assessing who else is interested in TQ in the same industry, or in different industries, making contact and visiting companies undergoing the same drive, will add breadth and avoid tunnel vision. There are many companies involved in TQ which would value others showing an interest. TQM managers devloping a 'support system' can help enormously and, at the same time, avoid pitfalls which others have encountered.

ICL breakfast workshops

ICL, which has been progressing TQ for some time, has arranged a series of free seminars and workshops demonstrating just what can be achieved. Managers attending these 'breakfast sessions' can learn a great deal.

British industry in general has never been renowned for sharing its secrets, even with companies in other industries. What we need are more TQM consortiums orientated towards avoiding the problems of implementation — but consortiums, composed of user organisations, will not create themselves. TQM managers committed to the TQM concept must make the first moves and create the interest. Companies like BP, British Telecom, Borg Warner Chemicals, Andrew Antenna, Dow Chemical, ICL, Unisys and others are pleased to help their suppliers and others on the road to TQM.

Personality and TQM, the TQM manager should have a powerful personality as he has to enthuse people to think and work differently. If you pick the right TQM manager to champion the cause you can move mountains. There is nothing that can't be achieved if you have committed and professional champions within the company.

Living in the real world

Developing champions within the company is all very well but organisations do not have unlimited resources from which to choose a co-ordinator to facilitate TQM. We can suggest that organisations should be sufficiently committed to select, develop or recruit the right person to do the job but, for many management teams, funding a TQM drive requires a shift in resources which should not be made unbearable on other demands. Neither can we solve all our problems by throwing money at them!

We are sure that, given time and money, we could develop the right profile of a manager suited to promote TQM and match it exactly — but we all live in the real world and recognise that the reality is that 'we have to achieve more with less.' However, please do not take this comment out of context. All organisations require some injection of 'prevention', however you define it, to reduce rework or at least start the trend. There must be an initial investment in 'internal resources' in order to demonstrate commitment — deeds, not just words, are the order of the day.

Recruiting a TQM manager is not the only answer

We all have to recognise that there is a limit to the resources we can allocate to TQM but increasing head-count and recruiting outsiders does not always change the culture. Head-hunting a manager who has nurtured TQM in one company is no guarantee that he will be able to do it in others. The company has to be prepared for change. Some are not. Recruiting an outsider may 'appear' to solve the immediate problem of finding someone to take responsibility — but the appointment of one man cannot by itself change the style and attitudes of the rest of the management team.

Here is where the commitment and the responsibility for TQM must lie. The TQM manager is the instrument of the management team. He implements policy — but he must not be seen as the only active adherent to TQM. He facilitates change, prepares the base and collects and disseminates data and information. The functional manager must be the leader who brings quality to his function. This is imperative because the functional head has the experience and wisdom to know the system and the way it operates and is aware of the major leverage points for change.

Who should manage change?

This is a general debate on the key players — but who should hold the responsibility? It should not be an external consultant, although he should have the major responsibility when the drive is first underway. Gradually, his role, his impact and his influence should recede. The time taken is determined by the speed at which others within the company take their roles seriously and reflect words with actions.

In Fig. 2 we can see that over time the responsibility for implementing TQM is shared between the internal TQM manager, together with the functional heads and external consultants. This proportion of 'responsibility' for implementation, however, changes over time. In Fig. 2 we can see that everything is going to plan. There is a close relationship between the internals who are accountable and the external change agent. As the external gives up roles and responsibilities, as the TQM drive progresses, we can see that these respon-

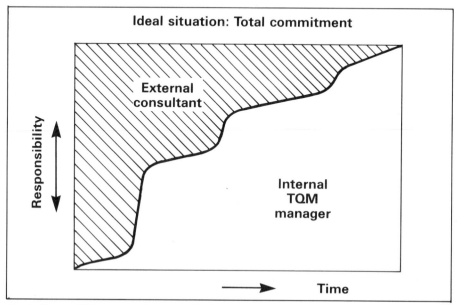

Fig. 2 Responsibility for implementing TQM

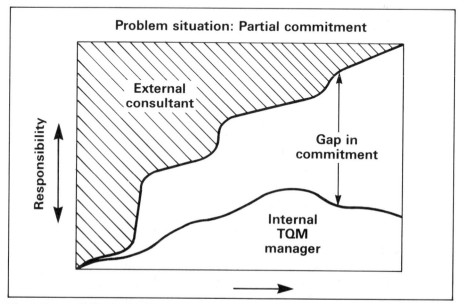

Fig. 3 Responsibility for implementing TQM

sibilities are claimed by internal staff. As we proceed we can see that there are 'step jumps' — most usually related to critical activities which have been completed. These activities include the completion of: senior management training; the diagnostic phase; completion of COQ measures; departmental purpose analysis; training trainers; staff training; problem solving; and corrective action teams, etc. Over time responsibilities and roles change and these should be taken seriously too, i.e. commitment. At the end of the intervention the internal TQ manager and his colleagues and associates take over full control and manage the process.

In Fig. 3 there are serious problems. After some time the internal staff fail to take responsibility. At first this may not appear evident but, as time goes on, we can see a definite gap or 'failure' to grasp the responsibility. As agreed responsibility and roles are taken from the external consultant, we can see that there is a failure by the 'internals' to take the reins. This can happen for a variety of reasons.

The typical way of solving this problem is to get the consultants back in to take over the programme or run more 'training workshops', hoping that enthusiasm and drive will be maintained by others. This is highly unlikely because, if a structured plan and agreement for implementing TQ are not in existence, they won't arise just by accident. Fundamentally, there should be checks and balances at each stage of the drive which must be maintained before progress to the next stage. This ensures that a rift is never allowed to develop.

We may be aware of who should do what, in terms of internal and external accountability, but who inside the company should drive it?

The QA manager is totally responsible for driving TQM!

Promoting the QA manager and increasing his/her range of responsibilities to take control of TQM creates difficulties. Others within the structure perceive this change as it appears. They may believe that TQM is just an expansion of the QA manager's remit and they may fail to accept fully the fundamental truth that Quality problems can originate in all areas of the organisation. This further becomes a problem when we hear the remark, "I thought we had BS 5750, why are we promoting another quality initiative?" This reinforces the mistaken belief that TQM is just another system.

In this way, managers who may administer service functions fail to appreciate the 'preventative' role of QA and see TQM as another sophisticated series of inspection procedures and routines.

All the mistakes originate in production — get them to drive it!

There is an inherent danger that those responsible for production are given the initial responsibility. Again there is a major concern that service functions such as sales, marketing, finance, personnel and others see the TQM drive relating to production facilities only.

Bear in mind that TQM is concerned not only with developing strategies, structures and systems, but also promoting behavioural change. This can only happen through providing staff with the skills, attitude and motivation to bring about change in the styles of management. This requires an individual who is genuinely sensitive to the behavioural issues.

A no-nonsense, results-driven individual may not fully understand the transitions and changes which others have to undergo in order to activate TQM. This does not suggest that the converse — a sensitive, feeling, process-orientated person — is best for the job. A mixture of these two broad 'types' is important if the change is going to be effective.

Human resource specialist as TQM manager

It has been debated whether the personnel or human resource specialist is a natural choice for TQM manager. There is some wisdom in this view, although this could be equally expressed for the commercial or sales manager taking over the role.

TQM is about creating change through attitudes and, for some organisations who wish to drive TQM utilising their own training resources, this is an interesting and productive choice. Obviously, the size and support of the training function is important as to whether this is a reality, but experience in a US chemical company, a US medical company and a UK brewing company suggests that, given adequate resources, this can be extremely effective — because the companies in question had a stronger than 'fairly high' commitment to change through people, *prior* to embarking on the TQM drive.

Status

Obviously, the higher the status of the TQM manager the better. In all honesty, a member of the board is a preferable choice, although there are circumstances when smaller companies have few directors and this is not feasible. Perhaps, if this is not a possibility, it is wise that the person selected is sufficiently close to board members that he has the authority to bring about necessary changes.

The chief executive should drive quality

It must be said that if the TQM manager is not a board member, with full responsibility to see TQM through to the end, there will always be doubts about commitment from other levels of management.

In all honesty, the TQM manager should be the MD of the company. I have heard MDs shout in horror, "I don't have time. I don't think that you understand my responsibilities — I'm very busy." It is for these reasons that the MD should take responsibility. Few will argue with him/her — unless there is a justified reason to halt TQM. He/she may not have time — but neither does anybody else. The MD leading the drive indicates to people how important it is and how they should allocate their time. Their time allocation should be no different from the MD's. If he has time to devote to preventative action there is no reason why others cannot follow. This is probably the single biggest factor which slows down the success rate of any drive failing to establish leadership for TQM. Getting this right first will create a key change in the culture.

If the MD has responsibility, this does not mean that he has to do everything himself. He can appoint or delegate duties to his people on the board and ensure that they have full responsibility for TQM in their functional area. However, on no account should TQM responsibility be cascaded down to someone who does not have an impact on corporate strategy and action. This is a sure sign of window dressing which fools no one.

Rotating TQM managers

Again, this is another possibility for board members to assume the role for a time period and then hand responsibilities on to others. The advantages of this approach are that everyone, at some time, has to get involved and drive the programme — and that the results of the actions of directors are observed and assessed.

The big disadvantage of this strategy is that one director or manager, who may not be committed or finds it hard to make the transition himself, may just 'breathe in and out' until others take over. Overall ownership of the operational side of the drive may be difficult to define — and time spent defining and, in some cases, allocating blame is time when TQM may be decelerating and reinforcing the prejudices of those who believe that it is only 'flavour of the month'.

TQM should be driven by the board at a strategic level. The question and practicalities of operationalising the TQM drive may be another question.

Management team responsibility

Setting up a management team to oversee and take specific roles and responsibilities can be a real winner as long as the key co-ordinator ensures that particular responsibilities are defined in terms of specific outcomes. In other words goals, milestones and objectives are defined in a realistic, achievable, measurable and tangible sense so that progress can be reviewed and action taken if ambiguity over ownership should arise.

Part-time TQM managers

Responsibility may be given to an individual to promote TQM with a corresponding reduction in other duties. Whether this becomes a reality is dependent upon acknowledgement of the time which has to be expended to do the job properly. In one case, a manager had so many responsibilities and production targets that he spent more time on the things for which he was 'being paid', rather than his peripheral duties of TQM. Success and advancement within the organisation was equated with achieving results and, knowing this, the manager naturally allocated time and resources in direct proportion to perceived rewards.

The organisation could have helped the situation by reducing other 'commitments' and understanding that TQM was not so easy to implement. The manager may have benefitted if he had been more assertive in his role but, of course, he had to consider how far he could rock the boat.

This is a very real problem for some organisations. Managers are given projects to complete but still realise that they have a career path to return to once TQM is established.

Compatibility

Team working and building relationships between internal and external consultants are extremely important. The time gap between meetings, especially at a stage when external consultants withdraw from the organisation are, for a short time, breeding grounds for misunderstanding. Being involved in other projects, in other industries and with other companies can lead to communication problems, but many consultancies recognise this problem and take preventative action.

The task force — sometimes a waste of time

Sometimes companies decide to pursue the TQ initiative by setting up a task force or TQM policy group. This can create a great deal of frustration for those on the team if there is little action. Having been introduced to some of the groups assigned to examining the applicability of TQ to their own operations I am not surprised that things don't seem to happen. This is not always the case.

The task force has a great deal of difficulty in defining its terms of reference. Without a very structured approach this sort of group will be feeding little back in the short or medium term. As in some areas of the public sector, the fastest way to kill an idea is to delegate it to a committee — this can be exactly the same strategy.

Delegating a strategic issue to a committee of people from all areas smacks of the promotion of inertia. Unless there are some key players on the team — with the status and charisma to make things happen — nothing will happen. The committee may have good intentions and its members will, perhaps, work as individuals or in sub-groups, visiting other companies who are practising TQM, attending conferences on the subject and having guest speakers, etc. However, unless this information, impressions and ideas, etc. are fed back and

Mission

- Develop a company-wide strategy to implement TQ.
- Provide direction and guidance to implement TQ at various locations.
- Ensure consistency in the TQ initiative but also ensure that TQ is tailored to location.
- Assess the present state of quality awareness within the company.
- Adjust the process to meet varying business needs.

Major activities

- Establish commitment.
- Publicity and communication.
- Assess COQ and agree a model and/or a consistent method of assessment.
- Ensure that TQM is consistent with other company-wide initiatives, i.e. MIP, SPC, MRP and JIT.
- Manage the process of change. Work on those factors which will hinder progress.
- Provide checks, i.e. communication and organisation structure, etc.
- Recognition issues.
- Ensure that a policy is created which is owned by everyone.
- Provide a service, i.e. pilots and feasibility studies.

Operational issues

- Develop a company-wide strategy to implement TQ. (Before this can be achieved it is necessary to build a committed team.)

Issues to discuss

- Composition of the team.
- Rationale to pursue TQ.
- Ensure that all task force members are aware of TQ. It may be necessary to develop an off-site awareness programme.
- Output of programme is remit of total quality task force (TQTF) feedback to company and approval for the next step.
- Agree goals.
- Assess current checks on readiness for change in locations and cultures.
- Provide direction and guidance to implement TQ at various locations.
- Ensure that culture of organisation and historical background determine the level of quality created.
- Communicate to all locations in a meaningful way.
- Develop company strategy and relate to every other function to check for consistency. Research and feedback recommendations to board of directors. Ensure an action plan with time frames is completed.
- Ensure consistency in the TQ initiative but also ensure that TQ is tailored to location.

Carry out checks

- Assess readiness for change. Attitude survey.
- Organisational structure and reporting relationships.
- Communication audit.
- Assess the present state of quality awareness within the company.
- Adjust the process to meet varying business needs. Decide priorities, i.e. existing and future safety, quality, schedule, quantity, cost and JIT, etc.

Fig. 4 The role of the total quality task force

acted upon there will be no move forward.

Few of these groups will meet on a regular basis. There has been only one example which we have encountered where members of the task force were allocated to their duties full time for a period of 3 months. Even with this commitment, 40% of this particular group appeared to be passive and willing to 'watch' while others started the ball rolling.

If you are considering developing a task team or force to assess TQM and its applicability to your company — pick your team carefully. Make sure you have a transformational leader who is committed to changing things. Ensure that he has plenty of support for administrative work. Ensure that a member of the team is sufficiently analytical to guard against the leader 'flying off at tangents'. Team composition and interaction are covered in chapter 11 but Fig. 4 gives a brief utline of a team's role.

Issues for debate

So where does this leave us? These issues are real. Many organisations have experienced these problems and many will confront them in the future.

We need to ensure that managers and consultants debate these points. We need to ensure that false 'assumptions' are not made about roles, responsibilities and expectations. We also need to recognise that there is no easy answer. This means that, in some cases, mistakes will be made and that remedial action will have to be taken.

Change is not easy. What I hope we will recognise is that mistakes can be made and that change is a 'learning process'. Standing back and examining the operational issues and learning from the experience of others, preventing problems arising, in this key area, will enable us to make the transition to TQM a smoother one.

Summary and bullet points

- Prepare the way for TQ. You can underestimate the amount of time needed to appraise the things that could go wrong.
- Success depends upon those whom you have chosen to take TQM forward. Don't give responsibility thinking that their 'status' is enough to see it through. You need to use your best people — not your worst!
- Ownership is the key and it rests nowhere else but at the top.
- If the MD makes an excuse of not having enough time to devote to TQM as a major responsibility — how can he expect others to take it as a key responsibility?
- Choose transformational leaders who can change things quickly. We need people who will take calculated risks and challenge the old ways.
- Don't give all the responsibility to external consultants to create change. If you do this, when they leave so will the concept.
- Ownership for implementation must be shared between internal people and outsiders. Draw up an agreement detailing expectations, roles, responsibilities and time frames for completion. If you don't have a firm route to achieve TQM it won't happen by accident.
- The TQM manager should be your best man — the guy who can establish rapport with your most awkward suppliers. A man of charm but who isn't afraid to say what he thinks.
- TQM can create other initiatives. Work with suppliers on the basis of developing 'preferred' suppliers. Jointly draw up criteria for evaluation. Keep records and ensure actions are taken by the purchasing manager after due consultation with suppliers.

- If some suppliers won't change — change them.
- Appraise your external suppliers. You will be surprised at how well your internal suppliers match up against the criteria which you impose on outsiders.
- Organise events of recognition when suppliers attend and are publicly praised for the hard work they put in to quality improvement — a practice employed by Jaguar and others.
- If you have a problem with a supplier and he takes no notice, ask for a member of his staff to work with you. Processing the inaccurate documentation and experiencing the receipt of faulty or damaged goods will soon get the message back to home base.
- Don't ask suppliers to do the impossible and then change your mind. They are supposed to be partners.
- Recognise that some of your suppliers are only as good as the guidance they are given by their customers, i.e. you help them to develop systems to make things easier for you and them and then costs will drop rapidly.
- Ask your customers what you are doing wrong. Encourage them to be critical. You can only improve things which you know are wrong. You can't improve when you have no feedback on performance. Encourage others to be self critical.
- Enthusiasm is the key. TQM is infectious. Choose people for TQM implementation with caution. You need a combination of vision and persuasiveness followed by analysis.
- TQM is a major change and it can sometimes force or pressurise managers to think in tunnel vision and concentrate within the company. Improvement comes from looking outside, and from talking with people who have done it before and made mistakes. You can learn from their experiences.
- We live in the real world and have to work within resources — but if you don't want your drive to fail ensure that you get more resources for the start-up.
- Don't feel that head-hunting TQ managers from other companies is the answer. One man cannot take the place or, all the responsibility, of the 'Management Team'.
- Ensure that clear responsibilities exist between internal and external change agents.
- Do not make the QA manager responsible for TQM. You will reinforce the belief that TQM is just another system and the responsibility of one distinct area.
- Don't give full responsibility to manufacturing managers. You will reinforce the belief that the service units have no part to play.
- Human resource director is the natural choice for TQM manager — just ensure he has the right status.
- Never mind the natural choice — the best choice for driving TQ resides with the chief executive.
- It is possible to rotate the responsibilities of the post among senior officers — but it can fail more than succeed.
- Part-time TQM managers don't work. When the pressure is on they tend to

concentrate on those things for which they are 'paid' — probably productivity at any price.

- Total quality task forces (TQTFs) can be a waste of time — if they have little guidance and those to whom they report have little idea of what they want. They can work — but it needs a good structure and a good leader.
- These issues are real. Don't discount them. There are many companies who wish they had explored these areas prior to committing themselves to TQM.

SECTION 3:
FEATURES OF TQM DRIVES

8 MEETING CUSTOMER REQUIREMENTS

TQM in any organisation, whether in the public or private sector, must focus upon meeting the requirements of customers in order to strengthen the competitive edge. This is the fundamental consideration behind any quality drive. Konosuke Matsushita, the founder and chief executive of Matsushita, one of the largest manufacturers of consumer electrical goods in the world, stresses in his book 'Not for Bread Alone' that we should strive to find out what our customers think about the service we provide.

The foundation of superlative performance rests on being self critical and asking others to comment on our performance. This means listening to what we do not want to hear. We should go to extraordinary lengths to explore the level of 'disservice' we provide. We should encourage criticism even if this is negative — because we should realise that the chance to succeed and provide superior service comes from us looking at all the occasions when we fail.

Focusing too much on the end user — the customer

Often this open approach brings to reality the things we would rather not hear, but it is the opportunity to really do something about the service we provide — to do things better. Matsushita thought this to be one of the real keys to long-term competitiveness. There can, however, be a danger that we focus too much attention on the customer and direct our TQM drive towards a customer service orientation, focusing too much on the perceptions of our external customer. This can be a danger because we fail to consider the implications of putting all our eggs into one basket. There is also a danger that a customer service drive is achieved through the means of 'Public Relations'. This is not improving customer service — it is manipulating and changing the perception of our customers and this may not be based on reality.

TQM must focus on the customer, the eventual buyer of the service or product which we provide — but we must be careful. Imagine running a training workshop for all grades of employee and focusing entirely on the customer. There may be a danger that people attending will switch off, for the simple reason that 95% of employees within manufacturing companies never even meet the customer. They might think, "This is all very interesting, but I never meet the customer. Therefore anything which is said is not applicable to me." This is where we turn the tables and get those attending to think of their colleagues as their customers — hence the orientation towards the internal customer.

It is difficult for people working at the same workstation everyday, whether they be manufacturing based, a secretary, an administrator in an accounts department, a draughtsman or a storesman. They all have an equal role to play in improving quality but fail to recognise it because they never 'meet the customer'. This difficulty can also be encountered in the service sector. Staff employed in clerical, supervisory and managerial positions within the health service, local or public authorities and those in the banking and finance sector all could interpret the customer as someone who purchases the end product or service. Clearly we have to enlarge this definition.

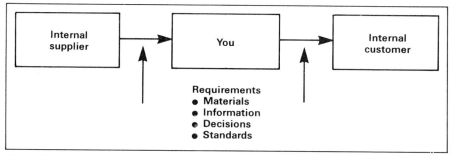

Fig. 1 Meeting customer requirements

Internal customer

We believe that everybody within an enterprise should consider the interaction between themselves and their 'internal customers' — those who are next in line. Failing to grasp this notion can kill the most effective TQM drive. It was for this very reason that British Airways introduced both a customer care service and a total quality drive. They recognised that you cannot have one without the other.

Everyday we are dependent upon the quality of information, decisions and resources supplied by others. The quality of information which personnel practitioners receive from line management will determine the success of personnel practice, i.e. recruitment, selection, appraisal, redeployment, manpower planning and training. We need to understand that the interaction between functions and departments is critical if we want to improve everything we do. So what action can we take?

Who are my customers?

Your customer is anyone who is dependent upon you for the supply of goods or a service. It is someone who can't complete their job to an agreed level or standard on time without your timely input. You provide the resources, information and decisions upon which others act. In other words, your customers are dependent upon you to provide a high-quality service. If you fail to deliver they in turn cannot provide a good quality service to their customers and so on (see Fig. 2).

- List your chief customers.
- What do they need from you? How can you ensure that you provide them with their requirements, on time, every time?
- When did you last discuss your requirements with your customers?
- Assume a meeting has been called to improve the provision of your services to your major customers. What issues would you debate?
- What three major factors stop you meeting the requirements of your customers on time, every time, without error, defect or omission?

Fig. 2 Negotiating with customers?

Who are my suppliers?

As we have customers so also do we have suppliers. Try not to think of suppliers as the people external to your business who provide you with raw materials, stationery, power and fuel and so forth. Think of suppliers as 'internal' suppliers, those people within the company who supply you with all you need in order for you to do your job. We can see that any company, no matter how small, has a network of suppliers and customers. This network creates a mutually dependent relationship. If there is a breakdown between internal customers and suppliers, then quality of service within the company will be poor (see Fig. 3).

> **Think of your suppliers. How can you ensure that your suppliers provide you with the necessary information, decisions, standards, services or goods on time, every time, without defect, error or omission?**
>
> - **How can you ensure that your suppliers meet your requirements?**
> - **What actions can you take to reduce ambiguity in the services they provide for you?**
> - **To what extent do your requirements, and the suppliers' perception of your requirements, match?**
> - **Why is there a mismatch? What are the major causes of ambiguity?**
> - **Have you and your suppliers jointly agreed objectives and information required? If not, how were these agreed and when?**
> - **What specific action will you take to clear up any ambiguities between your requirements and the suppliers' perception of your requirements?**

Fig. 3 Negotiating with major suppliers?

The customer/supplier chain

Let us look at a real example. Consider the mutual interplay between a sales department, a research and development area, where drawings are completed, and manufacturing locations. This example existed in a large engineering company. Sales staff spent a great deal of time with customers. Most sales people in this company had some level of engineering expertise but this had been gained many years beforehand. Due to some of the demands of their customers, sales people had to be pretty quick in responding to rush orders — otherwise this could mean lost business. Sales had to have a quote for its biggest customer almost immediately. It had very little lead time.

The major problems lay with the provision of new products. Increasingly, more of the business was of this variety because of the changing product which their customer was producing. Consequently lead times were reduced to the bare minimum.

Salesmen would return from the customer with a requirement to tender a quote for the business. Before the quote was assessed there was a great deal of information which had to be generated. If the information was incorrect the quote may be too high, thus making the firm less competitive against others quoting for the business. If it were too low, because of a failure to incorporate all costs, it would mean that the business was unprofitable. Clearly there was balance to be sought in order to generate the right quote.

Working in spite of each other!, salesmen who were keen for the business, promised early delivery to the customer of 'sample parts' for testing. This date was firmly set. The salesman would return and talk to the people in R&D, who would start generating plans for discussion. There are few R&D establishments which don't have a backlog of work and this company was no different. Consequently, other work in progress would be put to one side while the new priority work was slotted into its place.

Drawings had to be generated. These would be the basis for manufacturing set-up and assembly as well as the foundation required for design by the tool makers.

There was a failure to assess and develop customer/supplier relationships. One major problem was that few designers/draughtsmen had actually visited their own various manufacturing locations. There were 6 plants spread over a fairly wide area in the Midlands. Upon investigation, it became clear that some of the draughtsmen did not even know where the actual factories were located. Now, if draughtsmen were unaware of location how reliable was their understanding of manufacturing process within the plants? It soon transpired that there was little understanding.

Assumptions were made about techniques of assembly and the 'cost estimators', those responsible for working out the total unit cost of possible manufacture, were widely off the mark in their assessments. Consequently, some of the estimates provided little profit for the company. In some cases this created further problems. Priorities had not been agreed between departments everywhere so there was fire-fighting.

Drawings arrived late for toolmakers so toolmakers had to work 3 shifts to complete the tools for the manufacturing process. This cost a great deal and was passed onto the customer — eventually! Due to the constraint on time tools weren't tested, and this meant that, in the manufacturing process, that they did the wrong job, creating rework. Tools did not fit specific technology in some locations and soon broke in manufacture in other plants.

In addition, the toolmakers were unreliable and could not provide a back-up service. The reason for this was that the purchasing manager had been told to take 'toolmakers' from the cheaper end of the market. Toolmakers at the cheaper end existed because nobody else used their services and they did not have the up-to-date machinery on which to prove the tools. Consequently, their overheads were lower and they were able to provide a cheaper service — at least in the short term.

TQM is doing the right job, everybody was extremely busy but nobody was really being effective. There was a need to develop closer relationships between customer and supplier. Here the emphasis was placed on meeting the requirements of the external customer — however crazy — whereas some attention should have been placed on the 'internal customer' relationship. If we fail to get this relationship right we will not meet the needs of the external customer.

Get it right inside the company first

Agreeing to bend over backwards for the external customer is a grave mistake if it creates a great deal of chaos and rework within the company. This is not to say that we should not attempt to meet the requirements of our 'externals' — but we need to be realistic. We should not agree to the impossible if it creates more problems within the company.

Quality dialogue

In the company discussed above, a typical project meeting would go something like this:

Sales manager "I don't care whether you can make the production date or not. You said you needed 17 weeks lead time, but the customer wants it in 14 weeks. Is that so difficult? Listen, my guys spend a lot of time getting orders for you guys in manufacturing. We keep you in a job. It's difficult out there in the real world. You have to complete the order or we lose the business."

Production manager: "Well Ron, that's all very well for you but we have to make the product to specification. George in R&D tells us that he has not got enough time to do the drawings. He doesn't want to send them outside to sub-contractors — but he'll have to, to make your deadline."

Sales manager: "No way. They have to be produced in-house. We don't want those cowboys at ABC doing the drawings again. Last time the tools were wrong and it was all traced back to their drawings."

So the story continues. This is not a one-off occurrence but the norm for many companies. The secret is to get things right inside the company before going outside. The customer doesn't realise the chaos which is created, even though his product is delivered on time. Many say they don't care as long as they receive the product right first time, on time. However, this is nonsense because the product has been manufactured at unit costs plus reworked costs. The customer still has to bear the costs of inefficiency of the supplier. These costs have to be passed on otherwise many companies would go out of business. Many still don't realise this!

Major training initiative

There is a requirement for departments to work 'together' instead of 'in spite of each other'. There is a need to do things differently.

One approach, when TQM training is underway, is to create 'Supplier/ Customer Workshops', where a small number of people from different departments and functions are brought together to discuss problem areas, with quality of service and product in mind. This approach helps share stereotypes of each other, reject these as negative and discuss new ways of working to improve service.

Listing your chief customers

Often when managers attend these sessions they tend not to think of others around the table as being their customers. It is quite a transition getting people to appreciate that their customer has needs and requirements and that these have to be met first, before we attempt to meet the requirements of external customers. Getting people to generate a list of customers and suppliers is useful because we use this information to enquire as to the frequency of interaction between internal customer and supplier. We tend to find that suppliers of information tend to converse fairly frequently and spend 80% of their available time with 20% of their customers — what about the others?

It is all very well spending time with some customers but who determines the choice of customers? The suppliers do. Which means that they determine the choice and priority. There may be many instances when internal customers feel that their suppliers spend too little time with them trying to solve problems. They feel short-changed and this reinforces the belief "Those guys are not interested in improving things so let's keep clear of them." This can be a rift which creates untold damage between and within departments.

Personalise customer/supplier interface

Asking customers what they need is a question which many internal suppliers have never asked. They may be surprised by the answer. Let's look at a simple example.

Think of an internal customer with whom you have a particular problem. Write down the problem. Why is there a problem? Presumably this has something to do with the service which you provide to him or her.

Now, write down your perception of the requirements of this customer. What are they? Please be specific. Now think from your customers perspective. What are his requirements of you? Be detailed. Write down specific requirements. Now compare the two lists. Are they somewhat different?

This exercise is an extremely powerful tool when integrated as part of a workshop session. Knowing where problems are within the company, finding a known area for improvement and collecting data prior to a training session are prerequisites for improvement.

The information from the two perspectives is then used to generate lists from these different perspectives. Disclosing these lists to both parties, internal customer and supplier, creates disbelief. They are exposed to 'requirements' which they had never considered before. The misconception of 'requirements' then becomes the focus for discussing things and improving service.

Currently, in too many organisations, insufficient time is spent in this activity. It is critical that this is reversed in order to promote effective teamwork.

What are requirements?

The requirements are the standards by which the output of a person or unit can be measured. Requirements include time to do a job, a set standard of performance and the resources to complete work, including information.

Requirements also include decisions which have to be taken and passed on to others. Requirements are not just related to 'tangible' items such as resources and decisions — but also to processes, i.e. there is a requirement for draughtsmen to talk with manufacturing people to ensure that the methods identified for manufacture, and quoted in technical drawings, are feasible. This means the draughtsmen/engineers may have to talk with the people who actually do the job. Those on the shop floor are the customers of the draughtsmen and, likewise, the designer is the supplier to those in manufacturing.

As part of a TQM drive the personnel of a drawing office agreed to meet people who produce the product. This was a major step. Some designers and draughtsmen had been employed for over 5 years and had never been on the shop floor. Clearly their perception of how things were differed from reality. As part of an action plan for change, the visits to the shop floor were to be a regular occurrence.

It started with the designer/engineer introducing himself to the people who assembled the product. This introduction created an instant rapport with assemblers who asked designers why they did things in certain ways. They discussed scrap, manufacturing capability of equipment and failure mode effect analysis (FMEA), etc. (There was to be some staggering improvement in design and process FMEAs.) The designers learned from their experiences, changed the estimates for manufacturing assembly and discussed these with cost estimators. The impact that this had on morale on the shop floor was amazing. The designers and draughtsmen were no longer 'the guys with white shirts who live in ivory towers' but instead, had started to appreciate the value of conversations with their internal customers.

People took requirements seriously — for the first time.

What happens if we fail to meet the requirements?

It's pretty obvious. We deviate from the expected performance or level of quality of output. Things do not arrive on time. Production is slowed. This becomes even more of a problem in a service area because the 'intangibility' of what is offered is not as apparent as in a failure of parts not being manufactured or shipped late. If a lorry is waiting for parts and they are not ready, there would be an uproar. However, documentation — i.e. reports, annual appraisals, working party findings, accounts figures, drawings and many other things, which may be even more important for the organisation but do not turn up on time in the right place — does not appear to be of the same urgency.

There still seem to be dual standards between the product and the service sides of the business. Some may claim that this is a vast generalisation but this is what happens in industry in the 1990s. Figures and information can always be subject to 'guesstimates' but the product must be there — and it must be right.

It just so happens that companies can go out of business with a product which is defect free. Failing to provide a service or maintain internal controls, can lead to company failure probably more quickly than a poor product. We wonder if senior officers in business spend enough time and attention examining the perceived 'intangible' service between internal customers and suppliers and examine its consequences for competitiveness.

Is failing to meet requirements serious?

Yes. It can be very serious, especially if the deviation or error is not spotted and is compounded by others. Consider what happens in a production process if an error creeps into the product and is not spotted. A great deal of manufacture can take place before the error or deviation is discovered — unfortunately and, sometimes this does not happen until inspection after the final assembly stage. This can contribute to a huge cost if left unchecked.

This is even more serious in the service side of the business. Information which supervisors believe to be correct is passed to others who use this information for decision making. As supervisors are busy they do not question the figures, expecting others to have checked and so errors are compounded. This can be far more serious than we realise.

What can we do to avoid ambiguity in requirements?

The solution is easy but we can always find a reason not to do it. Meet, discuss and agree 'requirements' with our customers and suppliers. This is the preventative action on which TQM is based.

Common problems of not meeting customer requirements

Requirements are ill defined and/or inaccurate. Our customers can make too many assumptions and develop unrealistic expectations of the service we can provide as suppliers. If customers and suppliers fail to discuss requirements there is going to be a surprise when delivery of service or product does or doesn't take place.

Requirements are unrealistic. We often agree to the impossible and wonder why we suffer from self-induced stress. On the spur of the moment we agree to achieving things which are beyond our control. This self imposition of targets can act as a short-term motivator but, if it becomes part of day-to-day organisational life, sooner or later someone is going to be found out, hurt and disappointed.

Requirements are not achievable, measurable or quantifiable. Two or more people or departmental representatives can get together to talk about things in fairly general terms, fail to summarise an agreement in precise terms, return to their departments and wait for others to deliver whatever has been agreed. Here, there is too much 'flexibility' in requirements. There will be little likelihood in this instance of delivery of anything taking place.

As each person retreats to his respective department he develops his own general expectations of the overall effect. Failing to tie things down to specifics and measurable targets or sub-goals creates a great deal of room for error and false assumption.

Requirements are not discussed, tested or agreed with customers and suppliers. If there is no joint agreement on targets and priorities, again, too much is left to chance. People do not seem to have a clear idea of what is expected of them. Somehow, perhaps by accident, the defect-free service or product might arrive. TQM isn't like that — we need to work to eradicate misconception of requirements so that we are all working for a common goal.

Lack of commitment to your requirements by your customers and suppliers. Another classic problem. Customers and suppliers sometimes develop a departmental attitude which focuses upon their own needs at the expense of others. They fail to remember that other people have demands upon them and they tend to treat others rather badly. Others perceive your problems as yours alone and want to play no part in resolving them. This failure to develop team spirit kills TQM.

Requirements are not 'owned', managers fail to take responsibility and communicate requirements to their staffs. If nobody takes ownership for a problem nobody is going to solve it. Recognition of problems is something which is critical to success. Working together to solve problems and fix them once and for all is the key to success.

Meeting with customers and suppliers

Assume a meeting has been called to improve the provision of your services to your major customers and suppliers. What issues would you debate? These are the crucial issues which help develop the required team spirit. There is no reason why, during a project planning meeting, all attending internal suppliers and customers cannot generate a list of issues for clarification. These can then become the focus for customer/supplier workshops. Once we have developed the commitment to work together then we can examine the major barriers to working together (see Figs. 4 and 5).

20 factors which stop us meeting the requirements of our customers

What are major factors preventing you from meeting the requirements of your customers? It is relatively easy to generate a list of at least 100 items — but we

1. Who is my customer?

Your customer may be a person, department or unit which relies on you to provide goods, services, decisions, information or advice.

2. Who is my supplier?

Your supplier is a person, a department or unit, which provides you with goods, services, decisions or advice.

3. Procedure

Do you have a formal or an informal procedure between yourself and your customer(s) or supplier(s) for stated goods and services? Do you have procedures which are not used or are out of date? Identify them now. Do something about them.

4. Rating your customers

How would you honestly rate the service you provide to your customers? Score out of 10, where 10 is excellent. (Pick 5 customers with whom you know you have problems. Rate them now.)

5. Precision — customer

(i) Does your customer clearly state what s/he wants? (Think again of 5 customers and the services you provide. Rate them now.)

Yes:
Every time	score 3
Most times	score 2
Rarely	score 1
Never	score 0

(ii) Does s/he give you all the necessary information in order for you to meet the requirements? (Do this exercise thinking of 5 internal customers where you know you have a problem. Score for each customer.)

Yes:
Every time	score 3
Most times	score 2
Rarely	score 1
Never	score 0

(iii) Does your customer have an input to the request for the service? (Score for 5 customers.)

Yes	score 3
Quite a lot	score 2
Very little	score 1
No	score 0

6. Precision — supplier

(i) Do you think you provide adequate instructions to your supplier? (Think of 5 suppliers — pick some with whom you have problems.)

Yes	score 3
Sometimes	score 2
Not sure	score 1
No	score 0

(ii) Do you give your suppliers enough time to supply to your requests?

Yes	score 3
Sometimes	score 2
Not often	score 1
No	score 0

(iii) Do you regularly review the quality of service between you and your suppliers?

Yes	score 3
Sometimes	score 2
Not often	score 1
No	score 0

There is no profile against which to assess your scores. However, the relative figures should be sufficient to set up meetings with your most important customers and suppliers.

Fig. 4 Appraisal of customer/supplier relationships

Meeting customer requirements: Memo pad

To ....

From ....

Date ....

Subject ....

My requirements are:

1.
2.
3.
4.
5.
6.
7.
8.

Can you meet these requirements? If not could you note down alternatives for discussion?

1.
2.
3.
4.
5.
6.

Fig. 5 TQM Associates Ltd customer requirements form

think it is important to look at the top 20 items, from experience, and relate these to the majority of problems within companies. What is noticeable is that all these factors are behavioural. They are not strictly dependent upon resources and they can be challenged and beaten if people have the will to change their attitudes.

- Ambiguous instructions. There is no clarity between customer and supplier concerning what is wanted.
- Misinformation either by accident or 'guesstimates'. Too many use 'swinging wild ass'd guesstimates' (SWAG) as a method for calculation. Managers not wanting to be caught out by their internal customers or suppliers will use SWAG as an alternative to accurate information. The consequences are predictable.
- Agreeing to impossible deadlines because of fear or belief that imposing unrealistic demands upon themselves and others will create the will to achieve. This fear-driven strategy may work in the short term but will fail quickly with TQM. Attendees at workshops suddenly start using these examples of the 'counter culture' to discredit the drive. There can be another side to this example — that of the imposed requirements. This never works.
- Little understanding of constraints and demands of our customers. This unwillingness to explore the problems of others runs against TQM to such a degree that a joint problem-solving approach would be anathema.

- Lack of forward planning by ourselves and our customers. There is so much fire-fighting in industry and commerce today that customers and suppliers never have time to get together, or so they say. People can only forward plan when they involve others. The future success of companies is infrequently determined solely by the success of one solitary department, so it is important to spend more time working together, instead of against each other.
- Being insufficiently selective when defining requirements. Again, lack of perceived available time plays a part here as an excuse but not a legitimate reason. Being selective and precise is imperative in order to filter out the major points for agreement.
- Lack of training or inadequate training. We always find it amazing that people can be trained in TQM in 2 or 3 days but that they have never really received good quality training to do their job. Many cannot use the technology available, are computer illiterate and have never attended the most basic of management training courses.
- Lack of co-ordination. Failure to lead through teams and horizontal management will create a functional organisation where there is little interaction.
- Tunnel vision — "Let me do my job and you stick to yours." This is too prevalent and negative. Senior management is to blame for not doing something about this in recent years.
- Customers' inability to assess their own requirements. The customer may be ignorant of the service which can be provided for him by the supplier. The supplier must then realise that he/she has an educational role to play in helping the customer to assess his requirements.
- Suppliers' inability to help customers recognise and identify their requirements. Sometimes the supplier is ignorant of the help that he can provide to his customer or, even worse, is unaware of the ignorance of the customer. This is particularly the case with systems people when they talk with their customers — perhaps people in line management. Sometimes systems people have to treat their customers as suppliers, getting them to think about what they need in order to do a job. Systems people may have to say what they can do in order for line management to appraise what is available and possible.
- Poor time management and objective setting. Lack of time is a major excuse for failing to get together to discuss requirements. It is just an excuse because if managers really valued the clarification of requirements they would make time for it! If they do not value it they will find an excuse not to do it.
- Lack of warning about urgent requirements. This reflects the short-term drive of many businesses. Everything is fire-fighting or a surprise. Perhaps this keeps the adrenalin pumping round the system but it does not promote long-term effectiveness.
- Assumptions — "I thought you wanted it the same as last time," or, "I thought you would not mind waiting." Assumptions exist because there is a failure to be precise and to define standards or performance. Attention to detail is all it is!

- Poor communication and listening. "I hear what you are saying," is an over-used and pointless phrase. Passive hearing characterises too many managers who believe that they are the source of meaningful improvement. What is required is managers opening up and actively listening to what others are expressing. Couple this with the certain knowledge that precise notes on agreements between customer and supplier are not a thing we see often in an organisation. There are too many verbal agreements which are open to whatever interpretation managers choose. It is no surprise that there are different perspectives on requirements and no surprise that people do not live up to their promises.
- Poor understanding of priorities. It is interesting to note that too few people within companies are really aware of where the company is going. There is some misunderstanding about priorities and the means to achieve objectives.
- Unwillingness to bargain and agree. This is characteristic of areas where there is a great deal of rework generated between departments. Requirements tend to be imposed on the suppliers of goods or a service. Imagine the working relationship created!
- Passing the buck to other people and departments. This is common — "If X only provided us with Z on time." Rejecting this failure to share ownership is the foundation to the solution of this problem.
- Unaware of own responsibility. Often people can be ignorant of the role they can play with others. Imagine how strange the alternative would be to someone who has worked in a culture which has always operated on a strictly functionalised basis.
- Inability and unwillingness to criticise personal performance. This is a common trait in many organisations and can be the single biggest threat to getting customers and suppliers to work together.

Departmental purpose analysis

Although this will be examined in chapter 13, it is important to note that functional groups or departments do need to clarify the reasons for their existance. These goals and objectives need to be communicated to everybody within the function so that they have a real grasp of their 'missions'. Ideally, the departmental purpose analysis (DPA) will be created from the existing culture and the comments and views developed from those in the function. However, overall, people will gain a better grasp of meeting requirements when they have a better picture of what they should be offering to their customers. "If you don't know where you are going — any road will get you there," is an approach which we have to reject. There are plenty of instances, in both the private and the public sectors, which could benefit from asking some serious questions like, "What are we here to do and where are we going?"

Summary and bullet points

- Customer satisfaction is the fundamental motivation behind TQ — but too much attention should not be focused at first on the external customer to the detriment of the customer/supplier relationship within the company.

- Superlative performance relies on being constantly self critical and knowing we can do things better with our internal and external customers.
- Seek out criticism — 95% of success comes from examining the 5% of failures.
- Don't get involved in external customer care until you have satisfied yourself that you have an internal customer care programme.
- Don't ever equate customer care, and TQ with a public relations approach to corporate change.
- Everyone has customers and suppliers and the sooner we can work together the sooner improvements will be made.
- TQM is about challenging requirements, talking with our customers and agreeing new requirements. As business changes so do requirements.
- Requirements include information, decisions, resources, materials, time and standards. These should never be imposed upon others. It is much better to have joint ownership.
- TQ is reflected in the deviation from meeting customer requirements. TQ is about narrowing this deviation to zero — so that suppliers' and customers' requirements are the same.
- TQ attitude between customers and suppliers is not a matter of accident or luck. It has to be worked for.
- When there is disagreement with customers and suppliers, the emphasis should be on agreement, dialogue and joint problem-solving.
- Meeting customer requirements 100% of the time equates with competitive advantage.
- The relationship between customer and supplier should be strengthened by the interaction. Negative stereotyping of departments should be minimised and team-work encouraged.
- Avoid ambiguity when agreeing requirements. Ensure that requirements are specific, realistic and measurable.
- Reject assumptions and question woolly thinking.
- The factors which inhibit meeting customer requirements are behavioural in nature and are often self-imposed and self-perpetuating.
- Departmental purpose analysis, as a process, can be founded upon major discrepancies between internal customers and suppliers.

9 ERROR PREVENTION

Right first time and rhetoric

There is a real danger when we start using phrases like 'getting it right the first time' (RFT) that these are perceived by employees as no more than rhetoric and exhortation. Deming warns us about these dangers. Catch-phrases publicising the 'cause' soon become worn and meaningless. It can become even more pronounced when someone has the bright idea to have posters printed. Posters adorn the building, with the RFT slogan well displayed and it soon becomes a meaningless three letter abbreviation (TLA).

There is another danger, and that is that these phrases are used for the wrong purpose. Too often we have heard the phrase 'right first time' used in a negative context, to allocate blame and catch people out! RFT is a state towards which a company is moving. It can be used in too literal a manner when, instead, it should be used positively so that we can learn to do things better.

We have to be careful that phrases, which once had meaning, do not become colourless with little vibrancy or life. We have to ensure that the RFT mentality really is that. It must become part of the managerial way of doing things — managers and others in authority leading by example. RFT is, after all, the only acceptable standard of performance.

Right first time is a standard of performance

RFT is a performance standard. It is about performing and achieving work which is error free. This is the foundation upon which the positive attitudes towards TQM are made. Many traditional QA drives focus on standardising procedures and agreeing specifications for inspection. The RFT approach is concerned with surpassing the present performance standard and replacing it with zero defects.

The RFT approach is a 'performance standard' which we want everybody to gradually acquire. Please note the word 'gradually'. We do not expect people to change their behaviour overnight — as we would not expect the senior officers of a company to change the way they do things immediately. RFT is about only passing those things on to your customer which meet his or her requirements.

Error-free work

This approach is concerned with getting staff, whether internal suppliers or customers, to perform error-free work. This principle helps us forge the chain of quality between all functions, units and departments. Overall, the RFT philosophy helps us to reduce the requirement for expensive rework by preventing problems arising. Fundamentally, this is about developing a strong value in everybody so as not to pass something on which we know is wrong. This might sound easy but it isn't.

Right second time threatening TQM progress

One major US-owned market leader in medical technology had been developing a TQ drive for quite some time. The great majority of the workforce had been through the educational process and managers in plant locations were making some attempt to bring down the cost of quality by taking preventative action. Several years into the programme, the R&D boys developed a new product which would revolutionise a number of products in the industry.

Sales people did not waste any time. They saw this as a grand opportunity to consolidate market share. A great deal of fuss and hype was generated about the new product and, of course, the sales force went out selling. Before they realised it the sales people had accrued $20m-worth of sales — but, as yet, the product was still undergoing tests.

Although the prototype and the tests suggested that the product would be reliable, when the plant eventually went into production, some time later, the QA people discovered that there had been a design error which might lead to failure in 2–3% of the products. At first they were shocked, realising the impact that this would have on the TQ programme. Nobody seemed to question that the product would be released and there were many urgent meetings with senior staff from head office mulling over the possible consequences.

It was touch and go. Although this was a multi-billion dollar company, with a reputation for quality to protect, there was one school of thought that suggested that the product should be released into the market-place! It was hypothesised that, in the few cases where there was breakdown, the company could service the product, rework it or substitute it with a reliable model when a new, more compatible design was approved. Clearly an 'acceptable quality level' (AQL) was appearing. If 97% of the product range was okay, then ship the lot and put up with the rework. After all it would not cost too much. The company would still gain $20m in the short term and could put up with rework costs which wouldn't be too expensive. This was the argument. The only problem was that the 100% quality zero defect goal was being compromised, and who was to say it wouldn't happen again? Next time the AQL might be 96% or 93% but who cares —rework costs aren't high anyway. Clearly this violation of a major principle of TQM would kill the incentive behind the drive.

TQM heroes, the senior staff at the manufacturing plant stood out for the 'scrap it' option, much against the view from corporate headquarters. Some put their heads on the block. They were total advocates of TQM. Those risking their jobs for a 'principle' also recognised that this event was critical for the take up of TQM within the workforce. For some time, the workforce in some units had been looking for an excuse to confirm its prejudice that management was not serious about quality. It almost had its wish come true. The CEO entered into the debate and made the only choice possible. He scrapped $20m-worth of equipment and started again.

The company lost face with its customers — but only in the short term. Apart from the odd customer, most accepted the reason for withdrawal from the market and were happy to wait the extra 9 months for 'Error-Free Products'. This display of commitment reinforced the belief in the company that the senior officers were serious about quality improvement.

Most important of all, it created within the workforce a level of trust never before witnessed. The company was serious. People who had pushed TQM and put their jobs on the line were classed as heroes. Stories of how local managers convinced corporate officers of the wisdom of the TQM approach were told, with the resulting effect that morale and job satisfaction went through the roof.

This incident also acted as a catalyst to those who were doubters. Resistance to TQM fell.

Right first time is developed by example

The case above shows us that cultures need time to change and that critical incidents like the one described can act as either the death knell or the mark of success for TQM. Overall it reflects the phrase: "We do what we value and we value what we do."

Actions reflect attitudes and values. Attitude change mirrored in actions and behaviour is the foundation upon which quality grows and flourishes to become a way of life. This requires people at all levels who have strong values to lead by example. Those who possess a strong positive attitude are those who are committed to improving individual, departmental and organisational standards of performance. This attitude and the enthusiasm generated from it can take companies far above their competitors in terms of quality of performance.

Error-free standards

Work which is error-free is a statement of our own personal standard of performance. More importantly, it means that people with this standard will positively stop errors creeping into their work. They are their own inspectors. They do not require antiquated methods of control. They want to do things properly. They have pride in their work. However, although they are their own inspectors they want to do more than just check for errors. They want to prevent errors arising and this means looking for ways to stop errors taking place. People — if trained — also come up with lots of ideas to prevent problems arising. This is the approach behind 'foolproofing' which the Japanese have turned into an art form. Those interested in 'foolproofing' deliberately go out of their way to look at every possible combination of what can go wrong in manufacture and then take preventative action — just once — to eradicate the problem.

Foolproofing: the Japanese approach to prevention

When walking round Japanese companies it is amazing to see the level of sophistication in 'foolproofing'. From simple examples at Toyota, where cars are covered with plastic strips to avoid scratched paintwork during assembly, to Nippon Denso where the achieved performance standard for manufacture and assembly of brake drums and other automotive components is zero defects. It is incredible. Simple devices, developed by operators, are located all along the assembly line. Jigs are designed to reject metallic items which do not conform to a standard. Nippon Denso has not had a major problem with any of the car manufacturers it services for the past 10 years. British managers witnessing this experience have been amazed, have considered the behaviour of suppliers to the automotive industry in Europe and wondered what the performance standard would be in this country.

Quality improvement statistics

The devotion to duty is even more marked in Japanese manufacturing plants. There, we are told that employees constantly provide suggestions to improve everything they do. This does not include just manufacturing areas but clerical and administrative procedures too. It is quite frightening when statistics are bandered about. On average, the Japanese suggest that they get something like 100–140 ideas from each employee. The really frightening statistic is that, on average, they tend to implement 80% of these suggestions.

Why does this approach work? It is quite simple. Employees see a wonderful opportunity for quality improvement in the most general of senses. The idea may speed up production — but it does not have to. The improvement may be to do with cost reduction, quality improvement, health and safety, or ergonomics, etc.

Implement improvement — don't kill them with talking

On a trip to Mitsubishi, a group stopped beside the assembly line and talked through an interpretator to a shop floor employee. He was asked about the suggestions he had recently given to his manager and his quality circle. He talked about a suggestion of which he was most proud. This had to do with moving a button from the floor area of his workstation, just beneath the assembly line, to a place adjacent to his waist. The suggestion had been approved by the circle 7 days prior to the visit. Five days after the proposals were approved the button was moved. Movement of the button did not increase productivity or improve quality but it stopped the employee having to bend over every 3 minutes. He now felt more rested and was extremely grateful.

Can you imagine the effect that this action had on the morale of employees? It would encourage more suggestions and it demonstrates that the management of the company is really concerned about its people. The management doesn't just implement those things which will lead to significant cost reduction or productivity or quality improvement, it is prepared to improve everything. It is committed to zero defects, not just in manufacture but in people management.

Bearing this last case in mind, think about and honestly answer one simple question: In the average UK plant, what would happen if an employee suggested the movement of a button to ease the operations he performed? Would management respond and move the button? Would it feed back and tell the employee it was a good idea — but could not be implemented because of XY or Z — or would nothing happen?

It is most likely that nothing would happen or that there would be a response which discouraged any further involvement!

The average British company does not recognise the contribution the employee can make to improvement. Compare the British to the Japanese rivals. Just to push this point beyond credence, Toyota recently announced that in 1988 its Japanese employees made 1,903,858 suggestions of which 97% were adopted. Does anyone have similar figures for European industry? Don't think that this is a quirk of the Japanese culture. In Japanese-owned companies and joint ventures in Europe and the USA, quality improvement is just as high. This is not a feature of the 'Japanese' but a feature of the approach they use — which can work in all European and US companies given time, planning and patience.

Suggestions are not limited to manufacturing

Many suggestions affect performance in manufacturing areas but careful examination by Toyota has ensured that the hands-on approach by employees can be improved and continued in all areas. The results of this are increased efficiency, cost control and a happy, motivated and satisfied workforce. This approach is clearly desirable — so what action can we take in Europe and the USA to promote the RFT attitude?

Right first time must become a personal standard of performance

It means that the individual prevents errors from intruding into his or her own personal work. The errors which creep into our work and are passed on to our internal customers are compounded and passed on to the recipient of the service or goods — the external customer. The customer's dissatisfaction then becomes a significant quality problem. How long is it before the customer becomes sufficiently upset with our lack of attention to detail that he decides to go elsewhere — to our competitors? In markets which are growing slowly, an increase in sales for one company usually means a reduction in sales, work and job security for others.

Only when RFT becomes the expected standard of performance for everybody, can we ensure that errors are not compounded and passed on to the customer. We must understand that the results of failing to take preventative action are a loss of market share and a reduction in profit levels. There are some cases when the cost of putting things right can cost more than the revenue received for the product or service. This is not healthy and can lead to only one conclusion — customers learn quickly and do business only with organisations who are committed to TQ.

Personal values and standards

We would not expect airline pilots to adopt a less than 100% commitment to take off, flying and landing. Neither would we expect a dentist to adopt a sloppy attitude. We are very critical of others but not sufficiently critical of ourselves. We know that the sloppy attitude is indicative of others — but never ourselves!

When we do things wrong we often rationalise and find a reason for the error. When others use the same approach we claim it as an 'excuse'. For instance, many complain that they are 'so busy fire-fighting and extinguishing yesterday's problems' that they 'never have time, the resources or the support to work on preventing tomorrow's problems'. This is an excuse not a reason.

This is a strange attitude indeed because senior officers in organisations are aware that eventually they will have to fix things. So why not aim to get things right — the first time? Why waste all the resources failing to do things and create all that unnecessary rework?

The implications of this common problem are dire. When a TQ drive commences, the RFT phrase fills the lecture rooms. It is broadcast on posters — but still the dominant attitude is 'fix it after things go wrong'! How can we expect others to take us seriously when we don't practise what we preach?

Case study: Ship it!

Some time ago, a company starting a quality drive (QD) had a significant problem. People at corporate headquarters were not happy — neither were the shareholders — because managers in the plant did not seem to be able to get the product through the plant and to the customers on time. Strict financial controls were imposed upon the plant. It had to generate so much revenue per month that it meant shipping the equivalent of £1.8m of orders per month.

During the first stages of the QD there was a great deal of confusion. The company managed to keep to the projected target for the first 3 weeks of each month and then all hell broke loose! The company would ship anything — just to maintain financial targets. In some cases this meant that the company was shipping half-empty crates to customers — with an attached note stating that the rest of the consignment would follow shortly.

The invoices dispatched to corporate headquarters indicated that the company was on target but the shop floor told another story. There were areas allocated for work in progress and these were growing each month. How were the employees supposed to take the RFT mentality seriously when there were clear cases of this principle being violated and compromised?

We cannot expect a company to move overnight to a TQM culture — but why wasn't the management team honest enough to tell the workforce the truth? It's far better to talk about targets of RFT than to pretend they can actually be achieved.

Telling the truth about TQM — it's not a fairy story. In the example above there are two issues which need to be clarified — the commitment issue and the time issue. It is clear that the HQ staff did not share the same regard for TQM as the managers of the plant. A major question has to be answered. Should one then stop the TQ drive until everybody is on board or should one continue?

A purist would stop the drive and wait for conditions to be perfect. A realist would continue the drive but tell the truth. "We are aiming for zero defects — but you know we have a long way to go. We will make progress but we will not lie to you. There will be times when we are implementing TQM when we may slide back 3 steps for every step taken forward but we will inform you of when this will happen and why! We will also tell you immediately after that crisis is over. Overall, we expect in three months to be spending a decreasing amount of our time on rework. Preventative type activities will replace this over the rest of the year."

The other issue is 'time'. We can find that time can pass very quickly and that we seem to achieve little in terms of adding value, although we can be extremely busy reworking problems. This often has its cause in a failure to determine priorities — spending more time on short-term rather than long-term objectives, failing to plan ahead and letting the urgent take over from the important. Sooner or later, the prevailing culture accepts this 'right second time' attitude as the performance standard. This is testified to in policy documents, when companies proudly proclaim that they will rectify faults arising from their products within a set time period. This creates confidence in the warranty but does not actually do too much for the reputations of the product and the company.

We should reject the 'right second time' approach because it creates long-term problems for the company. New employees may witness the 'second time' mentality and consider it acceptable to work to this standard. This soon spreads to become 'right third, fourth or fifth time'.

One interesting issue concerns what action should be taken with a company which experiences a high turnover of staff. How can the company ensure that the culture always remains tuned to TQM despite the influx of new employees? There is no response other than a detailed training programme for all new employees. This could easily be integrated into an induction programme.

What is the relationship between right first time and zero defects?

RFT is simple. It is no more and no less than meeting customer requirements. Knowing what customers need, renegotiating if circumstances are not right and delivering to that standard are all it is and no more. After a TQM drive has been in operation for some time, meeting customer requirements and RFT will mean the same thing — zero defects!

Many managers get too carried away at first with the meanings of the exhortations and start questioning the validity of achieving zero defects. Some claim to tell others that this is the performance standard, although desirable, is impossible and demotivating.

Tell people that zero defects and RFT, as a performance standard, are not demotivating — because we don't expect them to start tomorrow. It isn't easy — but the standard is attainable if we can inculcate the attitude and want to stop errors arising. If we don't aim for zero defects we will never achieve this standard.

What inhibits right first time?

A great deal can inhibit the movement towards wanting to get things right. Chapter 4 looks at some of the issues on managing resistance to change and chapter 5 examines some of the factors inherent in promoting 'cultural change'. These comments will not be duplicated.

The really critical issues are related to training and managing on a day-to-day basis. Staff has to be trained in how to do the job — otherwise people have no standard to work to.

In one company it was noted that most of the supervisors had been recruited from the shop floor — not that this is a bad thing — but little attempt was made to encourage others to come into the company. Consequently, the people who achieved supervisory status were new to that job. Due to the nature of the company, very little basic training was given. Supervisors also had the use of computers but, over a period of a few months, it was found that nobody had been provided with comprehensive training. The use of the computer was geared to inventory control. It was never used. Supervisors never approached management to explain their problems as they perceived them to be personal weaknesses.

Failing to train, even in the basics, and failing to listen to real concerns are major problems for companies attempting to introduce TQM. TQM can still be achieved despite these setbacks but its effects will take longer to materialise and will be weaker.

Error prevention

Some companies decide that they are not going to progress the TQM drive quickly. They realise that there are many factors within the company which are inhibiting its growth. To start the ball rolling, they commence the error prevention process. Some companies use a variant of this to unearth major quality issues for immediate improvement after the training event. However, this does not have to be a major event. It can be regulated and used extremely effectively — but it must be controlled!

If a company was to distribute an error prevention form (see Fig. 1), which forms the documentary basis of the error prevention process, to all members of staff and ask them to complete it the company would probably be inundated

---

Name .... **Unit** .... **Date** ....

The problem below is stopping me from performing error-free work. Could we investigate this problem and get it right first time?

The problem is . . . . . .

The symptoms are . . . . . .

Probable causes . . . . . .

Action by unit manager

Date ....

Referral to quality director   Date ....

Fig. 1 Error prevention form

with responses. Unless the right structure is in place it is unlikely that the company could do much about improvement. Hence the need for control. Being selective and administering the form within discrete work areas can highlight the problems which currently exist.

The selective and constrained use of such a document, together with the formal structure to create change and respond to 'right the wrongs', is a good incremental approach to implementing TQM and promoting RFT.

Summary and bullet points

- Ensure that RFT is more than just rhetoric.
- Reject posters displaying messages if they are going to be the most powerful medium you employ to create change.
- Don't try to catch each other out and prove that others failed to do things 'right first time'. This is negative and focuses on the 3–5% of what people may have done wrong rather than on the 95% of what they did well.
- RFT is a standard of performance. It is about promoting error-free work. It is about surpassing old standards and preventing errors creeping into work.
- By looking for possible errors and taking corrective and preventative action we are guarding against compounding errors and passing them on to our customers.
- The 'right second time' mentality threatens TQM progress.
- Demonstrate your commitment to TQM by doing something which reflects the RFT philosophy. Do all you can to create heroes related to battling the old culture.
- RFT is leading by example: "We do what we value and value what we do."
- Everybody is his own inspector.
- Look for all the ways a process can fail and then fix it — so it can't.
- The people we employ know more about the operational side of the business than the senior officers. Develop strategies to release these energies. Don't argue with suggestions — just implement them. Ensure that you don't focus implementation on productivity and cost reduction to the detriment of other issues.
- The service side has many improvements it can make to improve procedures and documentation.
- RFT must become the standard of performance by which we are all assessed. It must become our personal standard.
- Implementing TQM overnight is impossible. Managers in companies will continue to do things the wrong way. Telling your people why and when the 'old ways' will stop gains more credibility than lying.
- 'Zero defects' is not perfectionism. 'Zero defects means doing things right the first time and is orientated towards meeting customer requirements. (ZD = MCR).

- A failure to train, communicate and manage TQ on a day-to-day basis can inhibit the RFT mentality from becoming standard operating procedure.
- Conduct controlled exercises identifying areas where errors are most prominent. Control the exercise, otherwise managerial inaction to put right what is wrong, because of the size of response, will fuel the negative rumours about TQM not working.

10 TAKING PREVENTATIVE ACTION

Preventative Action

Preventative action is an alternative to fixing things after they have gone wrong. Preventative action means solving a problem permanently. You may be surprised to find that most problems which organisations cope with prior to TQM are never really solved. Rather, the small problems are worked through but the really big problems, which create a great deal of rework, are never really solved.

We tend to react to events as they arise and fix them quickly, in many cases concentrating on the effects rather than the causes. Consequently, the symptoms of the problems are dealt with but the factor which created the incident is still there — ready to arise some time in the future.

Listing key problems

We sometimes ask managers to list the sort of problems which they will be confronting in the next 3 months. After this has been completed, we ask them to create other lists of likely problems they will need to overcome in 6, 12, 18 and 24 months.

What the lists have in common is that key 'problems' appear time and time again on different lists. We can establish from this evidence that most problems are predictable and, more importantly, many are recurring. If this is the case, many problems have never been solved in the first instance — if they had they would not arise again!

If you have control you can solve problems. If you don't, you can't

Asking managers to cast their minds back over the years we usually find that some of the 'recurring' problems have not been properly tackled so as to be solved once and for all. Resources have been allocated, effort expended and things fixed temporarily — but they were not fixed permanently. Many problems which plague managers never seem to go away and this is because nobody has really developed a long-term, workable solution.

Not unusually, we find that it is not the small problems which cause the trouble. Consider a problem which impacts solely on one department, i.e. an inventory control, accounting or personnel problem. These problems will all have been fixed, there and then, never to arise again. The reason for this is that the manager solving the problem and implementing a solution will have had control over most of the variables which impact on the problem. In many cases, the problem will not have been shared with other sections, departments or units or, if it has, it will have been relatively easy to fix. The smaller the number of departments experiencing the problem, the easier it is to fix. This isn't a matter of size — but of control. If a manager has authority and control in specific areas he can influence performance there. It is unlikely that he will be able to control the actions and behaviour of other units.

In comparison let's consider the problems which lead to rework. These are the really big headaches — but they may be no bigger than the problems which many managers face in their specific areas on a day-to-day basis. So what makes one problem different from another? It is not size. The determining factor, in addition to control, which influences the extent to which problems can be solved once and for all, is simply the number and variety of units or departments affected by that problem.

Ownership and problem-solving

Nobody will really 'own' the problem and take it on board as his responsibility. Let's face it, the really big problems don't have owners — one department blames another. Sales blames R&D for failing to develop drawing, R&D blames the purchasing department for failing to co-ordinate raw materials flow, and manufacturing blames everybody! Everyone passes the buck to somebody else. As the interaction of departments makes the problem appear 'complex' nobody knows where to start — nor do they want to get involved. The chance of a problem being solved by four or more individuals from different departments and different cultures is not high in many companies (although a matrix management/task culture can develop superb solutions — but these are rare).

In all honesty how many departmental heads or managers are going to volunteer to solve problems? Very few, because they recognise how difficult it is to change things in other departments — especially where they have no authority or control for creating changes. Problems may be discussed freely — but they have no real home. Nobody wants ownership (see Fig. 1).

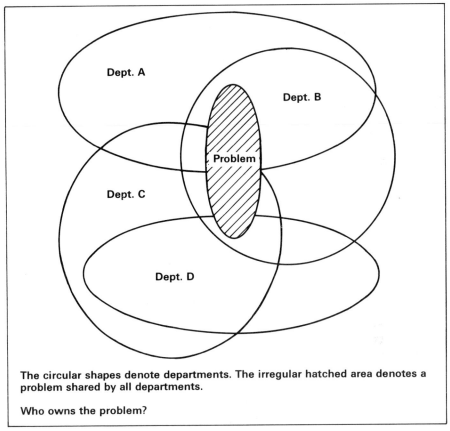

The circular shapes denote departments. The irregular hatched area denotes a problem shared by all departments.

Who owns the problem?

Fig. 1 Ownership and preventative action

The relief of shared ownership — nobody can be singled out for blame

To complicate matters when departmental managers experience a complex problem impacting upon all units at once — they can heave a sigh of relief! Why? They recognise that there are no clear lines between who is responsible for XY and Z problem in each department. If demarcation lines on 'ownership' are fuzzy — nobody can allocate blame to just one person. Knowing this, they are aware that 'ownership' is shared and unclear — so there is little incentive to create change.

Sooner or later someone has to attempt to solve what is wrong, but it can be too late and remedying the problem may cost the company a great deal.

The really big problems, as has been said, frequently occur between departments. For example, in some companies there are conflicts between sales and contract administration, between manufacturing and engineering and between personnel and line management.

Fire-fighting cultures

Two cases which illustrate the failure to prevent problems arising are given below.

(1) At a company producing heavy-duty catering equipment for hotels, hospitals, schools, colleges and the marine market, the problems were such that they created a tremendous amount of rework, and scheduling was appalling. There was little overview of the major company problem.

The company was experiencing severe cash flow difficulties. A short-term, short-sighted, decision was taken. In future all suppliers would be paid after the 30-day agreed limit and sometimes this was extended to 60 or 90 days. Customers were put under pressure to pay up although, as some of the customers were in the public sector, they were sometimes late with payment.

In the short term, some suppliers experiencing cash flow difficulties themselves put pressure on the manufacturer to pay on time. When the response was negative some suppliers stopped delivering and made it a condition that goods were paid for in advance. This created severe problems for the manufacturing areas which did not have enough components to make the product. Consequently, delivery of products was late which meant, in many cases, that the external customer imposed penalty clauses upon the manufacturer. This created even more cash flow problems.

This was serious. Work in progress was increasing and goods couldn't be finished or delivered on time. Customers, such as local authorities, were outraged. The kitchens in schools and colleges were incomplete, creating problems for them trying to provide a service for their pupils. The results were catastrophic.

(2) A company producing engineering sub-assembly parts had agreed to delivery dates which were not realistic. Lead times for manufacturing items were reduced radically. The company had completed the sale with the customer and, whatever happened, the goods would be delivered on time — but at what cost?

Due to the rush, technical drawings were sub-contracted and tooling rushed to manufacture without testing. Purchasing was pushed to reduce costs and, consequently, the quality of raw material was poor, rework was high and production control was in a spin. Extra shifts had to be arranged and delivery to the customer by outside contractors was necessary because of problems with scheduling delivery.

This sort of incident became more regular and, soon, a common occurrence. Every Friday afternoon was characterised by managers dashing about all over the place trying to ensure that goods went out of dispatch to be delivered on time. They did whatever was required and did a tremendous job, only to be deflated when the customer returned some of the items because of inconsistency or poor quality. This chaos and fire-fighting only got worse.

Changing to the preventative culture

Being critical of company organisation is easy — putting it right isn't! Changing from one culture to another is difficult. It takes time and a real devotion to company-wide problem solving. All the managers in the two examples quoted above were diligent and conscientious. They thought they were doing the right job. After all, they were rewarded for working in this manner and this was reinforced by the weekly fiasco. What was needed in both examples was a company-wide initiative with everyone willing to contribute to resolve these problems forever. The problems were so large that nobody had real responsibility for changing things, apart from the chief executive, and, in both instances, he was cushioned by line managers who did not speak up. In these two examples everyone was being defensive — the problem was 'somebody else's'.

Consider the consequences of not dealing with a problem like this in the proper manner. Time and resources are wasted, negative stereotypes are reinforced between departments and the 'pass the buck' attitude is prevalent. It was hard to believe that all the managers worked for the same company. Taking ownership and working things out together are the keys to preventative action.

Western problem-solving is fire-fighting

In the West, we have developed a reputation for putting things right after they have gone wrong. Organisations pride themselves on their 'no quibble guarantees'. We are proficient at setting up project teams to take corrective action but we spend little time on preventing these errors arising. Employees are rewarded for quick thinking and resolving crises but there appears to be little attention paid to those dedicated to prevention in the long term. We have the wrong approach to problem-solving.

Generally, too many of us spend so much time fire-fighting that we have little time left for prevention. How much time do people spend solving yesterday's problems rather than preventing tomorrow's? Could problems creating rework have been anticipated and preventative measures taken? More importantly, could your department or other functions have taken some form of preventative action and thus saved you doing the job 'twice over'?

Think about how you can start preventing errors. Do you consider likely problems before you start a new manufacturing or administrative process or do you adopt the approach that a run through will act as a useful pilot for further modification?

One hour of planning saves ten hours of chaos

The majority of problems can be controlled by understanding and developing clear objectives and requirements to cover all potential problems. Failure mode effect analysis (FMEA), of both process and design, is a useful tool to use to eliminate error. Requirements cover all the inputs — human, materials, decisions required, procedures and standards. A thorough analysis of meeting customer requirements (chapter 8) is essential and should enable most to solve problems before they arise.

Testing or using pilot studies is appropriate, provided that you can control the process. All variables must be regulated by you to ensure that tests and pilots are a true reflection of reality. It is of no value to run a set of tests on a product if the environment generated for test purposes does not match the real work conditions. This is true for product testing, for DP systems, manual systems and procedures. Like must be tested against like and conditions documented accurately. It is also important that circumstances be taken into account when we are examining results/conclusions of tests.

It is clear from the examples generated that in order to manage through preventative action, it is necessary to adopt the right attitude and concern for owning the problem. Training in problem-solving skills is also an inherent aspect of preventative action. Groups or teams of people may wish to get together to solve problems. They may have the necessary commitment but they do not automatically have the frameworks, the knowledge of problem-solving skills or statistical techniques which can help them.

Key issues in problem-solving

Talking about preventative action and putting it into effect are two different things. Most TQM initiatives have a formal structure where people come together to discuss the solutions to organisational problems. Prior to this they should have experienced the TQM 'educational process' and understand the philosophy, the key principles and the route the company is going to take to implement change.

At this stage, people become concerned about structures. Should our groups be voluntary, i.e. quality circles, or should they be firmly structured around the nature of a problem and be called corrective action teams and quality action teams, etc? The names and structures are unimportant at the moment (this is the subject of chapter 14). However, the process of problem-solving is the key.

Too many managers spend too much time concentrating on structure and neglect process. We will spend some time on process because it is critical to the solution of problems.

Everyone in the organisation needs to understand the techniques of problem-solving. People also need to be aware of statistical techniques. This is critical and cannot be over-emphasised. (Statistical techniques will not be dealt with in this book for there are plenty of good quality texts available.) Perhaps most important of all, people need to understand how they influence problem-solving by the way they work in groups, by understanding how they learn and reach conclusions.

Techniques are not enough: climate and rules for problem-solving

Personality characteristics are important determinants of a 'problem-solving' style which people will utilise. Some people are quite 'process orientated' and are concerned that the sequence of stages in problem-solving is explored and that everyone attending has the opportunity to contribute. Others, on the other hand, are extremely task centred and focus very little attention on people and the contribution they can make.

It is not surprising to find that the majority of people tend to be very structured (please note this does not mean logical) and orientated towards getting a right answer. It is necessary for people involved in problem-solving teams to understand fully the dynamics of problem-solving.

This does not mean that managers will be 'navel-gazing' but that they will be looking at the inherent features of problem-solving and generating a superior solution. Care and attention should be directed here because the success achieved by problem-solving groups will soon be transmitted through the structure to others and will indicate whether or not their efforts have been successful.

To help this process it is advisable to develop 'rules' by which business will be conducted. Rules help enormously provided that the group sees the wisdom in them and adhere to them. More important than this though is the learning or problem-solving style.

Some rules for problem-solving groups

We all need some rules to guide us when we are working as group members. These rules help regulate the behaviour of those in the team and facilitate progress. Ideally, the rules should be displayed in a prominent position.

Rule 1. Don't find 10 ways to make a good idea fail. Find 1 reason to make it work!

Rule 2. Don't be negative and say, "That won't work." Be positive and look for those things which unite members.

Rule 3. Don't do an 'over the wall' — don't pass the buck.

Rule 4. Listen to what others say and think through their proposals.

Rule 5. Leave your role and status outside.

Rule 6. Draw up a short agenda for each meeting and stick to it. Don't deviate. Agree action and take brief minutes to reflect agreement reached.

Rule 7. Be aware of your own problem-solving style and ensure that you look at problems from different perspectives.

Learning how you learn and solve problems

An excellent instrument for training in problem-solving is the Kolb Learning Style approach (see Fig. 2). This suggests that we each have preferences in methods of learning and solving problems. These tend to be reinforced during our professional lives and as we develop a preference, i.e., being practical and fixing things as they go wrong, we develop a strength in this area. This gaining of strength in one or two ways of learning and problem-solving reinforces our belief that the style works best for us. We tend to become specialised and increased use of one or more approaches means that we tend to neglect other relevant but less desired approaches.

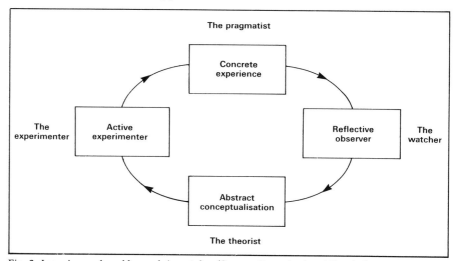

Fig. 2 Learning and problem-solving styles (Source: Organizational Psychology, 1984)

The Kolb instrument is extremely useful and one neglected by too many who believe that the answer to quality improvement is to get more people in a room talking around an agenda.

Problem-solving members spend a great deal of their time thinking through issues and trying to solve problems. The ability to think clearly and solve problems in a systematic way is what differentiates the successful group from the unsuccessful. Those who cannot solve problems quickly are those who either lack the talent, skill, knowledge, motivation or experience to do so. We are not born with 'problem-solving ability' — we have to practise it with others.

Problem-solving and making decisions

First of all, do not try to compartmentalise these two areas. They are not discrete — they overlap. You can attend a meeting and start applying the 'problem-solving' process to a particular issue but, if you are not careful, you will find others making decisions before the causes of the problem have been identified!

We can all jump to conclusions, make unreal assumptions and peddle our latest pet solution, all in aid of saving time. We may do so in the short term, i.e. dealing with an agenda quickly, but will we have solved the problem once and for all? It is unlikely. We may be so concerned with shortening the time allowed for the discussion with others, that we do not solve the problem. In fact, we create further problems for ourselves because we have not got it 'right first time'.

How can we avoid jumping to the wrong conclusion?

Sit down and think through the main issue. How do we normally solve problems? Do we debate at length and then vote? If that is the case, the decision is not based upon consensus, and it is likely that the decision reached will not have been gleaned from the whole range of alternatives.

Do we automatically think there is one right answer? This might well be the case when dealing with accounts, production and distribution schedules, etc., but most problems do not have one solution, they have many! What we have got to do is plan our resources to consider the best options.

Convergent and divergent thinking

When we think of problem-solving we tend to examine a logical approach to understanding the underlying causes of problems — but this is not the only approach. The logical approach is referred to as 'convergent thinking'. The alternative, creative approach is known as 'divergent thinking'.

Convergent thinking resembles the rational, systematic approach adopted by many managers. There is nothing wrong with this approach but sometimes a more creative, intuitive process of divergent thinking helps us look at possibilities and relationships.

The strength of convergent thinking relates to relying on 'what has happened', the information collected and the sequence and process of enquiry. The divergent approach is based on 'possibilities and relationships' and reflects the intuitive, creative element of problem-solving.

We can benefit from both approaches. Let us examine the rational, convergent process first. Later we will explore the divergent approach of 'creative thinking' and 'brainstorming'.

The rational approach demands that we tackle problems in a number of sequential steps. This is the way we should think about the problem but how often do we really think through the key stages and activities which we need to pursue in order to find a right answer? Not as often as we would like to think. Sometimes we jump to the first answer which comes into our heads — or we pursue our latest interest or hobby-horse. In reality there are many cases, because of time constraints or other pressures, where the rational approach to problem-solving has been neglected and a quick solution chosen — which can have dire consequences for the individual and the company.

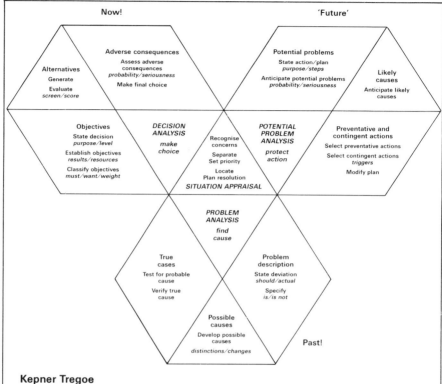

Kepner Tregoe

The Rational Manager

A large number of Fortune 500 companies has used this approach to great effect. Four basic processes comprise the KT model. Before we start we need to assess the present — the here and now. Situation appraisal is where we start every time. It helps us to make decisions about the routes we should follow — that is why it is central to the KT model.

Situation appraisal is a systematic approach to sorting out 'concerns' or those issues which need to be resolved in an organisation. This is separating the wood from the trees and trains people to prioritise their concerns and then choose which of the other three processes to follow.

Decision analysis — which is following a rigorous and systematic process for making a choice and reaching decisions.

Problem analysis — for finding the cause of a problem.

Potential problem analysis — for anticipating problems and preventing problems arising, or protecting existing plans or actions.

Fig. 3 Resolving concerns through rational process (Source: The New Rational Manager)

It is essential that all members use a logical sequential approach to problem-solving. Kepner and Tregoe in their book 'The New Rational Manager' outline the framework for logical problem-solving (see Fig. 3). This structured approach to problem-solving helps highlight the key stages we ought to consider before jumping at the first solution which appears. Few managers really adopt a rational approach (see Fig. 4). This approach is an excellent way of introducing problem-solving and decision-making to members of corrective action teams, etc. In past TQM interventions this has always been an extremely powerful tool for generating quality solutions. Time spent on these activities pay back dividends.

The rational approach to problem-solving.

Stage 1 is problem definition. A large number of problems are never really solved because group members do not spend sufficient time defining the nature of a problem. This means looking at the cause of the problem rather than the effect.

To illustrate this point, consider a visit to your doctor. You have found that you have a rash on your chest. The doctor gives you medication to relieve it. The rash eventually fades and the condition subsides. A week later the condition recurs. You pay another visit to the doctor and are prescribed the same

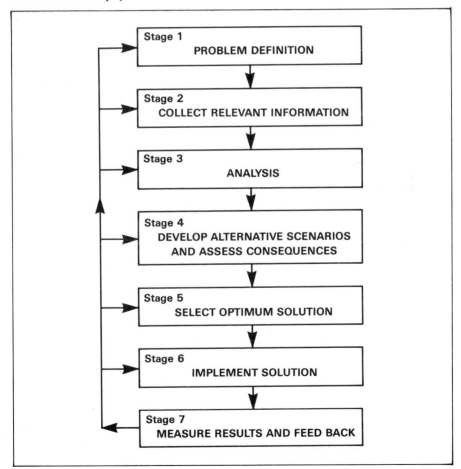

Fig. 4 Logical approach to problem solving

medication. This remedy clears up the symptoms of the problem but does nothing to eradicate the cause. Relate this to company problems. We should be certain before we pursue a course of action, not take a wild 'guesstimate'. Experience tells us that treating the symptoms will never solve a problem once and for all!

Stage 2: Collecting relevant information. Some group members try to solve problems without asking themselves what information they need to do a good job. They let their prejudices guide their judgements. They let their preferences structure the solution. Even worse, they have a kit bag of solutions which are just ready to be applied to problems, whether or not they are appropriate!

Some people spend all their lives 'trying to find problems which will fit their solutions'. Do not join them.

The classic mistake is to look at the broad parameters of a problem and then relate these back to information or 'similar' situations which we have confronted in the past.

We are all aware that the more information we have relating to the problem, the more accurate our diagnosis will be. Some, unfortunately, make a grave mistake. They do not look at the information and say, "Is this relevant?" Instead they say, "How can I use it?" They are confused. They equate available information with the information required to solve a problem! How easy it is to use all the information collected, rather than that which is really needed to solve the problem!

Collecting too much information. A problem which many experience is collecting a great quantity of information but failing to have any regard for quality. We can sometimes confuse the two and feel that quantity can be traded for quality! It can never be — and this is demonstrated in the number of problems in organisational experience.

Measuring everything and understanding nothing. Some people display a compulsion to measure everything which can be measured while neglecting other important variables which may not be so easily measured. These factors may be important but they are neglected and this can lead to inaccuracies in problem-resolution. Collecting vast quantities of data is somehow reassuring — whether the information will be of practical use does not seem quite so important a consideration.

Making too many assumptions. We all tend to make too many assumptions. Most are based on our own many and varied experiences within a given situation. We can generalise and this creates problems. The worst area of generalisation is when we make assumptions between cause and effect.

Stage 3: Analysis. When analysing cause/effect relationships, ensure that there are no significant intervening variables.

Be aware that all the facts will not 'jump out' at you all at once. You may need to pursue other lines of enquiry to establish intervening factors. Be careful and do not make too many assumptions.

Stage 4: Assess consequences. While working through the analysis phase and establishing cause and effect relationships, remember not to look for 'one right answer'. It is possible to develop a number of options which should help to achieve the goal.

Think through a number of alternative approaches and assess the consequences of each strategy. Think of the benefits in the short and the long-term. Think through the disadvantages and the costs of the actions. Then, progress to the next stage.

Stage 5: The optimum solution. At this stage problem-solving and decision-making merge. Perhaps a formal group meeting may be required in order to achieve the optimum solution. Ensure that those most affected by changes are involved. If they have to live with the solution and put it into practice, surely they have a part to play in contributing to the overall approach and finer details?

Stage 6: Implement solution. This is one of the most difficult stages in problem-solving and requires more action than words. Solutions, when written on paper, seem to work fine but, when implemented, can create all sorts of problems.

Most of these problems are human in origin and require new ways of working. 'Change' can create resistance. It is worth considering the 'people problems' before implementing new ideas. Ask yourself, "In how many ways can this idea fail?" Address the doubts you raise and be prepared to take corrective action. (See chapter 5 on managing cultural change.)

Managers achieve results through others. However good the idea generated by managerial staff and colleagues, if others will not put it into practice and accept the solution or innovation the solution will remain a good idea and never become a reality!

Stage 7: Measure results and gain feedback. It is all very well creating change and moving onto the next problem but, to ensure that you got it 'right first time', gain feedback on the practicality of the solution which has been implemented. Seek the views of those people who are most affected by your 'solution'. Their feedback is an important element in the problem-solving and decision-making processes. Without their consent and input, how can you hope to win their support to implement your solution?

Alternative problem-solving techniques. We have referred to the logical, sequential approach to the solution of problems and paid little attention to the more creative approach. 'Creative Thinking' and 'Brainstorming' are approaches which have helped many companies solve complex problems. This more creative alternative approach is particularly useful when there is not one right answer.

There may be a variety of answers 'close together', or one right answer, to production, accounting or engineering problems. Using the same approach for open-ended problems can be disastrous. You will spend a tremendous amount of time trying to find the one right answer. It does not exist, so why look for it!

Let us look at more creative problem-solving techniques and examine their applicability within problem-solving groups.

'Brainstorming' and 'Cause Effect Analysis' have helped particularly in quality improvement initiatives, where those who produce a component can meet together and 'solve' a production or quality problem.

What is creative thinking? Creative thinking, an aspect of divergent thinking, is 'relating those things which were previously unrelated'. This means that the mind has to 'free-wheel' and overcome the self-imposed barriers which can stop us moving towards innovative solutions. Edward De Bono, in particular, has spent many years teaching his variant of the creative approach to problem solution, called 'Lateral Thinking'.

Creative thinking is concerned with developing innovative solutions to traditional problems. It is also a set of techniques orientated towards extracting a large number of ideas from a group of people.

For instance, if you wished to use the brainstorming technique, the first thing you have to do is define the nature of the problem and express it in one statement. For instance, let us assume that productivity within a department is falling. We may define the problem thus: "In how many ways can we increase productivity within the department?"

Restatements, do not jump at this question and seek to find a solution. Are we really sure that we are dealing with the overall problem? What we need to do is develop restatements of the problem:

- **"In how many ways can we increase group productivity?"**
- **"In how many ways can we reduce unnecessary costs?"**
- **"What action can we take to ensure that we always provide a high-quality service?"**
- **"What manpower strategies can we use to ensure that both satisfaction and productivity remain high?"**

Clearly, we can make as many restatements as we wish but the overall purpose is to walk around the problem and look at it from different angles. This is most important. Otherwise, we tend to pursue the old 'tried and tested' techniques.

Having a group of employees restate the problem in 10–12 restatements is the first stage of a good problem-solving/corrective action team workshop. The next activity is to agree to work on one 'restatement'.

Free-wheeling, think through a trivial problem which faces the group and get them to brainstorm ideas quickly. This activity is not yet concerned with solving the problem but with giving those attending the confidence to develop new ideas, however wild! Results from brainstorming sessions indicate that some of the wild ideas, which appear outrageous at first, can generate some of the most innovative and effective solutions to problems.

The rules for brainstorming include:

- Do not try to find one right answer. It does not exist. There are many answers which might be of value.
- Build confidence amongst the team members and stress that they should try to generate as many ideas as possible. These ideas must not be evaluated, but listed to be discussed later. Do not evaluate, otherwise a lot of good ideas will never be expressed. The ideas should be presented and documented quickly. Speed is of the essence. Brainstorming should not last longer than 5 minutes.
- Avoid tunnel vision. Think through areas to take the group away from established practice. Do not dwell too much on old solutions.
- Reduce the inclination of members to analyse suggestions too quickly. They must avoid statements like, "That will not work," or "We tried that at my last company and found it to be too expensive." Evaluation is left for later. At the moment, the key activity is the generation of ideas.
- Many attending brainstorming sessions feel uncomfortable, fear appearing foolish and so do not contribute. We must break down barriers and encourage ideas, however outrageous they appear!

Agreeing criteria for evaluation, now that the session is over, the group has to get together to agree criteria by which the ideas can be judged, e.g. cost, administrative convenience, long-term impact and economical and technical feasibility, etc. Once these are agreed, it is a comparatively easy process to evaluate your list of ideas.

Logical thinking and brainstorming, now to evaluate we move away from divergent to convergent thinking, where we evaluate the brainstormed proposals. This is the process we would normally go through if we always used the rational method of problem-solving, except that we now have the value of lots of creative ideas to evaluate.

This approach helps us develop new, innovative approaches to solving problems.

Cause effect analysis, this technique is used a great deal by teams of workers and staff involved in quality improvement initiatives. The technique has a logical structure and framework which is easily understood and it incorporates elements of creative thought.

Cause effect analysis is a good, simple technique for examining the major factors which impact upon a particular problem. A 'fishbone diagram' (see Fig. 5) illustrates the relationship between cause and effect.

Defining the symptoms of the problem is the first step to developing a

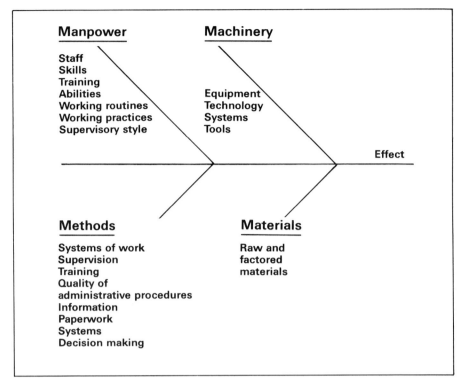

Fig. 5 Cause/effect analysis

'fishbone', asking, "What is the impact of the 'effect' on employees, the depart-ment and the organisation?" Describing the effect in detail is important. Listing the consequences, walking around the problem and considering it from dif-ferent angles are all aspects of the creative approach.

A team of staff should get together to brainstorm the possible and probable causes of the problem relating brainstorming and the listing of causes to the 4 Ms outlined below.

The way to build up a 'fishbone' is to brainstorm and generate a list of all the possible factors, without evaluating, which could create the effect. After you have listed the probable causes, it is then possible to add them to the 'fishbone'. Now key areas have been identified for investigation, target setting and review dates.

Using the 'fishbone' will not, by itself, solve the problem, but it will help examine the inter-relationships between the 4 Ms and give sufficient informa-tion on which your action can be based.

The 4 Ms is a simple and convenient method for isolating the probable causes of a problem under four headings:

Manpower — includes staff skills, training, abilities, attitudes and working routines and practices.
Methods — includes systems of work and paperwork routines, etc.

Machinery — includes equipment, technology and systems, etc.
Materials — includes raw and factored materials, statistics and information, etc.

Taking action

Problem-solving techniques, by themselves, will not solve all the problems. They will, however, provide a basis on which it is possible to make a balanced decision. In all honesty, if a problem has existed for a long time, one cannot assume that action to solve the problem will succeed 'first time'. The short-term, intermediate and long-term steps must be considered.

The approach adopted will be determined by the urgency of putting right what is wrong, the resources at your disposal and the speed at which results are required.

Routine and complex decisions, though problem-solving and decision-making are inextricably linked, we may ask how we should organise our time to make the best quality decisions.

We must also look at the decisions and ask ourselves whether they are complex or routine. Routine decisions can be delegated to others. You, personally, have to deal with the more difficult ones. Usually decisions are difficult to make because you lack the necessary information to act in the best interests of everyone. As the decisions become more difficult, and the solutions to the problems become more complex, you will need the support of other people. They will give you different perspectives and information which you do not already possess.

This means that your 'people' skills will be brought into play. Think through the criteria by which others will judge your decisions and, if in doubt, remember that planning is the best way of ensuring that errors do not arise.

Choosing solutions with a chance, although corrective action teams or problem-solving groups may have adhered to all the principles associated with problem-solving, one of the most difficult jobs is to put ideas into practice. Many corrective action teams give feedback on their progress to the senior management group. Before this can be achieved it is worth considering the strategies used for selling ideas to others. It is at this stage that resistance to new solutions may be in evidence. Resistance exists because others may perceive the ideas, actions and recommendations of others as some sort of threat.

There are certain actions that can be taken to ensure that solutions, or preferred action, stand a good chance of being accepted by others. Assessing the criteria by which others will judge your proposals is a good start. Looking at four areas should help:

● Is this idea administratively convenient?

- Is the recommendation technically feasible?
- Is the idea economically viable?
- Is the idea politically acceptable to the organisation?

If any of these has a negative response, spend some time developing alternative strategies for change. Seek the opposing arguments from your colleagues and address their objections.

Handling objection is the most important aspect of having ideas accepted. This requires a great deal of preparation, taking into account the personalities and roles of the people involved.

Now that you have assessed the criteria by which others will judge your proposals, it is time to assess the degree to which there is congruency or incongruency between proposals and the objections of others. Address these objections before presenting a case, order priorities and listen to what others say.

Build bridges and present your case in a non-threatening way. Look for win-win solutions. In other words, situations where all those involved benefit. This replaces the old idea of if one person or department succeeds, others must lose — reject this old approach and recognise the benefits and value of the team approach.

Communication and information

This is perhaps the most important aspect of implementing TQM. Failing to communicate intentions, hold regular briefing sessions and inform on progress will hinder success. What is sometimes surprising is the speed at which organisations undertake TQM drives — even those which failed when introducing briefing groups. The role of communication and briefing can't be underplayed and is part of the focus in chapter 11 on team building and participation.

Summary and bullet points

- Preventative action is the only alternative to constant reworking.
- We tend to react to events rather than manage them. We resolve short-term concerns but never really solve long-term problems. We emphasise dealing with 'symptoms' rather than causes.
- Many of the problems we encounter are predictable. Managers can forecast and generate lists of things which they will have to resolve in the future — but still fail to fix them.
- If you have control over problems you can fix them. If control is shared with others problem-solution is more difficult.
- If problems are owned they are solved. Too many problems are not owned and consequently no one does anything significant to put right what is wrong.

- If problems are shared it is difficult to allocate responsibility.
- Fire-fighting is a natural state in many companies. Many enjoy fire-fighting — it is exciting. It has to be replaced by a calmer, more regulated pace and concern for planning.
- Sometimes one visits companies and wonders how departments function in spite of themselves. It would be nice to see energy being expended in working together rather than wasted pursuing disparate goals.
- Changing to the 'Preventative Culture' requires a major change and promotion of problem-solving from being quick fixes to long-term company-wide affairs.
- Companies are pretty good at putting things right after they have gone wrong. Why is it so difficult to work on what we know will go wrong and fix it, rather than wasting resources to do things right second time?
- A genuine commitment to forecasting, planning and sharing information must be desirable to replace the 'wild guesstimates' approach.
- One hour of planning saves 10 hours of chaos.
- If we genuinely value our people and want them to solve problems, they need to be trained in problem-solving techniques. Process is more important than structure.
- Providing techniques for problem-solving and decision-making is all very well — but you must generate a climate in which people want to do things. It will have a bigger pay-back.
- Develop and keep to rules of behaviour for groups involved in promoting new solutions to old problems.
- Learning about personal problem-solving style is a good first step and probably tells you more about how you make managerial decisions than attending courses on structured problem-solving.
- Managers like to think they are rational, logical, systematic and methodical. The evidence of managers using 'guesstimates', following their intuitions and feelings suggests that everybody could benefit from studying the rational process.
- Managers solve problems using a combination of logic and feelings. Is it not then wise to provide them with training so that they can become more logical and more creative at the same time?
- Spend plenty of time defining the nature of problems rather than jumping to quick solutions. Base decisions on accurate and reliable information. Analyse cause/effect relationships, assess consequences, select the optimum solution, implement ideas and seek feedback.
- Use creative thinking as a tool to generate a vast number of ideas from many people and make use of the fishbone diagram to isolate cause from effect.
- When taking action, ensure that all factors have been considered. Is the idea administratively convenient, technically feasible, financially sound and politically acceptable? If it is not, you will stand less of a chance of having it implemented.
- Don't give up on the difficult decisions. They take longer to implement and you have to have more of the culture with you to agree action.
- The accurate transmission and reception of information is critical to

implementing TQM. Ineffective communication leads to inconsistent messages and conflict. Work on improving information and communication through the most powerful medium — management style.

11 TEAM BUILDING AND PARTICIPATION

Fire-fighting to prevention

Chapter 10 concentrated on the actions necessary to move from a fire-fighting culture to a TQM preventative culture. In particular, it was stated that having people trained in problem-solving techniques was important. However, just as important is examining the 'style' which each person uses when involved in the process of generating workable solutions. Personal style determines the route of pathways taken to solve problems.

Everyone can be trained in using cause/effect analysis but the effectiveness of those working on the solution can be inhibited if they fail to grasp the importance of personal problem-solving style. Each of us is driven by a preference to work, to confront and tackle problems in a certain way. This is usually determined by our experience and reflected in the way that we manage. Some can be locked into 'one best style' and fail to consider other ways of working. These personal preferences can sometimes be adopted, reinforced and rewarded by senior officers as the 'company style'. Having a number of people sitting around a table discussing problem areas using the same approach as their co-workers will fail to generate the spark needed to create alternatives and change. Preferring and using one method of problem-solving suggests that other ways have been avoided. It is for this reason that it is fitting to look at contributions of people working as a team.

Difficulties moving from the telling role to the listening role

There is little point talking about the joint approach to implementing company-wide improvement through TQM, when little effort is made to ensure that the drive is based on company-wide participation, where it is discouraged by strict demarcation between functions and departments.

We talk a great deal about team building and team effort but in many instances we don't give people a chance to contribute. Some time ago it was identified that over 100 people of one company were to be trained in problem-solving style over a series of weeks. On one occasion the engineering manager attended and took part in exercises. In every case he took over from those in his group and made the decisions for them. He adopted the same approach which he would use in the plant. He spoke, they listened. This was a major problem. Although the manager was committed in principle, it was very difficult to get him to drop his leading and directing role in order to listen to others and give their opinions a chance.

There needs to be a fundamental change in management style for this to work. If we fail to attempt to change style and examine the impact which managers have on others in groups, problem orientated or not, then we are failing to change the culture. Employees find that no real change has taken place. If the engineering manager doesn't change and listen more to others, avoid making his mind up before others speak and ask others for genuine solutions before contributing, then employees will witness no change at all. Some managers are frightened to change their 'style' because they think that this means abdication or giving control to others. It doesn't. It is giving others a chance to contribute from their perspective.

Achieving results through others

It is understandable that managers and supervisors do find it difficult to 'restrain' themselves from their normal roles of giving direction, but it is essential that they examine their approaches in order that ideas from others can permeate the structure. Before examining the routes organisations can take to unleashing the potential of their people, it is wise to look at the key issues in the team concept.

We all recognise that we are employed, not so much for what we can do individually, but for what we get others to achieve. Chapter 6 on leadership looks at the role the manager can play in leading this process. Enabling others to contribute is fundamental to TQM. When we look at Japanese companies practising the TQM leadership philosophy we see that we are a long way behind.

Employee involvement: West v East comparisons

In the West the probable response to a customer receiving defective components from its supplier would be that the supplier's salesman/engineer would visit the customer and try to remedy the error. After several discussions, the manufacturing process may be changed to avoid future error but this is not always the case. More inspectors could be employed to find the faults or extra staff trained to fix things after they have gone wrong. Let's be optimistic and assume that this complaint has created a change in the manufacturing process. Who will have been involved in the discussions? It is unlikely that the operator, who probably knows more about the product and possible defects in manufacture than anybody else, will have been consulted. In Japanese companies, however, this process is different in form and content.

The Nippon Denso approach

In Japan, an alternative approach is used. On receiving a (highly unlikely) complaint of a defective component being shipped to a customer, the management team, of Nippon Denso for example, would take immediate action.

A production engineer, together with the employee who made the component and his direct supervisor, would drop everything and travel to the customer. There, the three would conduct a problem-solving session focusing on how to ensure that the error did not arise again. The operator would play the key role. His contribution would be of much higher value than that of anyone else. He would then work with the production engineer to improve the process of manufacture, by foolproofing, so that the error was eradicated.

Clearly this is the only route to continuous improvement and zero defects. The solution is examined by those who operate the technology which makes the component. The operator has the knowledge and expertise in that operation and will have a multitude of ideas about how to stop problems arising.

Employee involvement in action in a UK plastics plant

The Japanese approach was put into effect in the plant of a major manufacturer of plastics in the UK. As in most plants, maintenance engineers are continually busy, fixing technology after it has failed. They recognised that many of the operators had a good working knowledge of the technology. After talking with the operators, the engineers came to the conclusion that variation in performance of production technology could be predicted by 'sound' coming from the machine. Instead of running the technology to 'breakdown', operatives were encouraged to shut down equipment temporarily, on hearing the sound, and to contact the engineers. Engineers could then begin to work on the equipment before significant damage occurred. This culminated in 'operators' suggesting periodic checks on equipment prior to breakdown and in the formation of a 'Preventative Maintenance Programme' (PMP).

In particular, this meant that down-time was decreased. When operatives using 'dicing machinery' (used to separate a continuous flow of hardened plastic into fine pellets direct from manufacture) were involved, it was possible to predict with some certainty the cause and time of potential failures. This was further analysed. From these data, a PMP for the 'dicers' was established. This would have been impossible without the help of the operator.

With this input it was possible for the machinery to run continuously 24 hours per day. This minimised down-time maintenance and made life a little more predictable for the engineers. What is surprising is that the plant had been running for 25 years without this input or suggestion ever being put forward. TQM had helped unlock the potential of employees.

This is not to say that operators did not care previously — it was simply that their views had not been sought at this level. Similar ideas worked wonders for this plant. Groups of committed employees would meet as corrective action teams to prevent problems arising. Their experiences were tapped and many disasters were averted. The operators possessed the body of knowledge to make continuous improvement a way of life.

Following this and other successes, a corrective action team was formed at the request of the operators, to look at water utilisation within the plant. From initial investigations and analysis it was found that the company could re-route water, at no great cost and, thereby, reduce operating costs by an amazing £80,000 per year. These successes do not come about by accident but because operators feel that they have the opportunity to contribute and improve performance. This, in turn, is 'learned' from their managers.

Alan Hughes: results through people, although these examples were a direct result of TQM, this plant had a fine reputation for 'improvement' in its most general sense prior to the drive. In the past, staff at all levels had met to establish employee involvement and produced many suggestions to reduce costs, improve productivity and so forth. Staff had a major input into the design of machinery, its location and its use. Alan Hughes, the plant manager, had established the practice of involvement and TQM was an extension of this process. Alan had created the involvement culture over a period of 11 years. First he had established briefing groups. Then he ensured that his managers met every day to discuss events which had taken place on other shifts and progress for the day ahead. The emphasis was not just on making better production targets. These '10 o'clock' briefings and his weekly 'tufty club' sessions were the keys to keeping rein on what was happening within the company.

Alan was also promoting horizontal management through cross-functional training. He and his management team were committed to retraining the 19 key supervisors in skills in 3 discrete areas. At any time, these supervisors could assume duties in other areas. It created flexibility, but this was not the real purpose behind the training — it was to get supervisors to understand problems from a proper systems perspective. Previously, rigid job demarcation through technology had created a sub-system mentality where there was little understanding of things apart from on an area basis. What was required was a 'plant perspective'. Within this framework, supervisors and operatives did things differently. This illustrates that TQM is a continuous process which links in well with other employee involvement initiatives.

Final assembly creating engineering changes

George was the final assembly foreman in an engineering company producing high-quality exhausts for cars. He had a great deal of rework with one component. On this component, a zinc plate had to be welded to an aluminised tube. This was a difficult process and created unpleasant and noxious fumes as well as a poor weld. Welders wanted to change the material of the plate to something which was more compatible with the pipe. George put in a suggestion to replace the zinc plate but was told that the customer liked it that way. George persevered and, together with the salesman who serviced the customer, sought help from the designer who, in turn, negotiated with the customer. The customer gladly agreed to the change.

This change reinforced the belief that the opinions of people on the shop floor were valued. It also helped to create a change in internal quality procedures. A new 'Change to Engineering Design Form' was developed to facilitate the speedy flow of ideas from the shop floor to designers and others. This was just one suggestion which helped to create the TQM culture in the company.

Architects serving beer

A similar example in non-manufacturing also deserves attention. During an intervention to help a major brewing company establish TQ in all areas of operations, a group of architects was spoken to. Nigel, one of 68 appointed internal TQM trainers, was a new recruit and gave an example of TQM in action. Architects were employed not just to help in designing and building new pubs and restaurants, but also to design and co-ordinate the refurbishment of older public houses. Nigel talked of the induction process he experienced. At first he had found this of little value. He had to spend 2 weeks in a number of pubs where he performed a wide variety of duties. He washed glasses, helped with deliveries to the cellar and aided in the general running of the pub. He found this experience to be invaluable later when he was involved in design work. His job had been made easier. He no longer saw the public house as a 3-dimensional model but as a place of work. He understood more about the design of shelves for glasses, the design and location of the cellar (it was rumoured that some cellars in the past had been located in areas unsuitable for storing beer) and kitchen layout.

This is only a simple example of employee involvement, the precursor of TQM. Here the publicans helped the professional designer to understand the constraints in which they worked. He now understood the pub was not just a building but a working environment where design should be focused on the movement and interaction of people, rather than imposing structures around which people must work.

Involvement is not obstruction!

There are scores of examples where employee involvement can help companies. However, there are also many instances when the views of employees are seen as no more than obstructive to 'business as usual'. Douglas, now an insurance executive and partner in a small business, looked back on his training in a large insurance company. There, he stated, he came across many forms which were inefficient in design. The information required was routed around offices and agents with no apparent structure. Obviously, the management services people had never considered talking to the end user. When Douglas suggested improvements, his immediate supervisor told him to 'mind his own business'. Douglas did not want to give up so he mentioned his ideas to others. He was greeted with indifference and vowed never to make a suggestion again!

It is clear that the secret of making TQM part of the organisational culture requires the involvement of everybody. Given the opportunity, people will contribute — but only if they see something happen. Once people are involved or start contributing, the worst thing that management can do is to stop it! Management can do this by ignoring ideas, by telling people that ideas only come from management, by failing to do what it says it will do, and by negative reinforcement. Obtaining suggestions for improvement can be accelerated through positive reinforcement. Failing to recognise contributions will kill quality improvement.

Find someone doing something right and tell them what a good job they are doing!

Hersey and Blanchard in the 'One Minute Manager' suggest that managers and supervisors spend too much time finding fault and telling people what they do wrong. The style of management which motivates people is orientated towards concentrating upon finding something good and telling people what a good job they do. This does not mean manufacturing a reason or generalising and telling everybody they are doing well. It means being specific in praise and ensuring that positive feedback is as close as possible to the desirable act which has taken place. This is the key to the motivation and the team building required to promote the TQM culture.

Reinforcing positive contributions through managerial actions is the quickest way to ensure that employees come up with ideas to make TQM work.

Communication is the foundation for real employee involvement. Few recognise the value of informing employees of progress or do not recognise how little their people are aware of company communications. Some companies value 'communication' and set up briefing sessions. These are usually organised to communicate top-down.

Briefing groups

In recent years, the briefing process has increased in the UK. Much of this is founded upon the work of the Industrial Society. Despite this push many companies have not really benefitted to the degree to which they were able to put briefing groups to work.

Briefing focuses upon the accurate transmission of information through the organisational structure and upon the role that employers can play. Many changes take place daily in an organisation and it is important that these are communicated effectively throughout the company. If a formal line of communication is ineffective, rumour and gossip will fill its place. Briefing rests on the 4 Ps — policy, purpose, people and progress. Inform employees about policy, purpose, people and progress. There are other variants of this approach but, generally, this is a structure upon which to communicate.

Failing to listen

The great danger when 'briefing' is to spend too much time telling people about changes and too little time listening. This is crucial, for failing to listen and act is the quickest way for things to fail. Obviously some communications are very formal and have to be passed on in a fairly structured manner in order to avoid inconsistencies in transmission. Such briefs must not be deviated from and are usually read to employees, but the majority of briefs should be interactive affairs where managers pass on a message, listen to the reaction and feed this back up through the management chain. Unfortunately, this is where too many briefing sessions break down.

Because of lack of time, managers transmit information one way but fail to listen and feed back the reaction of their people. In some cases, the briefing approach fails because the system falls into disrepute and 'briefs' are simply pinned to notice boards. The communication ends there. Although it would appear that the activities associated with briefing have been accomplished to some degree, the true spirit is lacking. Clearly a TQM intervention requires a sound briefing and communication system to be in existence. How can companies promote TQM with any hope of success when they cannot create a sound briefing system?

Team building and organisational culture

Creating a culture receptive to TQM is dependent upon creating the right management style, communicating and informing employees and developing team spirit. The team spirit must permeate functions and departments. There is little point having highly cohesive teams on strictly functional lines. That produces straight line solutions. Team spirit must be based on good horizontal principles with joint problem-solving in mind. Nowadays there is a constant requirement in many organisations for functional experts to work together on

Chairman/co-ordinator

As a team role, specifies controlling the way in which a team moves towards the group objectives by making the best use of team resources; recognising where the team's strengths and weaknesses lie; and ensuring that the best use is made of each team member's potential.

Company worker/implementer

As a team role, specifies turning concepts and plans into practical working procedures; and carrying out agreed plans systematically and efficiently.

Completer — finisher

As a team role, specifies ensuring that the team is protected as far as possible from mistakes of both commission and omission; actively searching for aspects of work which need a more than usual degree of attention; and maintaining a sense of urgency within the team.

Monitor — evaluator

As a team role, specifies analysing problems; and evaluating ideas and suggestions so that the team is better placed to take balanced decisions.

Plant

As a team role, specifies advancing new ideas and strategies with special attention to major issues; and looking for possible breaks in approach to the problems with which the group is confronted.

Resource investigator

As a team role, specifies exploring and reporting on ideas, developments and resources outside the group; creating external contacts that may be useful to the team; and conducting any subsequent negotiations.

Shaper

As a team role, specifies shaping the way in which a team effort is applied; directing attention generally to the setting of objectives and priorities; and seeking to impose some shape or pattern on group discussion and on the outcome of activities.

Team worker

As a team role, specifies supporting members in their strengths (e.g. building on suggestions); underpinning members in their shortcomings; improving communication between members; and fostering team spirit generally.

Fig. 1 Belbin team types (Source: Management Teams, 1981)

a project basis. However, after the project is over the experts revert back strictly to the interests of their departments. We suggest that more time is spent developing cross-functional groups to appreciate the company-wide perspective. In the real business world few problems have impact upon only one department —they have impact upon many — so it makes sense to develop this type of culture (see Fig. 1).

Rejecting the 'us and them' approach

There is a great deal of negative stereotyping between departments and within companies in general. There is too much of the 'us and them' or the 'win-lose' attitude in general, whether between trade union and company, or shop floor and management. If one department wins — it is usually at the expense of others. What we should be trying to develop is the 'win-win' attitude where people work together. The only real way to change is to improve personnel policy and practice. This means changing the systems of remuneration, appraisal and staff development.

Career progression can be horizontal

People become slotted into a career structure which is functional in nature. We end up breeding specialists who are very good at their jobs but who find it difficult to relate to those in other functions. Changing the career path — incorporating lateral development, valuing and rewarding cross-fertilisation is the only way to promote 'Horizontal Management'. What we have at present is the ridiculous situation where technical specialists have only one route to follow for promotion and an increase in salary, i.e. upwards. Technical experts then hold the most senior positions within a company. Whether they can actually manage is not questioned.

Consequently, we end up with good 'technicians' becoming poor managers in charge of other technicians or experts. We may lose our best experts and 'gain' a mediocre manager! It is a fact of life that there are not enough places at the top for everybody. So, not everybody is going to make it to the top but what do we do with people who can go no further?

The traditional hierarchical structure will only accommodate a few, so what happens to everybody else? Is this the end of a person's career? It shouldn't be but it usually is. Organisations should revise 'career structures' and build them on horizontal rather than vertical lines. Career progression should be based upon managers changing functions when possible. This is not to suggest that the MIS manager should become the engineering manager but that there are many opportunities where horizons can be broadened.

Many companies already do this. A notable example is Ciba Corning Diagnostics where the policy is to provide challenge for its people. They do a remarkable job and the managers benefit as well.

Hugh, a successful sales manager was being groomed at one stage for personnel manager. Now he is responsible for UK acquisitions. His company, a US manufacturer of medical technology, recognises that the best way to obtain the best from people is to provide them with continuous challenge. This does not mean throwing people in at the deep end. It means considering career and succession planning on a horizontal basis.

Breathing in and out

After being in a senior position for some time, many managers lose their drive and enthusiasm. It is not unnatural for managers to slip into the 'fat and happy' state when they know they are going no further. They start to wind down. Yet the most successful people in the company, those that have risen to senior company status, still have a great deal of experience and enthusiasm to offer the organisation. In many cases this is not channelled, little action is taken and we are left with a manager whose experience can be measured in time rather than quality. Is it any surprise that some managers go through the motions each day, breathe in and out without making mistakes and then go home on the dot? They contribute little, fail to motivate others and create the 'non-achieving' environment. The good, aspiring manager leaves the company — leaving the future of the company to be run by managers 'dead from the neck up'.

A TQM presentation was given to one engineering company where the manufacturing manager, Bob, was alive, alert and keen to promote change. He said, "We need to turn this company upside down. We need TQM, otherwise they will kill it." Who were they? The managers. Bob couldn't have been more right. The management culture was one of longevity. Who could stay the longest? Bob had taken on the responsibility of making changes through TQM and had inherited a senior team, 40% of which had been in the same company, in the same function, although at different status, an average of 32 years! The rest of the team was equally divided between 'long-servers' and 'new blood'. We are now promoting change, slowly, through the 'young blood' but we have a long way to go.

Most employees are creative, committed and achieving — except for the eight hours when they work for you!

An example from Tom Peters illustrates this point well. If we take a sample of ten employees we will probably find that at least one is a keen and active member of his local church, another runs a Boy Scout group, another is a leading actor in a local repertory company, others are involved in running a business and one may lead the local youth football team, etc. What we can deduce is that in many cases employees, whether they are staff or managers are enthusiastic, keen, creative, organised and achieving — except during working hours!

There are still too many organisations where staff at all levels have occupied their roles for too long. Their drive is blunted and a large percentage will be past their peaks. The fault lies with senior officers who have wasted the talents and experiences of their most precious resources — their people. Is it not sensible to capitalise on the strengths of experienced and successful managers and staff, share these with others in different functions who can benefit from their input and maintain a high level of overall company-wide motivation? The alternative is a structure which is doomed to extinction.

Bearing in mind that the team building and succession planning issues are important — the real impetus can only come from a management team which is committed to change. Management has to be able to acknowledge weaknesses within the company and do something about it. However, first, the orientation must come from the top and that means being self critical.

Team building — right at the top

TQM requires a complete turnabout in the way senior officers look on their companies. They cannot expect all the changes to come from below. They must provide the examples for others to follow. Challenging assumptions and the role that the senior management team plays in promoting success through TQM, can only come from looking inwards first and then looking at how members of the 'Team' work together.

It is not sufficient to look at performance at a superficial level, it requires some depth. Looking at personal strengths and weaknesses is a route which some management teams promote with pride. Some of the most successful interventions have taken place because the senior officers wanted to examine their impact on others. For these teams, the route was team building based on psychometric profiles. This is an extremely powerful and under-utilised method for creating significant change.

Unfortunately, many still feel the role of the psychologist in management is solely to aid recruitment and selection. Analysis of strengths and weaknesses may lie in pursuing the same route — but with a different purpose.

Psychometric profiling and team building

There are many common misconceptions of psychometric profiling. Some managers focus on the use of 'psychometrics' as tests which can be passed or failed. This is a gross under-simplification and is not true. A profile will give a good indication of 'what is'. It is then up to the manager and his colleagues to assess whether the profile fits the needs of the job.

What must be borne in mind is the validity of the profiles and their general credibility. There are too many profiles entering the market which are not valid — they don't measure what they say they do or they are unreliable and poorly researched.

Instances of the positive use of profiles follow. Although some instruments will be referred to, this is not an exhaustive list. Overall, the companies which have used this approach have believed that there was a causal relationship between assessing management style and developing company values which are reflected in a new managerial approach, which influences the TQM culture of team building and participation.

Developing trust at the top, a number of companies has decided to promote the psycometric profiling approach. Needless to say, many of the managers involved were concerned that the 'results' would be used for other purposes. A few general points should be considered. If managers are sufficiently trusting to undergo the 'rigours' of profiling they should be fed back the results confidentially. Results should not be on general display. Sharing of results with others on the management team should be determined and paced by the managers themselves, not an occupational psychologist. How can one expect to achieve a change in culture and promote trust and concern for others if feedback is less than confidential? Finally, profiles should only be administered, interpreted and fed back by qualified specialists.

Changing style through Myers-Briggs, one profile design is that of Myers Briggs. This is an extremely rigorous approach to looking at the differences which exist between personality types. All too often we come into contact with people who do not reason as we reason, or do not value the things we value, or are not interested in what interests us.

The objective of using the Myers Briggs type indicator (MBTI) is to examine personality differences and deal with these differences in a constructive way (see Fig. 2). For instance, certain personality 'types' are attracted to specific professions. Their personality characteristics fit best with their roles or posts (although some claim that post develops and reinforces type). Others in different functions may find it hard to understand them.

Let's look at some examples. In order to do this we need to look at some stereotyped views of certain functional managers. It should be noted that these stereotyped images are for clarification of the MBTI principles only.

Hypothetical profiles, let us look at a marketing manager and make some general assumptions. He/she may tend to be strongly innovative in outlook. He or she will probably move quickly from one subject to another and will be good at looking at relationships between unrelated subjects. He/she will probably have difficulty concentrating on one subject for a long time, dislike activities requiring detailed and routine analysis and make quick decisions.

Now let us consider a technical manager in a laboratory. People employed in laboratory work may be strongly sensing, trusting only their senses and what they can see or feel. They tend to relate to all that is concrete and tangible. It will be unlikely that they are strong extroverts preferring to associate with a 'select' few. They may be good at analysis and systematic and logical thinking. They will not be quick to make decisions because they value their technical competence. They will be objective and will not be swayed by opinion.

Putting these two individuals together in a close working environment may create difficulties. Although we are told that opposites attract, this is unlikely. People tend to be attracted to similar people, those who portray similar traits and viewpoints. Although people differ it is extremely unlikely that exact opposites will work well! Each may value the characteristics which they consider lacking in their colleague. Bringing together a number of people with strongly contrasting characteristics may create some friction and a failure to work together. Imagine the impact of this on temporary task or project groups.

It is important to examine the differences between people and the actions we can take to promote team-work. Mixing the differences and understanding the 'gifts' which each member of the team has is a sure way of promoting a common team approach — but it is easier said than done. The Myers Briggs approach looks at four dimensions.

Introversion and extroversion. The first dimension is a measure of introversion and extroversion. The introvert tends to be more interested in the 'inner world' of concepts and ideas and the extrovert the 'outer world' or relationships and possibilities. Clearly a strong preference either way creates certain strong behaviours which have an impact on others. These also may be indicative of certain preferential managerial careers.

The second dimension is concerned with perception. Perceiving means the way people become aware of things, people, occurrences and ideas and how they absorb information from the environment, etc.

We can perceive the world in two ways, sensing and intuition. Sensing is becoming aware of things through our 5 senses. Intuition is indirect perception through our unconscious, incorporating ideas or associations. These may range from the masculine 'hunch' to the feminine 'intuition'.

Readers of this chapter who prefer sensing will concentrate on the words, readers who prefer intuition will read between the lines. Overall, we tend to favour one process over others. We neglect the other, which we enjoy less. We probably neglect a 'process' because we are not too skilled in its use. If a certain process has been encouraged in our work life then it is natural for us to favour or prefer it. If we favour one method we avoid the use of other ways. Over time, and with experience, the preferred process grows more controlled and more trustworthy. This enjoyment of a 'process' extends into activities requiring that process and we tend to develop the traits that come from looking at life in a particular way. We each develop along different lines.

The third dimension is judging and includes the processes of coming to conclusions about what we have perceived. Together, perception and judgement govern much of a person's outward behaviour. Perception determines what people see in a situation and judgement determines what they do about it.

Judging is the way we come to conclusions. One way is thinking, that is by a logical process, aimed at impersonal findings. The other is by feeling, that is by appreciation — bestowing on things a value based on personal subjectivity. People tend to trust one process over the other.

A thinking reader will judge on the logical process of what is said. The feeling person on ideas which are pleasing or displeasing, supporting or threatening. The person who uses feeling is more alert to developing human relationships whereas the person who is more adept at thinking grows more skilled in the organisation of facts and logical analysis.

Finally, the last dimension refers to your approach to life. If a person is judging in outlook he probably prefers an organised existence and plans well in advance. Others, with the alternative approach, are perceptive in nature and prefer to do things as they arise. They are probably more spontaneous and prefer to be flexible.

Consequently, people who share preferences for doing things find each other easy to understand and get along and work well together. Those who don't share preferences have difficulty understanding each other. This opposition can be a strain if these people are members of the same management team.

Characteristics frequently associated with each type

	Sensing Types		Intuitive Types	
	Extroverts / Introverts			
Introverts	**ISTJ** Serious, quiet, earn success by concentration and thoroughness. Practical, orderly, matter-of-fact, logical, realistic, and dependable. See to it that everything is well organized. Take responsibility. Make up their own minds as to what should be accomplished and work toward it steadily, regardless of protests or distractions.	**ISFJ** Quiet, friendly, responsible, and conscientious. Work devotedly to meet their obligations. Lend stability to any project or group. Thorough, painstaking, accurate. Their interests are usually not technical. Can be patient with necessary details. Loyal, considerate, perceptive, concerned with how other people feel.	**INFJ** Succeed by perseverance, originality, and desire to do whatever is needed or wanted. Put their best efforts into their work. Quietly forceful, conscientious, concerned for others. Respected for their firm principles. Likely to be honored and followed for their clear convictions as to how best to serve the common good.	**INTJ** Usually have original minds and great drive for their own ideas and purposes. In fields that appeal to them, they have a fine power to organize a job and carry it through with or without help. Sceptical, critical, independent, determined, sometimes stubborn. Must learn to yield less important points in order to win the most important.
	ISTP Cool onlookers — quiet, reserved, observing and analyzing life with detached curiosity and unexpected flashes of original humor. Usually interested in cause and effect, how and why mechanical things work, and in organizing facts using logical principles.	**ISFP** Retiring, quietly friendly, sensitive, kind, modest about their abilities. Shun disagreements, do not force their opinions or values on others. Usually do not care to lead but are often loyal followers. Often relaxed about getting things done, because they enjoy the present moment and do not want to spoil it by undue haste or exertion.	**INFP** Full of enthusiasms and loyalties, but seldom talk of these until they know you well. Care about learning, ideas, language, and independent projects of their own. Tend to undertake too much, then somehow get it done. Friendly, but often too absorbed in what they are doing to be sociable. Little concerned with possessions or physical surroundings.	**INTP** Quiet and reserved. Especially enjoy theoretical or scientific pursuits. Like solving problems with logic and analysis. Usually interested mainly in ideas, with little liking for parties or small talk. Tend to have sharply defined interests. Need careers where some strong interest can be used and useful.
Extroverts	**ESTP** Good at on-the-spot problem solving. Do not worry, enjoy whatever comes along. Tend to like mechanical things and sports, with friends on the side. Adaptable, tolerant, generally conservative in values. Dislike long explanations. Are best with real things that can be worked, handled, taken apart, or put together.	**ESFP** Outgoing, easygoing, accepting, friendly, enjoy everything and make things more fun for others by their enjoyment. Like sports and making things happen. Know what's going on and join in eagerly. Find remembering facts easier than mastering theories. Are best in situations that need sound common sense and practical ability with people as well as with things.	**ENFP** Warmly enthusiastic, high-spirited, ingenious, imaginative. Able to do almost anything that interests them. Quick with a solution for any difficulty and ready to help anyone with a problem. Often rely on their ability to improvise instead of preparing in advance. Can usually find compelling reasons for whatever they want.	**ENTP** Quick, ingenious, good at many things. Stimulating company, alert and outspoken. May argue for fun on either side of a question. Resourceful in solving new and challenging problems, but may neglect routine assignments. Apt to turn to one new interest after another. Skillful in finding logical reasons for what they want.
	ESTJ Practical, realistic, matter-of-fact, with a natural head for business or mechanics. Not interested in subjects they see no use for, but can apply themselves when necessary. Like to organize and run activities. May make good administrators, especially if they remember to consider others' feelings and points of view.	**ESFJ** Warm-hearted, talkative, popular, conscientious, born cooperators, active committee members. Need harmony and may be good at creating it. Always doing something nice for someone. Work best with encouragement and praise. Main interest is in things that directly and visibly affect people's lives.	**ENFJ** Responsive and responsible. Generally feel real concern for what others think or want, and try to handle things with due regard for the other person's feelings. Can present a proposal or lead a group discussion with ease and tact. Sociable, popular, sympathetic. Responsive to praise and criticism.	**ENTJ** Hearty, frank, decisive, leaders in activities. Usually good in anything that requires reasoning and intelligent talk, such as public speaking. Are usually well informed and enjoy adding to their fund of knowledge. May sometimes appear more positive and confident than their experience in an area warrants.

Fig. 2 Myers Briggs type indicator (MBTI) (Source: Consulting Psychologists Press Inc., 577 College Avenue, Palo Alto, California 94306)

There is not a good or bad type, understanding some of the differences between colleagues helps us to understand how we and others organise our working lives and how we manage others. We can also find out more about preferences for planning and decision-making.

Some managers, the analyst type, may be highly logical and systematic and find it difficult to get on with the visionary who trades on ideas and moves from one subject to another. Management development is all about understanding these differences and working through the conflicts.

Profiles and examples, with the MBTI there are 16 basic profiles. Understanding a personal profile and working to understand others with whom we interact ensures that a real team effort is achieved. For instance, an ISTJ who is quiet, thorough, practical, organised, dependable and who can work on projects independently, may have some difficulty understanding the views of an ENFP who is high spirited, friendly, ready to help and feels able to contribute to situations even if not an expert.

Knowing that certain occupational profiles attract certain 'types' may give some indication why there can be conflict between say personnel managers and systems analysts and marketing managers and researchers, etc. Understanding the reasons for these differences is critical to effective team-work. Types suggest certain leadership styles and leadership behaviours.

Saville and Holdsworth, in their OPQ personality profile, also indicates ways of working in groups and leading others. It is one of the most powerful instruments on the market and has been designed to generate information and relate to other 'managerial' profiles such as Belbin's team types.

There is a great deal to be said about profiles but I will concentrate here on their value to the management team. The profiles help us to understand why we and others behave as we do. Failing to understand and deal with personal differences suggests a rigidity in management style — which is not conducive to TQM.

In a successful chemical company this approach helped the senior team to understand the conflict behind planning the roll-out of TQ. Some of the managers wanted a planned, detailed approach while others wanted to try a few 'flexible' pilots and others wanted to think about it!

The senior officers in a major finance house concentrated on their managerial style and the impact their style had on others. The majority tried to vary their natural styles in certain circumstances. This was all in aid of gaining balance in managing the process of cultural change.

Many critics of this approach feel that this is too 'touching and feeling'. Some managers prefer the rigours of strategy, systems and structure. The team build-ing approach rests with staff at all levels, providing them with the skills, chang-ing management style and leading by example in order to create shared values or a new culture founded on TQM.

This approach is pursued in order to better understand behaviour and actions. This understanding is the cornerstone for creating long-term cultural change. The use of profiles is gaining ground in most companies and it is only a matter of time before this is the central focus behind many major change strategies.

Summary and bullet points

- Senior officers can only move from the fire-fighting to the preventative culture through changing the 'styles' of their managers.
- Don't underestimate the changes necessary. Getting people to move from a rigid 'telling' culture to a 'listening' culture does take time and extraordinary effort by senior people.
- Moving to a 'listening' culture does not equate with abdicating managerial responsibility.
- When we identify defective services or products we should call in the person who may have the best solutions — the person directly and physically responsible for the delivery of those goods or services. Remember we employ people from the neck up, not down!
- Remember you only get results through others. Give operators and service people the responsibility and the scope to create changes. Leave them to it and get out of the way.
- Create opportunities all the time to involve people. If things go wrong, don't blame them — ask them for suggestions for improvement. If you are developing a new product or service, ask for their viewpoint. It's free and effective.
- If you find there are managers who are obstructive to initiating new ideas and improvements, give them the chance to change. If they don't change — change them!
- Try to motivate your people. Research tells us that positive reinforcement which is specific and delivered as soon as the desirable behaviour has taken place promotes motivation. Spend less time telling people what they did 3% wrong and congratulate them for what they did 97% right. Ask them for detailed plans on getting the whole 100% right next time.
- The effective transmission of information through briefing groups creates a climate of trust and co-operation. Fail to communicate and people will think you don't trust them.
- If you can't make briefing groups work up and down the organisation you'll never achieve the full benefits of TQM.
- The organisational culture reflects team-work. A frightened, fear-driven culture will be reinforced by win-lose team tactics both in and between departments. A TQM culture is founded upon win-win relationships.
- Reject the 'us and them' attitude. The more you recognise it the more you reinforce it. It belongs in the 1890s not the 1990s.
- Senior management teams deserve the managers who work for them. Career development is a strategic issue and should be taken seriously. The people who work for you now are the products of your human resource policies of previous years. If you don't value your people — they won't value working for you.

- Don't believe that all career progression is vertical. Move to a philosophy which promotes, values and rewards managers working across boundaries.
- Most people are creative, committed and achieving — except when they work for you. Develop human resource strategies to promote the use of talent at work.
- Start team building right at the top. Explore differences and learn to adopt styles.
- Don't reject psychometrics as 'mumbo jumbo'! Reject the negatives and learn how you interact with influence and lead others.
- Understand that change begins at the top.

12 YOU CAN'T LET THEM LOOSE UNTIL YOU HAVE GIVEN THEM THE BEST TRAINING YOU CAN . . .

The role of training, development and education is probably the most critical aspect of any TQM drive. Training workshops should be designed to stimulate, challenge and provide attendees with all the knowledge they need to make TQM happen. If this experience is a failure, then those attending the sessions will gain little and you have reduced your chance of success.

Too many management teams think that their enthusiasm for TQM will be shared automatically by other employees. They believe that fantastic changes will come about when the training takes off! We know this will not always be the case. Many people will look upon the change as a threat to the security of their positions and will avoid creating the necessary changes. This attitude is difficult to hide in training sessions — when case studies and action plans are explored.

Success comes from examining the reasons why TQM training initiatives have not been as successful as they should have been. Too often, management teams think that a spell of training will work wonders. Yes, it will — if it is planned properly and is tested and owned by more than the guy who stands at the front and trains!

Let's look at the ways in which training can fail and the action we can take to avoid failure. Each of these points will be explained and tentative solutions proffered. However, first let us start with the most basic of problems — examining the role of training in organisation development.

Misunderstanding what training and development is about!

Let us be realistic, the role of training is one which is not always valued by all companies. Perhaps the reason for this is that we may find it so difficult to relate to specific training events with particular organisational success. Too many managers see training as a luxury, undertaken only by larger companies which can afford to spread the costs over many functions and locations. This is nonsense.

Many managers discount the role of training because they find it difficult to relate training exercises to the bottom line. A fundamental point needs clarification. A great deal of investment in training may not be gleaned in the short term for a variety of reasons — but this should not be an excuse for not doing it.

Relating training initiatives to specific outcomes has never been easy —that's why too many personnel practitioners appear to have little power — but it is not insurmountable. Spending time and energy in planning can enable us to relate specific outcomes to training inputs.

One excuse used by many trainers is the intangibility of training and relating this to business results. If we know why we are training we should be able to monitor progress. If we can't measure success, then little thought has gone into training design.

Training managers who have specified their objectives, designed drives to meet them and have carefully monitored progress are those who have gained most. A 'hit and miss' training affair does not create the required cultural change. Training as a method of change can be extremely successful if managed properly. However, we must reject the generalised training event characterised by inappropriate material, irrelevant case studies and video presentations delivered by trainers who are more committed to their own interests than to the well-being of the company.

Not all responsibility falls on the trainer though. Some managers, when asked about their commitment to training, suggest defensively that the selection process is geared towards bringing the best calibre people into the structure, so there is little need to devote resources to training.

There is an implication that new recruits have received all the training they require. This may be true on a professional basis for today — but what about tomorrow? The really interesting question which is never answered, relates to existing employees. Do they magically acquire the skills and abilities to cope with changes in the organisation? Are they able, through a process of osmosis, to acquire skills so they can fulfil senior roles in the organisation? No, of course not. Managers have to be developed within the company to meet the challenge of the future. Companies that fail to do this had better start investing in the future — otherwise they won't have one.

Training in professional and technical skills only!

Unfortunately, in too many cases, in the UK, training refers directly to professional and technical training only. As long as employees are trained in the latest state of the art or techniques of their specialisms or functions, the 'management process' can take care of itself! The only problem is that the 'management process' is critical to the success of TQM and, if not properly planned and implemented, can create havoc and destroy a perfectly good initiative.

Too few organisations value training — look what has happened to the training function when there is a downturn in economic activity. Those activities which fail to bring in tangible results are sacrificed in the short term. The long term, in many cases, is made up of short-term fixes or decisions which are geared totally towards reducing costs and maintaining profit on the bottom line. It is not surprising that, in the long term, training issues are never fully addressed.

Consider the value of trainers in organisations. Do they process high status or is their position basically a job-share with a production role? This is true in too many cases. Consequently, few managers have the same level of commitment towards training as in the 'excellent' companies. Training is something which can be left to another day.

I am glad to say not all companies portray this image. For instance, IBM is renowned for its commitment to training. Each manager receives at least 5 managerial training days per year. Other companies committed to the TQ culture do likewise but they are few and far between. Without doubt, the companies which value management development tend to be the more enlightened UK companies, most US-based multinationals, East-West joint venture companies and the Japanese.

Of course, many readers will dispute this view as a vast generalisation but the reality is that too many companies fail to provide even the most basic training. Evidence for this viewpoint can be seen if we explore employment in the 1990s.

Demographic trends

Estimates suggest that in the near future, the numbers seeking employment in industry and commerce on a professional basis will fall. This is primarily related to the falling birth rate in the '70s. We understand that in the 1990s 50% of the workforce will be made up of women returning to work and, of the remainder, 50% will be young females.

Alarm bells are starting to ring. Traditionally, most European and US companies drew, rightly or wrongly, upon the male population for recruitment for managerial staff. The reality is that young men will be in short supply.

To attract this scarce resource companies will need to prove that they walk with the giants. Companies will have to take serious note of this challenge. Young graduates are in demand. They will go to the company with the 'excellent' image. They will not be interested in those which have little commitment to training, development, career development and succession planning.

Too few companies have considered the severity of this problem. If we have not prepared ourselves for the immediate future, including equal opportunity, what preparation have we made for TQM?

This is bad news as we move towards 1992 — but if little movement is taking place on the generalised training front you can be sure that too little time has been put into training for TQM.

Companies committed to training as a catalyst of change, both organisationally and individually, will find the transition to TQM relatively easy. Does your company project this image?

Training: We are the best — we think!

In one company in the finance sector, the opinion expressed by many managers was, "We are the best at providing training in the business." This was hard to believe, because many supervisors and managers had not attended a training workshop for years! The statement, 'the best in the business' had come about because of a specific comment made about an objection-handling workshop run for salesmen. This was translated into a general belief that the company provided the best training in the industry!

Questionnaires to explore the reality of the situation requested managers to be specific about the workshops and focus of training provided by other companies. There was a general belief, founded on no more than prejudice and company loyalty, that their company was the industry's best at providing training. Although tremendously loyal, this attitude, if shared by all, does little to move the company forward.

Quality of people

Training and development is one of the 3 most important investments any company can make, the other 2 being technological innovation and research and development. Organisations fail to realise that the quality of their people is determined by the *experiences* to which they are exposed within the company. If these experiences are all short-term outcomes and production orientated, with little opportunity for development, then we cannot expect people to come up with innovative ways of doing things and solving old problems.

An old culture geared to production, with no time devoted to critical review and development, will create employees who are solely geared to production with little foresight.

Comparing UK company commitment to training to that of our foreign competitors is an embarassment. While many companies, renowned for the ways they do things, invest as much as 3–5% of sales turnover on training, many spend considerably less. Talking with managers from a company in the whisky industry, it was surprising to learn that they did not base their financial commitment to training on a percentage of sales turnover, but on the wage bill. Apparently, resources devoted to training exceeded 1% of wage bill the previous year. However, most of the money had been spent on a training facility — which had not been used for training but for meetings!

Great TQ training — pity about their inability to manage!

To demonstrate the attitude of some companies to training consider the following instance. While we were working with an engineering company, a senior manager told us how pleased he had been with the training that they had received. However, he had some reservations. After discussion about the good points of the course, he stated that his supervisors were still deficient in leadership and team building. He explained, "They know what they should do but they still don't know how to delegate, plan activities, hold meetings and motivate."

This was quite a shock. What was learned most from this encounter was that a 2-day course on TQ does not even start to redress the failure of management over many years to provide employees with even the basic management education.

Companies need to realise that training is the key to an improved culture. The prescription is simple. Become committed today to spending double, triple and quadruple on training. If not, you get what you deserve.

First learn how people learn, then develop the training initiatives

There are some similarities between training in athletics and management. The more successful athletics coaches tend to be those who have been through similar experiences to those whom they train. This is also true for managers. The coaches understand how skills and abilities are acquired and recognise that the major obstacles to training have to be overcome — these are usually self-imposed and related to attitude. The same applies for management. A coach would never design a training programme which would take an athlete to Olympic competition without making some appraisal of past performance. Coaches need to understand what turns their athlete 'on' and 'off' and design programmes with this in mind. This is also true in management circles. The past performance of managers, identified in appraisals or reviews of training courses, will give some indication of strengths, weaknesses and potential. Failing to review the past performance of managers and supervisors before designing a training event is tantamount to disaster. Clearly, we can benefit from looking at past actions to help us predict future behaviour.

Deal with the stress issue first!

Many people attending training workshops, on any subject, experience some level of stress. This is fine if that stress is perceived as being a positive motivator, i.e. they are looking forward to the challenge, the stimulation, the excitement and the debate, etc. However, what happens when the negative elements of stress take over and the training event is perceived as being negative and punitive?

People don't learn if they are afraid

In some cases, people believe their reasons for attendance on a course is because of their poor performances. They are doing things wrong. It is not unheard of for managers to state that attendance on a one or two day course will instantly eradicate undesirable managerial or supervisory performance.

Training in the negative sense, and in the Dickensian culture, is something you do to people! What are the consequences? Many trainers find that some attendees are extremely tense and anxious. It is not surprising that the first half hour or so of a programme can be a lonesome affair for the trainers, with the trainees sitting rigid and afraid to speak up.

In one or two instances, fortunately too rare to suggest that this is the industry average, courses have included managers and supervisors who have not been briefed on the purpose of the course or their expected contribution. Clearly, lack of organisation and commitment to the event are holding back TQM.

Trainees need to be relaxed to take new ideas on board. Learning cannot take place in a climate of fear. Some have the belief, not shared by all, that training should be an enjoyable experience. It should challenge the previous experience of the participant and build upon a commitment to do better in the future. This is critical in any quality improvement initiative.

In order to learn, considerable unfreezing of attitudes has to take place prior to the training experience. Any 'fear' associated with training has to be dispelled. Whose responsibility is unfreezing? Most tends to fall upon the shoulders of the trainer but we believe strongly that the line manager should be coaching the potential course delegate on the purpose and objectives of the course and expected contributions. Obviously, this can only be achieved if the training course has been discussed at all management levels.

Let strategy lead training

One of the most common failures in training for quality is that too much emphasis is given to the role of training as the activity which will create the TQ culture by itself. Experiencing a meaningful course on TQ will not necessarily generate TQ behaviour. It is the foundation upon which to work. There is a natural tendency to roll-out training before the management team is really aware of what it wants to achieve in specific functions and departments.

Training as part of TQM seems to be an activity which is encouraged because it is tangible — something is happening. The question asked is, "Is it happening at the right time?"

We all know that training has costs — people will be away from work. Others should fill in for them. Those attending sessions should not be penalised by finding mountains of work on their desks when they return.

We all know that in order to reduce waste and rework we need to prevent problems arising and this includes putting time aside for planning and training. Trying to make the transition without some commitment to additional resources puts stress and pressure on the workforce and reinforces the belief that the company is not really serious.

The solution to this dilemma rests with senior management. The training of staff in TQ and related techniques has to be thought through at a strategic level and training designed specifically for the future of the company. That is why it is critical that companies plan the implementation of TQ and spend some time considering exactly where they would like to be in the next few years and what resources they will commit to the transition. It is a waste of time committing resources to external consultants only. The major investment should be inside the company. This means the company has to know where it is going and how each department fits into the picture.

The approach which many companies use is departmental purpose analysis (DPA) (see chapter 13) which focuses the attention of departmental and functional heads on specific objectives. This planning exercise can be an important prerequisite to roll-out of the training programme.

Training should address changing attitudes

To reap the full benefit from the experience, trainers should spend some time talking about attitudes and change. There is little point giving out a great deal of interesting and highly entertaining information if you want people to concentrate on 'doing' rather than 'knowing' things. Trainers often have a conflict of interest between using training material with which they are fully conversant and that with which they are not — but which meets the real needs of the company.

If in doubt, ask a trainer for specific objectives which will be achieved at the end of the session! What will people be able to do? What can they define? What methodologies will they use for solving problems? What are the likely outcomes? Where will the major problems arise? What action will they take to promote TQM over the next 3 months?

Establishing rapport: interested people listen and act

Establishing rapport is never easy, particularly with a new audience, but the rift between the trainer and trainee can be considerably reduced if material is strongly participative in nature.

However, formal inputs tend to be the order of the day. 'Mass baptism' can take place in large halls. Information is projected one way with little opportunity for meaningful discussion. In some cases, participative material can be discouraged — with the phrase, "They are committed, they will fly with it. Just tell them."

Material which is presented in a lecture type environment, which does not require feedback or questioning from the audience, will achieve little except for those who make detailed notes or who have a long attention span.

Recognising that the average span of attention is not long — perhaps 10 to 20 minutes — suggests that the medium whereby we instil the message has to be changed frequently, to take account of those who have 'fallen off' the learning curve. Lecturing for hours on end will not create a great deal of learning. Although we all learn and absorb knowledge and information at different speeds, we can maximise learning by changing, fairly frequently, our means of delivery.

Although this is not a book on 'learning' it is useful to know that most of us retain information in our short-term rather than our long-term memory. Bearing this in mind, it is not surprising that we have a great deal of difficulty in recalling information we have absorbed some time ago.

We can all look back at examinations we have taken years ago and remember the cramming techniques we may have used. We may have managed to remember sufficient to get through the paper but, come a week after the exam, I doubt if many of us could have recalled 2–3% of what we could the previous week.

We know that simply exposing people to information is not learning — recall is low because we tend to take information into our short-term memory. If this information is not continually analysed, questioned and assessed in the immediate future, then we lose it for ever. It is never transferred to the long-term memory.

Failing to consolidate information effectively destroys it, so it is hardly surprising that a week or so after attending a course, we have little recall of the events which have taken place. Does this have any direct relevance to training for TQM? Of course it does. A solitary training event, poorly designed and delivered, will have minimal effect. The effect can even be negative, confirming the worst fears and prejudices of those present.

Even the best trainer, the most interesting material and riveting case studies will fail if the event has not been planned properly and there is no follow-up or encouragement from line management.

Learning techniques

Techniques which have been developed by Tony Buzan and others have helped many to assemble information and retain in the long-term memory.

We must give serious consideration to the training issue and not take trainers at face value. We need to be critical of our performance. We are willing to put our most important and precious resource, our people, in the training arena and sometimes, only sometimes, fail to maximise the experience — either because of failure to plan or insufficient enthusiasm to make things happen quickly.

Is it asking too much to put that extra 20% of effort into planning and preparation to make the experience the best it can be? Perhaps if we reverse the question. How can we expect those attending training workshops to put into practice those things we value as important, when we have put little effort into the training experience itself?

Manage the learning environment

It is worth remembering that some psychologists tell us that we forget over 98% of information we take in over the relatively short period of 48 hours. What impact does this information have on training design of TQM workshops?

We need to manage the learning environment. What we should be doing is spending equal time on two key areas:

● Learning how others learn, prior to embarking on developing training materials.
● Ensuring that the design of the learning experience is focused on the 'customer', i.e. the learner.

Maintaining interest

Understanding learning difficulties, addressing obstacles to learners, must be a priority, before absorbing ourselves in the choice of learning materials.

We should address ourselves to maintaining interest, inviting participation and giving concrete and visual illustrations. Tom Peters, guru of quality and customer service, understands this well. His training materials present a picture which is memorable. His enthusiasm and clever choice of anecdotes, examples and quotes reminds us all that the training experience can be considerably enlightened through presentation skills and understanding what turns the audience 'on'. He puts equal emphasis on the content and the process of delivery.

Relying on a package

Training packages are an excellent vehicle for projecting a coherent message. A large number of people can be trained to use the material and it ensures consistency. Regardless of who uses the package roughly the same impression should be projected, but this is not always the case. So many companies are moving away from the packaged ideas on TQM towards a more tailored approach. Packaged approaches provide consistency in message, because the package has worked well in other companies. Beware, however, as there is no guarantee that it will work in every context. Material which goes down well in one environment can be a disaster in others. Using the same material within companies which differ greatly can be 'fatal'.

Another consideration is that using the same package for sales staff, production personnel and R&D departments can have its shortcomings. If the training is designed for a mix of individuals from different functions then the material must be excellent. It has to involve all and relate to all functions present. It is unusual nowadays to segment training to specific functions, but this can be a real danger when companies have several locations separated by many miles. Clearly the more cross-training the better. The quicker the walls between functional specialisms tumble, the sooner internal customer and supplier start working together.

Avoid lowest common denominator

Material which is sufficiently general in nature as to be applicable to all, smacks of the lowest common denominator (LCD) approach which has its drawbacks. Reprinting a quality manual with the exception of a few pages is not the best way of demonstrating that management is serious in its intent on the design of training materials.

It is for this reason that a systematic approach to training can be developed. This approach is not new, but focuses upon five key areas.

This model is a useful tool for helping think through the key issues in training and development.

Training often fails to challenge attitudes

Training has been defined as providing 'the attitudes, skills and knowledge in order to perform and achieve a task'. If this is the case, why do so many training programmes focus entirely upon information and knowledge? Few courses are 'doing' in nature. Even fewer really get to grips with the attitude-changing issue.

Addressing the attitude of trainees and getting them to do things is critical. It is pointless having someone leave a course knowing a great deal but being unaware of how to put it into practice. This opposes all TQM principles.

What we say and do is paramount in making people feel differently about their roles in promoting quality. We need to attack the very fabric of 'resistance' to create a real movement in doing new things — getting rid of the old culture.

The training experience should be focused on changing the feelings of those attending. The role of the trainer is to challenge old views and replace them with new, tangible and concrete behaviours.

We want to send people away from sessions with the hope, enthusiasm and commitment to doing things right — first time.

Line management should reinforce TQM behaviour

Focusing too much on information and quoting facts and figures, to the detriment of action, will never promote change. The right approach is to get people to do things differently in one small area of their work, so they can feed back at some later stage, preferably at a follow-up workshop. This action should be reinforced constantly so that it becomes a way of life. The trainer cannot always be around to reinforce the TQM beliefs, so line management has to take the message and ensure that consistent behaviour is promoted within the workforce.

This is not as easy as it sounds. Often the supervisory grades will not fully understand the changes required to develop a TQ culture. They themselves could be fighting the cultural change, which in turn requires a significant change in their supervisory behaviour. (See chapter on managing change.)

Employees may also doubt that TQM will change the culture of the organisation. Comments reflecting this are common. "We have heard all this before. They said things would change when briefing groups were introduced — what happened? Nothing. They said exactly the same 5 years ago with quality circles. What happened? Nothing! Why should TQM be any different?"

Morale is not improved when supervisory staff fuel the mistrust by stating to shopfloor employees, "Don't concern yourself about TQM — you'll be back fire-fighting tomorrow."

If employees leave a workshop session committed to TQM this is extremely satisfying. However, the degree to which this can be maintained on their return to the shop floor is ultimately determined by the behaviour of those with whom they come into contact most frequently — the supervisors. Get commitment from them, and success will follow.

Success in TQM is related to the requirement to lead, communicate and train in that order.

Cascading TQM down through the structure

TQM slogans, expressed on posters, will never create the necessary changes to promote TQM. What is required is a major change or shift in how people think about what they do. This can only come about through systematic training and reinforcement of behaviour through supervisory and managerial staff.

Some have described this change in thinking as a 'Paradigm Shift' implying that we have to adopt a different way of perceiving and understanding what we do each day.

A classic example of a 'Paradigm Shift' is Copernicus's rejection of the flat earth idea. This revelation forced people to think differently. Many resisted this new knowledge as heresy. This change in perception changed our view of time and space, a viewpoint requiring a re-evaluation of our science, philosophy and theology.

In a similar fashion, TQM changes the way we see things and how we perceive the way organisations should function. The TQM initiative should fundamentally change the way we structure and pursue activities within the organisation. That is why, when designing training and development workshops, we concentrate on changing attitudes.

We have to change attitudes towards flexibility. We want there to be more cross-fertilisation between departments, functions and individuals skills. We need more horizontal management, with managers spending a great deal of their time co-ordinating work — rather than building thicker walls between functions and responsibilities.

We have to reject the belief that there is an acceptable level of non-quality. Zero defects should be our purpose in everything we do.

We have to promote team-work and encourage people to discuss their differences. Conflict is endemic within any organisation. Using conflict to build a positive bridge between units and functions is critical — if we hope to develop the climate of trust reflective of a TQM culture.

We need to change attitudes towards the resolution of conflict. In too many organisations, the purpose behind finding out what is wrong is allocating blame. This has to change to a culture where things are identified as being wrong and, where they are put right straight away.

Avoiding blame can be a lifetime ambition for some people in organisations. Analysis of internal memos generated by some managers suggests that too many are written with the sole purpose of covering their backs. TQM is about improving something every day and this cannot be achieved without taking a few risks. TQM has to challenge the risk-averse culture.

Doing what you value and valuing what you do

What we find difficult to understand is that most people have developed a value system of RFT in their personal lives. We witness it in most daily activities. For instance, we all expect that car drivers will maintain their good driving behaviour and avoid driving on the pavement or knocking people over. Thankfully it is a commonly shared value.

Equally, we expect most people to be disciplined when drinking and driving. Our value system demands it because of the harm and damage which could result from failing to do so.

When visiting the doctor we expect that he or she will be committed to prescribing drugs which will help alleviate the symptoms of illness and help us to recovery. We do not expect to have to check the prescription with a pharmacist. We demand and expect a 100% commitment to quality.

Likewise, when we travel by plane, we expect the pilot to be 100% committed to take off, flying and landing. A commitment to less than 100% will create anxiety or, perhaps, death.

It is clear that we have common expectations which are reflected in social attitudes but often we fail to apply these to work situations.

The training experience must bridge the gulf between social behaviour and values and work behaviour and values. Training which fails to get people to think about their value system, the effect this has on their attitudes, their work behaviour, beliefs and actions, is clearly too wide of the mark that TQM is all about.

TQM workshops and action learning

To overcome many of the criticisms associated with the poor provision of TQM training, a number of steps can be taken. Overall, the training should be relevant and based on the real needs of those attending. The material should be specifically designed for the participants and plenty of attention should be given to the 'medium' or the method of imparting learning. Case studies designed around the problems experienced by the company should form the focus of attention.

One of the single most important factors is the structure behind the training. For instance, in one engineering company there was awareness of the major criticisms of the training input. In particular, there was concern about a number of issues which fell within 2 key areas. First, how much would the participants learn? How much would they take away with them to their work? What would be the key points of the sessions that they would remember? How long would it be before all the information they had picked up in the workshop would be all but a distant memory? The second area was related to relevance and application of principles to the work. 'Words and workshops change nobody' is a phrase which sums up too much training nowadays.

Participants have to be aware that the ideas to which they are being exposed, the concepts they will explore and the structures they will investigate, all have one thing in common — these are the features of TQM which are to be placed and planted within the organisation. It must be emphasised that nothing learned during the workshop will be a waste of time. Everything is geared to application.

In our workshops participants are aware, from reading the objectives right at the beginning of the workshop, that they will be expected to formulate an action plan for change before they leave the session. Even on a 1-day course, lasting 7 hours, there is always a 2-hour period allocated for action planning. Before the session ends, everybody will have spoken and explained precisely what they are going to change when they get back to work.

The action plan is composed of 3 or 4 pages, and typical questions ask participants to identify their key result areas, activities where a great deal of rework takes place and areas where waste is evident. If they have difficulty working through this aspect of the plan they have to identify the 'service' they provide to their internal customers. Requirements are defined in many cases and this is an attempt to bring customers and suppliers much closer together (see Fig. 1 and Fig. 2).

Mary Smith, an accountant, decided that she would work on reducing the amount of rework in administration and processing of expense claims from managers. She defined the problem she experienced as being due to many managers putting in individual claims for lunch and travelling expenses, even though these were incurred in a group and only one receipt was being handed in for processing. This caused considerable rework in tracing back through the claims, often months apart, to extract VAT/sales invoice numbers.

Mary talked to her boss, George, about her action plan. George thought it too big a problem to tackle, so suggested that she contact the Department of Customs and Excise. It must have experienced problems from other companies and, perhaps, had a solution.

While the Customs and Excise officials were on site they helped Mary look through other issues and came across a real anomaly. The company purchased raw material from a sister company in Spain and paid duty on the purchase. The company machined the product and sold it back to Spain — neglecting to claim back the duty. The company had foregone this expense for 15 years — losing £2,500 per month!

In this example, Mary made progress on her original objective but exploring in her area also uncovered other problems which had been disregarded for years.

Fig. 1 Action planning: The ripple effect

Gerry Wilson is a maintenance engineer who was continually harassed and spent most of his time fixing things as they broke down. His company had a clear policy. If it breaks — fix it!

Gerry had had enough of the production manager, who never gave him enough time to do even the barest of preventative maintenance. So, Gerry concentrated on one machine and recorded the true cost of breakdown. On average the machine broke down once every 2 weeks and this was always caused by the same component. This cost the company an incredible £12,000 per year.

Gerry reset the machine to run at its correct speed and production was re-scheduled. Result — the machine has not broken down since then. Gerry is a hero.

The production manager now wants Gerry to look at other machines with the purpose of developing a preventative maintenance programme. It looks like Gerry has changed the culture!

Fig. 2 Action planning: Reversing a philosophy

Those attending are aware that they have to come back for future workshops and their purpose is to work away and report on progress when they return. As the workshops are restricted to 10 people at a time there is a requirement to talk in some depth about possibilities. Action planning must be flexible. Those attending must have the opportunity to talk with their colleagues and their direct superior in order to ensure that their plan is achievable, measurable (otherwise how can progress be assessed?), realistic in the time-frame and compatible with the aims and objectives of the department. Clearly, the action plan must be negotiable, otherwise people may be working counter to each other. The small goals must complement the overall picture and should fit in nicely with the results from the departmental purpose analysis (DPA).

Participants have a commitment to make things happen, as do those who supervise them. You can image the embarrassment for attendees of attending a follow-up session where participants state that they have been too busy or that they have been blocked in their progress by others. One can see instantly where the blockages to TQM are within the structure.

The follow-up sessions should be held between 6–12 weeks after the initial session. As the first session puts TQM in perspective as a strategic imperative, the second series of workshops concentrates wholly on action and the experienced problems with implementation. It is not surprising to find that the focus of this session is on 'managing change'.

Prior to any formal input, it is best to structure feedback of the group on progress. This can take up to 3 or 4 hours, but the focus is on recognition and recounting success. There are many benefits from taking this approach. Overall, the major feature is that people from all aspects of the organisation can assess the progress which is being made in different areas, locations and functions. This feedback is a powerful motivator. It is also found that there is a great deal more recall of what happened in the first session because people have been engaged in putting theory into practice for some time.

Finally, at the end of this session, further emphasis is given to action planning for the final workshop which will take place 6–12 weeks hence. The focus of the last session is problem-solving, especially in groups. Here, participants are given the structures and some techniques for working as members of teams: CATs, QITs or whatever.

What happens next. Well, managers at all levels should now be well acquainted with the process of action planning and there should not be a requirement to formalise sessions in quite the same way. This 'process' should become part of the culture. Managers and staff should meet frequently to discuss action plans for quality improvement. This should become part of the everyday way of doing things.

To aid this process, it may be advisable to formalise the action planning in a twice-yearly appraisal exercise — but great care should be taken here. Organisations may be moving ahead in some areas, but many carry with them some old habits/techniques. One of these may be an appraisal system which was designed for other times. Ensure that the appraisal system really does complement the TQM initiative.

This action-centered learning approach is extremely powerful.

Feedback and cultural change

We are all aware that creating a TQM structure takes time, and the problem here is that results will take some time to show. Tangible feedback has always been a problem when creating real strategic change but this approach helps to focus attention on quality improvements which will have some impact in the short term. It acts as a tool to reinforce the drive for TQ and stimulates enthusiasm. Maintaining enthusiasm is probably the most difficult aspect of

TQM to control when promoting changes orientated towards stimulating long-term cultural change.

Many of the action plans have a ripple effect. People recognise those things between functions and departments which inhibit effectiveness. They also stimulate interest in new areas which are ripe for quality improvement (QI).

This approach to QI also encourages members of departments to work together to solve joint problems. Breaking down functional and departmental barriers is one of the objectives of this approach.

Many of the ideas and action plans achieved can be transferred to other parts of the organisation. For instance, a large company distributing beer and lagers nationwide found that many ideas derived from manufacturing or distribution areas could be used in other locations on other sites. For the recipients, QI was free.

The importance of sharing success should not be minimised in action plans. However, this all comes down to thinking about TQM training using the planning methodology described at the beginning of this book. Looking at training failures helps us examine the action we can take to train people thoroughly and improve performance by leaps and bounds. From the 10% of failure comes 99% of success.

Summary and bullet points

- Learn to value and love training. Training is not a luxury. It is a necessity.
- Training is the most important vehicle in creating cultural change.
- Training should not be the sole responsibility of external trainers — but the real responsibility of the line manager.
- People don't go forward under their own power. They need to be energised by others and be provided with the opportunities to develop.
- You get the people you deserve. If you don't help people go forward and develop — they slip backwards.
- Training is not only about professional and technical issues. Real change takes place when people feel competent to manage the process of getting people to do everything better.
- Don't debate the issue — double, triple or quadruple the size of the training budget. There are fewer known cases of over-training forcing business failure than of under-training.
- Find out what other companies are really doing in your industry. Emulate their best practices. When you have achieved this, move on to emulate the best companies in other industries.
- Only compare your training with the best. It's easy to be the best at training when you compare yourself with failures.
- Recognise that if training is new, then those attending may be anxious. Dispel their fears.

- Ensure that there is no excuse for non-attendance at training courses. Always put prevention before production. Arrange for others to do the work of trainees. If all else fails, do it yourself. Don't penalise people for attending courses by failing to reallocate their work.
- Line managers should play their parts in training. The more they attend training events, the more trust is generated by their staff.
- Design training workshops to change attitudes.
- Remember, people who are interested and involved listen and act.
- Employ everything you can to keep attention during training workshops. Keep the audience motivated and they will learn.
- Don't put too many eggs in one basket. Just because someone has attended a training event, don't expect that you don't have to reinforce behaviour on the job.
- We forget things quickly. Come up with bullet points reflecting TQM. Tell your people about them, communicate and canvas them. Most importantly, live by them.
- Encourage note-taking. Have posters designed with bullet points in mind.
- Understand the learning difficulties of others.
- Design your own programme and ensure it meets your requirements.
- Ensure that line management reinforces the 'beliefs' in day-to-day behaviour.

SECTION 4:
CONTINUOUS IMPROVEMENT

13 READINESS FOR CHANGE

It is critical that an in-depth analysis of the company is pursued prior to the commencement of a TQM drive. Responsibility must be allocated between internal and external agents of change. (The responsibilities of a TQM manager have already been discussed in chapter 7.)

Commitment determines the speed of success

Obviously, every company will want to see results from their TQM initiatives fairly quickly — but they are going to have to be patient. The larger the company, the longer the time-span required for TQM to take hold. However, time is not the most important factor — more important is a willingness to promote cultural change. TQM can be rooted within the culture of smaller companies quite quickly; the dependent variable here is not size but commitment. In a medium-size UK company with 100–200 employees and a turnover of approximately £10–20m, TQM should be well assimilated within 2–3 years. Larger companies will take longer.

Currently, we are working with a financial 'service' company with 800 employees. The chief executive considers that the 'cultural change' programme will take anywhere between 5–7 years to take hold. When he says this he is not relating to the running of training workshops but to the change required in management style. This is not unusual. Ciba Corning has suggested that 7–10 years is the time-scale to consider. British Telecom suggests even longer with estimates of 15–20 years.

Tailored drives

TQM is not a package that can be taken from the 'shelf' of one company and dropped neatly into another with the same impact. A package which is suitable for one organisation might lead to failure for another. TQM cannot be uprooted from one culture and grafted quickly onto another. It must be tailored to fit an organisation's special demands and circumstances. Organisations differ on a number of dimensions. Every company has a special history, culture and management system which make it different from others. These will determine the speed of implementation.

Feasibility studies and planning

Feasibility studies are critical to the effectiveness of TQM. If more time was devoted to planning there would be fewer mistakes compounded. Nobody would genuinely wish to leap, head first, into a TQM drive without a thorough analysis and diagnosis of the special problems which impact upon the organisation. It is desirable at this stage to form a small team of internal practitioners and external TQM consultants. The team should agree parameters for research and design and data collection should be started.

Feasibility studies *v* quality audits

'Selling' the benefits of change to a company is never easy because the people expect quick results. TQM philosophy is not tuned in to the quick fix but the drive can be structured so that there is continuous feedback as milestones are reached and targets are achieved. This means that wanting to change culture is not enough. We need to structure a systematic framework to which we can adhere. This framework should be communicated to all and is generated from the first stage of the drive when we concentrate on feasibility studies.

Some people refer to the feasibility studies as an appraisal of where the company is in terms of quality. Some prefer the audit approach. However, these are vastly different from feasibility studies in nature and scope. Audits are all very well but they smack of checklist management with a focus on the hard Ss, (strategy, structure and systems) to the detriment of staff, skills, style and shared values. In other words, the 'audit' approach has an ideal of what quality should look like within a company. The auditor then assesses the deficiencies of a system. Quality audits usually refer to vendor appraisal, product liability assurance, product certification, process certification, quality system audits and product quality audit, etc., whereas a feasibility study focuses on the 'total organisation and the integration between the parts'.

This approach examines the dynamics of organisational life, concentrating on specific interactions between functions, symptoms of conflict between departments, management style, communication and briefing system and rework in product and service areas, etc.

Purpose of feasibility studies

The output of the feasibility study is an outline of the major problems experienced in TQM terms, the assessment of the predominant management style and its impact upon human resource management, communication and information systems within the company. Within the feasibility study report there is a plan or critical path which provides senior staff with a sequential step-by-step approach to implementing TQM. The senior officers then have a period of 2 weeks to review the plan and consider related issues before they meet to agree action to be taken. The feasibility study then becomes the vehicle for change.

The feasibility study becomes the focus for the second stage of the drive, which is often termed the diagnostic phase. Managers will have had feedback on their operations and have a good idea of rework and waste, etc. Some may have difficulty with the proposals or feel that quality is not their responsibility and reject them. Assuming the facts are accurate, the major problem here is resistance to change. Perhaps the manager cannot or will not perceive the errors passed on from his department or perhaps he does not want to appear to lose control over his function. Whatever the reason, the diagnostic phase is the forum and the opportunity for real debate.

The diagnostic phase

The purpose of this phase is to win commitment to change from all areas. Each manager should agree with the plan or come up with an alternative approach which will convince every other manager present about his commitment to implementing TQM in his discrete work area. If there are dissenters in the management team then this is the time to discuss alternatives or reject TQM as an inappropriate strategy for the company. From this stage on, departmental managers will be held accountable for progress within their own areas. Part of the responsibility will be geared towards promoting COQ measures, communicating the purpose and progress of TQM throughout the company, the pace of TQM and how and when it will filter down through and between departments. These are some of the many aspects of planning for TQM which have to be agreed. We can only assess progress when we have developed a flexible plan to implement TQM.

Departmental purpose analysis

During the diagnostic phase, the formation of 'Departmental' or 'Function' groups is organised throughout the company to appraise the purpose of individual departmental objectives. These are then assessed in terms of how they best fit with the objectives and purposes of other departments. This is basically an approach to examining the efficacy of internal customer/supplier relationships with a focus on clarifying requirements.

IBM has termed this 'approach' departmental purpose analysis (DPA). It should be driven from within a function to assess the services which are provided to the internal customers. The purpose behind DPA is that in some organisations the purpose and objectives of departments can become vague and fuzzy.

DPA helps isolate their 'Key Result Areas' and identify where the department can add real value to the work of the overall company. To do this well, internal customers have to be identified, questioned and results assessed to develop a realistic picture of service. It may take some time to develop a suitable DPA but, if all functions are pursuing this with equal commitment, there should be a number of areas identified immediately for the work of CATs.

As the DPA is being completed, managers should be working on COQ measures. This information should come together and give departmental managers a better appreciation of problems which they have to overcome. This exercise, together with briefing sessions, should have gone some way to communicating the message among the workforce. TQM should not be a surprise!

Training workshops

Training workshops should be designed specifically around the needs of employees (see chapter 12) and should be based on sound action learning techniques. Training should be provided for all staff.

Some managers ask whether everybody has to attend sessions. Recently, an accountant with a large company questioned the sense of having 20 girls from the key punch area attend training sessions. He stated, "The job is boring and they only work for the money." His perception of the girls and the contribution they could make was patronising and inaccurate. The girls did have a major role to play in helping identify COQ measures. They regularly came across a large number of inaccuracies in their work and were a rich source of information. We were surprised to find that the manager had such a negative attitude about his staff. Changing this attitude would help to release the potential of his people and liberate them from the roles he had assigned them as thoughtless automatons.

All service employees should attend workshops of the same duration. A one- or two-hour session will barely cover the basics. It is strongly suggested that all training activities are measured in trainee days, rather than trainee hours! This training initiative is probably the most important that anyone could attend, because it is geared towards harnessing the potential of the people and driving them all in one direction.

During training, emphasis should be on customer-supplier relationships within the company. Everyone should develop a personal action plan for implementing quality within his or her immediate area of work.

All managers and supervisors should attend their workshops but limit themselves to attending sessions for their staffs. The presence of managers at workshops for others helps to reinforce the belief that the management group is committed to TQM. At recent workshops held with the market leaders in brewing in the UK we had a senior director to open every workshop for all levels within the organisation. Other members of the senior management group turned up at lunch and talked honestly with participants about changes in organisational culture. The managing board within a leading finance company pursued the same strategy to equal effect. This version of 'managing by wandering about' (MBWA) is critical if TQM is to be taken seriously.

Participants will have questions which only senior officers can address. Their attendance gives credibility to the message.

Why train service and shop floor people differently?

It is also critical that shop floor employees have similar training to service staff but there is a danger that some managers feel that production people should have more training than their clerical counterparts. This is founded on the belief that all errors originate in 'manufacturing'. This attitude must be changed. If this was the case it would reinforce the old stereotype that shop floor workers create all the problems.

Composition of workshop groups

Composition of workshop groups is also critical. We have found that the best results come from a genuine mix of all functions. Although this can create headaches in administration when working on many sites, it is the right thing to do. It is probably the first time that many people from different functions will meet. It gives them an opportunity to work together on exercises and case material and discuss the problems they have on a day-to-day basis. The effect of talking openly breaks down some of the negative stereotypes which have existed in some companies. Through one workshop, 2 people, who had been working for the company for 7 and 5 years respectively, met for the first time although they were on a shared site — and they were married 6 months later! TQM brings people together in many ways!

There are always instances where people have worked in one location for a long period of time and have little idea of what other people do. It is hard to believe that people who have worked for a company for in excess of 15 years still do not know others on a 250-person site. However, this happens and it says much about management commitment to communication, joint problem-solving and running the company.

Meeting for the first time in fifteen years

At the end of one session the production people present agreed to arrange a plant tour for the accountants and purchasing people. Some of these had been with the company in excess of 15 years, worked 20 yards away from the manufacturing plant, but had little understanding of what happened there! This is not an unusual occurrence — we have worked in breweries, insurance companies, chemical plants and so forth, where there had been little attempt to intermingle, interact and generally get to know other people.

There usually seemed to be a strict demarcation line structured on functional and geographical terms. Some of the clerical and supervisory staff had, in some cases, little apparent loyalty to the company. They could have been working anywhere — as a DP operator, systems analyst, secretary or typist on an occupational level and as a company employee second.

It is quite an interesting experience to ask some of the administrative people what the company produces or in which market it operates, etc. Many have a very poor idea of the range of the company's operations. We cannot blame the employee for this and we know that it has not been a deliberate policy of senior staff, but it is the outcome of failing to communicate and involve others. In too many companies this is the norm!

Implementation

Words and workshops can influence behaviour in the short term but their impact on individual performance is dependent upon the memory of the trainee and the pressure in the company to put the ideas into effect. For TQM to really work it is necessary for companies to set up structures to put the principles into practice. Passion has its place in any change but systems and structures are also required to demonstrate a framework for making things happen.

Quality improvement teams

It is necessary from the design phase to form a senior management quality improvement team. Some companies abbreviate this to QIT or quality improvement team. This is the group of senior people which meets frequently to discuss progress. These people oversee and take necessary actions to promote TQM. If the company has an internal consultant or TQM manager facilitating the TQM initiative he will report directly to this group.

There are problems with titles of such groups. Some companies create 'Quality Improvement Teams' to solve problems but often they do not have the executive authority as the group referred to above. There can be problems with terminology and it really isn't important if we call different groups different things, as long as we concentrate on roles, responsibilities and actions more than titles. This must be communicated to all.

Internal and external change agents

The quality improvement team co-ordinates events. The TQM manager is the catalyst who will probably work with an external consultant. We should be aiming to use a person with both levels of expertise, but often these people are in short supply. First, you need someone who is well acquainted with TQM practice and who understands the process of managing organisational and cultural change. It is a distinct advantage if this person has a 'behavioural' background. The whole concept is based on changing peoples attitudes — it is unlikely that a systems person will have the same degree of understanding and, more important, empathy with the difficulties of managing change. The external consultant need not be a TQM expert but, obviously, it is desirable. Whatever the characteristics of the external resource, he or she must have good grounding in organisational development and understand or have worked with companies managing change. It is far better working with a person who understands the dynamics of change and has little understanding of quality systems than working with people who have used TQM packages — but have a poor grounding in managing organisational transitions. The ideal is a marriage in both areas.

It is obvious that there should be a high level of integration between the QIT and the internal and external consultants. Meetings should be held frequently, should not be too lengthy and should be designed around sharing information about COQ measurements and supervisory training, etc.

Maintaining enthusiasm and morale

Enthusiasm is something which increases and decreases during a TQM drive. The role of the management team is to ensure that people are constantly given feedback on performance. Understanding that positive rather than negative reinforcement is more powerful in motivating people is obvious. Keeping enthusiasm for TQM high is quite easy, but there is a danger that the QIT might think that sufficient messages and examples have been set by it and it then backs away gently from its responsibilities. This is just the sort of action to kill a TQM drive.

When TQM first arrives on the scene the management team may be 'turned on' by the whole approach. Although there will be sceptics at first, generally TQM sounds like a good idea. Enthusiasm increases and, with it, the perception that things will change for the better! They will change but not overnight. The dawning reality that change will take time and that it can be painful can reduce enthusiasm. Sooner or later, management makes the change and starts moving along the 'Transition Curve' (see chapter 5). Meanwhile, middle managers may have been kept in the dark and are wary of the concept. Attending training workshops may encourage them. They can witness the success of others and start to create change. Their enthusiasm for TQM rises until something gets in the way — such as senior management standing in the way of change.

Middle managers may come up with brilliant ideas for preventing problems arising but resources may not be available or action not quick enough. Whatever happens, it has an effect on enthusiasm and morale. We don't have to go through all the scenarios to paint an accurate picture of what happens to man motivation.

In the real world all sorts of different personalities run large and small organisations. Rationality does not always guide behaviour and there are times when managers pursue interests other than those of the company. The problems to which we have referred do happen. Knowing that they might and the impact they can have on others should be sufficient to want to do something about them.

Plans should be made to inject enthusiasm into the drive every 6 weeks. Many people balk at this being too frequent, but if you aim for every 6 weeks there is a chance that you might get round to doing something within every 3 months!

Quality improvement process and publishing results

Running workshops and setting up action plans (see chapter 12) are only the start of the drive. Putting the philosophy into practice takes some effort. Depending upon the size of the company it is desirable to start the implementation phase after everybody has been through the training process. Implementation can take a number of routes but it is advisable to stick to a form ula that seems to work quite well.

Bearing in mind that all functions are generating information on progress through COQ measures, it is reasonable to assume that some of the major problems which a company faces will have surfaced. Work can begin straight away to resolve these problems.

Consider the example used previously — a manufacturing company producing hi-tech products. There are problems between the sales, research & development, production and purchasing departments. Salesmen can sell all they can, pleasing the customer by adapting to his specific requirements. (There is nothing wrong with this approach.) More companies could recognise that they have to be customer rather than product led. However, the specifications from the customer are not fed back to materials management R&D or production. The sales team promises delivery dates which are incongruent with the lead time for production, reinforcing the viewpoint that service people create the majority of quality problems within companies. The scenario is obvious. Similar problems are experienced by many within manufacturing. What is required is a bringing together of those who are sympathetic to a TQM solution, to work towards resolution.

Failure: Problems which are too big are tackled first!

Solutions would have impact upon everyone, so everybody needs to change. The interesting point about this example is that the 'problem' probably has not just arisen, but has been with the company for many years. Bringing representatives together from different functions may help to solve the problem but there should be desirable conditions created for genuine solution. One mistake which is made frequently is the assumption that the organisational culture has changed! It may not. Those solving problems should try to win small successes — not go for the biggest problem which creates the most hassle, conflict and rework for the company. Trying to change these things takes time.

The conditions for effective solution of problems are probably not in tune with the present culture. The preconditions for success follow. Everybody working on the problem should leave his role, status and position outside the problem-solving forum. Each participant must be committed to coming up with a workable and realistic solution. The politics, which kills companies and destroys the morale of too many company people, should be left outside the session. Senior officers within companies should recognise that 'solutions' will only develop from an atmosphere of trust. Working under political constraints will produce a win-lose solution, where someone gains at the expense of others. Those attending problem-solving sessions need to be 'self critical' about their performances and that of their sections or functions. Failing to meet these conditions is enough to send too many companies on to a 'quick fix'.

Already, the conditions set for effective problem-solving appear to be in excess of what happens in the real world. What is important is that at least this approach should be given a try, or the initiative may fail. It may fail because the assumptions which are made about the styles and attitudes which people bring to the problem-solving session are far from realistic. People really do attend sessions to protect the interests of their departments, they do say things they do not mean and they do not live up to promises, etc. This pessimistic belief is founded upon experience. Doubtless there will be critics who suggest this viewpoint is negative — but at least it is realistic.

Experience and comments in this book which reflect the pessimistic view do not arise from the experience of TQM within a small number of companies. They come from a viewpoint shared with many people who have had difficulty implementing change. Can anybody prove that this perspective is distorted? An attitude survey conducted in any company after the introduction of TQM usually highlights major factors, such as those outlined above, which should be addressed straight away. (This is examined in chapter 14.) Nevertheless, let us look at a way out of this problem. The first major issue is that people are tackling the biggest problem the company faces. This is wrong.

Pick the little issues first

The first major objective of using problem-solving and corrective action teams (CATs) is not the solution of long-term problems but rather to prove that problem solving works. It is also a test of management commitment to implementing the solution. It is to prove that people live up to their promises and that the expectations of all company people, regarding the implementation of TQM, are met. The alternative is to jump at the first problem and hastily develop a solution which is poorly implemented. Plan some wins. Ensure that the small successes are implemented. This reinforces the belief among employees that TQM is here to stay.

We should pick upon small problems, bring small groups of committed people together to work through the solutions and implement them quickly. We should initially spend 80% of our time implementing changes which have 20% impact on the bottom line. This may appear to go against all the teaching of the 'quality gurus' but, in fact, it does not. They talk of dealing with the vital few, rather than the trivial many — but only when the programme is in full swing.

To starting off dealing with the minor problems and putting things right has a profound effect on the organisation. For a start, people see things happening. Solutions to small problems might not create such significant savings in money but they do at least reinforce the idea that change is taking place. If implementation of solutions is speedy, and it must be so, people start believing that TQM is having some impact. If this is reinforced by senior officers proclaiming that overnight success is improbable while working on solvable problems, at first the morale of the workforce could go through the roof.

For instance, dealing with a niggling paperwork problem or sorting out business expenses claims and increasing the speed of payment will have most impact on those most affected. This gives people confidence and belief in TQM. Working initially on those problems which are small in nature is incredibly important. Management should capitalise on solutions and publicise their success. If managers fail to do so then they might as well forget all the effort they have expended. Newsletters should be written and published at regular intervals. After working on smaller problems, those in the company committed to TQM have concrete examples of changes which have taken place. This creates the momentum to continue the drive. Generating enthusiasm and momentum is critical for success at the beginning of any TQM drive.

Starting off the quality improvement process

Very few companies will have the need to 'generate' problems to solve but, for some strange reason, they find it difficult to get started. The problems that any company faces must be identified, not by the managers but by the people who do the work. This is important because, if TQM has been developed to solve the problems of a small number of people at the top, there may be little support for TQM from the bottom. People below the managerial grades must feel that the company is dealing with their problems. If you can make life easier for an hourly-paid employee or for a clerk working in purchasing or acccounts, the word will soon spread. Working on operational problems is where companies should start. Strategic issues should wait.

Japanese companies have maintained their successes through implementing the ideas which come from the shop floor. They seek continuous innovation and work on the mass principle. The more ideas accepted and implemented, the easier the job gets. Work becomes safer, more interesting and less routine. People feel that they can actually influence events. Job satisfaction increases and people take more interest in the drive. It is a fairly simple motivational formula. Ask someone to take the hassle, rework or problems out of their job and they participate. The suggestions which are forthcoming probably have an impact on the 'bottom line'. People who feel that their managers listen to them are going to be more interested and contribute more to their work. Having suggestions made and implemented is tantamount to telling the guy with the suggestion that his idea was valid — so much so, that the management team took note and fixed things. This is not the usual practice of European companies.

Toyota implements 5,000 ideas per day. These ideas come from the 68,000 employees. Each day they become better at everything they do. Can we say that about our companies? It does not need to be said that people are the most important resource which is available to every company. This is often stated in company reports but the real truth is that we don't really value our people. We tend to hire them from the neck down! Listening to people, implementing their ideas and structuring things for them makes the job efficient and enjoyable.

One approach, which is used to start off the scheme on promoting company-wide improvement works incredibly well. Let us call it the company wide improvement process. In some ways it is similar to a suggestion scheme so it cannot run counter to one that is already in existence. It can, however, be integrated with it over time.

Suggestion schemes can run counter to quality improvement

Suggestion schemes rely on people generating ideas to improve the ways they do things. The criteria for suggestions are quite general. Often schemes are not well received and there is an understanding that employees will receive a reward for coming up with ideas which save the company money. In the UK, the Industrial Society has publicised the use of suggestion schemes to great effect and with success. However, the problem with such schemes is that they create a psychological bargaining situation, implying that if ideas do, for instance, reduce costs, then the employee will share in the saving. This is all very well but it has been witnessed that an employee kept an idea to himself until he was guaranteed a substantial figure in remuneration. There is nothing against sharing the gains but the idea of individual competition is against all ideas on TQM. We are pitting the wits of each employee against another rather than generating a 'collective' responsibility. Consider when employees draw the line between ideas for continuous improvement and those from which they can gain financially. This may reinforce individual competition and kills team spirit, unless the scheme is based on group sharing.

Paying employees twice!

Employees are paid not just to do a job but to think of better ways of doing it. Unfortunately, human resource practice in too many companies treats people as no more than a necessary evil — a resource which has to be paid for in order to achieve results. On the other hand, many managers and supervisors believe that, when they come up with improvements, these are incorporated in what they receive in their pay packets. We tend to treat employees differently. We can pay them twice! First we pay them to a job, then we pay them an additional amount for improving that job!

Corrective action teams

CATs are groups of committed individuals who are keen to improve quality. Members are selected from different functions and departments to work together. CATs differ quite markedly from QCs.

Circles are formed from a natural work unit and usually work through a facilitator who may also be the direct supervisor. The facilitator will have been trained in problem-solving techniques and, in the more enlightened companies, this will include advanced statistical techniques, such as SPC as well as fishbone diagrams. QCs are composed of committed volunteers who meet either in their own time or the time of the company. It is common to pay for attendance of QC members if they meet outside work.

CAT members are selected from a number of departments to solve a common problem. The selection of CAT members is determined by the nature of the problem. Enthusiastic volunteers are encouraged but selectivity has to come into play. There is a requirement to choose from the group available and an important criterion is 'knowledge' of the problem under scrutiny. CAT members can work in different ways but the orthodox method is to explain the nature of the problem with a facilitator available. He ensures that the group has rejected all departmental and personal preferences and predjudices prior to commencing the problem-solving.

CAT members are encouraged to adopt the logical approach to problem-solution, spending sufficient time defining the problem and deciding on methods of data collection. This approach guards against jumping to a preferred solution. The group may then allocate responsibilities to individuals and agree to collect relevant information which may help the group seek a solution. It then decides to meet again within a fairly short period of time to discuss the data collected.

At the second meeting the group may get involved in the 'creative' aspects of problem-solving and look for alternative ways of coming to a solution. In a fairly short period of time the group should be able to come up with a list of probable options. It will need supervision and the help of a facilitator. It should not, at first, be left to its own devices. The solutions should be tested for practicality, addressing the questions about technical feasibility, administrative convenience and political acceptability, and financial viability of the conclusions must be discussed. If the group's work is at the beginning of a TQM drive it should be set problems which have a solution. Scoring successes early on is important. The more difficult problems can wait until later.

One major flaw in the use of CATs is the setting of too difficult a problem for solution. If problems have plagued the company for some time they should not be considered for work by CAT members. When the CAT has developed a workable solution this should be condensed into a simple report, of no more than 2 or 3 pages, with a presentation arranged for senior management. For those who have never given a presentation before it is important that the facilitator gives guidance. The success of recommendations will be determined by the manner in which the report is delivered and its reception by the senior group (usually a QIT).

It cannot be over-emphasised that the QIT should look favourably upon the recommendations rewarding effort by implementing ideas quickly. Failure to take note, recognise a contribution and act immediately lead to failure!

News travels fast

News travels fast. If a CAT recommendation is taken in the spirit in which it has been given and implemented quickly, instant reinforcement to the rest of the company is acknowledged. A failure to implement ideas and workable solutions will justify the scepticism felt by some employees. This reinforces the belief that problems chosen for solutions should be carefully vetted. When starting the process of problem-solving, the initial problems should be chosen carefully before work begins. Successful implementation and the progress of CATs is determined by the management, which should be patient and not expect instant results to the major problems creating rework for others.

CATs should be carefully managed. The enthusiasm of QIT and CAT members can set an unbearable demand and pressure for results. Senior officers should be careful to manage the progress of no more than 2 or 3 CAT groups at first. A company pursuing solutions to problems with CATs choosing too many problems to be solved all at once will create an unrealistic demand on resources. The 'quick fix' should be rejected and careful, patient progress should be monitored. It is better to win 100% success early on by working with 2 small groups, than to fail with 6 or 7 groups because of lack of resources.

Quality and improvement proposal process

The generation of ideas for solution by CATs should not be too difficult but, bearing in mind that TQM is based on employee involvement, it is wise to get the workforce to generate the problems for solution. Encouraging the workforce to participate in a short programme of identifying 'Improvement

Proposals' is important and forms can be designed to facilitate the process. This process, although resembling suggestion schemes, should be quite different.

The suggestion scheme approach relies upon setting up a separate structure for improvement. This implies that suggestions can be submitted without consultation with others, especially line managers. Some justification for this may exist in companies where employees feel the solutions to problems may be blocked by their direct supervisors, but rejecting this practice is the price paid for genuine company-wide improvement.

Improvement proposals should use the existing structure. It is an admission of defeat to develop a new communication network especially designed for creating quality improvement. Employees who come up with proposals should first talk with their direct supervisors to discuss the feasibility of their ideas. Supervisors will have attended courses promoting quality improvement prior to the commencement of this process —so there should be some level of mutual understanding. The supervisors should take 'ownership' of the problem and take what action he or she can. This process is equally applicable in service and manufacturing environments. If the supervisor can solve the problem he should inform the QIT or TQ manager of the progress made. If he cannot find a solution he should refer the problem to the TQM manager or the QIT.

These processes are easily maintained through a procedure which is quick and responsive. The individual receiving the problems can categorise them and refer them to the senior management team (or QIT) and seek its commitment to the solutions of problems. Once this is given, CATs can be formed to start work. The QIT members must give whole-hearted support to any initiative, otherwise it is pointless in giving their approvals to problem solutions.

This process works remarkably well. It is unlikely that there will be a 'block' to implementation if QIT members have given their approval. Any resistance to analysis and implementation will demonstrate a failure to commit on the part of individual QIT members.

This process should be fairly easy to administer but caution should be exercised when the number of proposals exceeds the capacity of organisational members to seek and implement solutions. When the limit is reached everyone should be informed that CATs have sufficient to tackle. For instance, if 550 ideas for improvement are received, the TQM manager can use these valuable data to develop a Pareto Chart identifying the 20% of problem areas which create the 80% of rework problems for solution in the long term. After the success and implementation of CATs' work on 2 or 3 projects, then the larger projects can be tackled. It is imperative that managers manage the process.

Calling a time for a natural break in 'improvements' is important because too many problems identified can create major problems for the TQM drive. We should not take too much on at once. Each of the problems identified should be discussed and assessed. Progress should be immediately fed back to employees. If an employee gives ideas for improvement and has no response it confirms his major concerns on the credibility of such a drive. However, if an employee receives feedback, even negative, on the infeasibility of the project he will at least have been informed. Failure to communicate success or otherwise can be a major stumbling block to company-wide initiatives.

TQM newsletters

The TQM newsletter should address these points but is no substitute for 'personal feedback'. Personal feedback should be formal, not a comment voiced in passing. Newsletters succeed or fail by the commitment mirrored in the leading articles of the newsletter. If the same person writes articles every week, employees are soon aware that the TQM drive is only taken seriously by enthusiasts. Newsletters should reflect progress and praise the work of employees in any roles they have taken.

TQM integrated into every process

Starting a TQM initiative through quality or improvement proposals is good in the short run but what about progress in the long term? Although the process explained should become part of organisational life there must be a major attempt to inculcate TQM into the fabric and culture of the organisation. Action planning (chapter 12) and the improvement proposal process are two ways but they are insufficient to carry the drive through forever.

Attempts should be made to integrate these processes into the appriasal, recruitment and training policies. This is not a difficult task and will ensure that people perceive TQM in general organisational terms. It will be necessary to develop an induction package for new recruits and ensure that succession plans are based upon the principles of TQM. This task should only be encouraged after success in the previously mentioned processes.

Every meeting, whether it is departmental or project planning, in progress should have an item on the agenda entitled 'Quality Improvement'. There should not be anywhere for people to escape from the commitment to improve everything which is done. Requests for capital investment should be based on TQM initiatives. Resources allocated on this premise will do more for TQM than will hundreds of posters and newsletters exhorting TQ.

Partnerships

This should extend beyond the company including suppliers and customers. Adversorial relationships should be turned into partnerships. In other words companies, even in the same industry, should work together to improve industry standards and protect their joint market from external predators.

There is no reason why relationships cannot be developed with competitors to discuss mutual interests, except when this is morally or legally inappropriate. Companies can set up supplier Ddvelopment programmes and work with preferred suppliers trying to develop JIT relationships. Companies should encourage involvement in new product development where the input of suppliers can be valued and profitable. The limitations are only created by tunnel vision. Working together, creating win-win relationships, has pay-offs for all and further promotes the vision of TQM as the binding philosophy which enhances the competitive edge of all.

Summary and bullet points

- Success in TQM is not determined by the size of the enterprise but by the level of commitment demonstrated by the quality improvement team (QIT).
- TQM has to be tailored to the special needs of the company. It cannot be taken from one company and dropped neatly into another.
- The feasibility study should concentrate on company-wide improvement and examine management style, communication and the resolution of conflict.
- Quality audits differ from feasibility studies quite markedly. Audits tend to be organised around a checklist of what 'should be' and tend to relate to quality systems rather than the management of company-wide quality improvement.
- The diagnostic phase should be jointly owned by the QIT and the external consultant. At this stage it is important that all agree to an action plan which is realistic and achievable. It must be company-wide.
- DPA is a natural outcome of the diagnostic phase. Departments should question their objectives and assess the services they provide to others — their internal customers — and the services they receive from others — their internal suppliers.
- Managers should seek to attend as many training workshops as possible to reflect commitment to those attending.
- Devotion should be equally spread in the training of service and manufacturing personnel.
- Training workshops may be the first time that some people have met. This should be capitalised upon by structuring sessions so people can learn not just from the training material but through developing relationships with others from different units.
- A TQM manager should have a good understanding of people. It is desirable that he or she does understand how people work in organisations. He should also have a good knowledge of organisational dynamics and the management of change.
- When starting problem-solving with CAT members ensure that they work on establishing small wins. Do not pick the biggest problem you have encountered.
- Success by CAT members should be speedily communicated to all, otherwise the effort may have been in vain.
- The major characteristic of a CAT member should be that of being 'self

critical'. Politics and other negative pastimes should be left outside the problem-solving forum.

- Suggestion schemes rely on setting up a separate structure for improvement. Quality improvement should not reject the formal structure but should reinforce it.
- Newsletters should have a large number of contributors. Readers soon pick up the 'hidden message' when some functions fail to feature in the improvement process.
- TQM cannot exist solely through the improvement process and the work of CAT members. Real success comes from integrating TQM into selection, recruitment, training, manpower planning, capital investment proposals and appraisals, etc.

14 IMPLEMENTATION CHANGE AND REVIEW

Monitoring progress

Implementation of TQM takes time and requires managers to monitor progress. Undoubtedly a manager internal to the company will have responsibility and this will be shared, at least in the short-term, with external advisers. However, there comes a time when progress has to be reported. It can be quite a simple affair relating back to the action plan or critical path developed in the feasibility stage. For instance, the criteria used for assessing progress could be quite simple and focus on COQ measures, quality improvement, quality structures and the supporting infrastructure of communication and leadership by the QIT.

Periodically the internal TQM manager should review action on COQ measures. In many cases these may appear to be going well in production areas but there will probably be problems in the service areas. Knowing the likely blockages in advance, the TQM manager should have spent sufficient preventative time with purchasing, R&D, data processing, sales and other functions to ensure that measures are in place. Information should have been collected and displayed openly and be available to all people passing through the work area. For instance, some companies encourage all employees to develop their own

COQ measure/s which relate to their personal performances. This may be as simple as looking at the number of times late for meetings over a period of a month, creating unnecessary rework for others, or monitoring occasions when instructions to employees have had to be given more than once, etc. Although these measures may be difficult to quantify and relate to a financial COQ measure they are a reflection of a desire to improve personal performance. This commitment should be encouraged.

COQ measures displayed

The TQM manager may wish to visit known locations of COQ measures and check for fairly simple clues. Are the measures visible? Are they accurate and up to date? Do they have meaning to the people who work on them and work in the immediate area? Is the area where they are located clean and tidy? If not, this may show a lack of concern and commitment to the overall goals of TQM. Are COQ measures displayed in corridors or in service areas or are they hidden behind filing cabinets? Monitoring COQ measures does not finish here but there should be sufficient visible information to indicate whether these are being taken seriously.

Moving from the physical location of COQ measures to understanding and meaning — how did the measures arise? Were they selected exclusively by the manager concerned without reference to the work group, or did the group have a part to play in generating measures?

Attitudes and costs of quality

Stopping people at random and asking them the following questions may be helpful:

- Do you know what COQ measures there are in your location?
- Can you tell me why we are using COQ measures?
- What do the measures mean to you?
- Do you know where the measures are located?
- How often are they updated?

This is all useful data and, if used diplomatically, can bring a department, which may have slipped backwards because of other work pressures perhaps, back on-stream.

TQM should become a common language

On a day-to-day basis it is important to introduce TQM into the business and for TQM to become the common language. If the only time that TQM is discussed by supervisors and employees is when they are trying to arrange attendance for future TQM training programmes it is clear that TQM will not have too much credibility. TQM must become the common language of the business. Supervisors and managers should attempt to talk TQM as often as possible.

If we cannot communicate, forget TQM

Nobody should miss an opportunity to discuss progress on TQ. Developing a common language, reflected in the culture, takes time and is the responsibility of all managers. Readers may recall the example given earlier, in chapter 5, when a management team agreed to meet with its supervisors and charge-hands individually. The task was to speak with any 2 supervisors each day and note comments in a diary. The focus of the 10-minute conversations was to be non-operational issues, in other words issues related to the future growth of the company. Only a small percentage of the team members managed to complete the task in the allotted time. It is disturbing and of real concern that people find it so difficult to 'talk' with each other for no more than 20 minutes per day and report back. Even the embarrassment of having little to say in front of their peers was not sufficient to generate a half dishonest answer from the members. They said they did not have enough time!

The management team had agreed that these actions were necessary and would be of value. However, despite their best intentions, less than half of the members achieved their objectives. There is a genuine worry about the ability of companies in Europe to grasp the ideas of TQM and to catch up with the Japanese, when we have intentions which evaporate as soon as they leave a room. If we cannot perform a simple task, structure a talk with our people and feed back, what chance is there that real cultural change can be managed through communication?

Communication is simple — Taguchi methodology, JIT and SPC really do require commitment in actions to make them work

There has to be a genuine drive to communicate, communicate, communicate. If we fail in the simple things how can we hope to succeed with TQM related initiatives like JIT, Taguchi methodology and SPC, etc., which require more thoroughness and supervision to be managed successfully?

Directing questions to operators, clerical staff, supervisors and managers gives a good indication of how well the TQM drive is going. The responses give scope for remedial action to be taken. There may be a further requirement than asking people about the 'frequency' of communication when we focus on 'specifics' which have been relayed. For instance, it is hoped that the managerial and supervisory group members will have given a great deal of thought to the roles that their people can play in TQM. If they have not done so, how can they measure progress?

Knowing what to do

It is essential that everybody knows what is expected of them, even if it is recording data and progressing this on a chart. People can only achieve results when they have performance measures outlined and agreed with their direct managers. There is a danger that people develop unrealistic expectations of others. The disparity between expectations of managers and managed can soon erupt when a review is in progress. Conflict can arise and statements such as the following can occur:

Manager:

"You know I expected you to develop COQ measures and meet regularly with your work team to assess progress."

Member of staff:

"You never told me that. You said we should think of what we could do. You did not specify any actions."

Manager:

"Do I have to tell you everything? Don't you have any initiative?"

Member of staff:

"This is just as we thought. It is another opportunity to devolve responsibility. This is abdication. We do not know what you expect."

We can see that this discussion is changing quickly into an argument. If we are not careful these individuals will develop their old negative stereotypes of each other and take two steps backwards.

This process must be managed. A tremendous responsibility is on the manager to manage the process of TQM with his or her people. This means he has to think of his people as his 'internal customers'. In order for his people to meet his expectations he will have to develop 'requirements' which are communicated to them and tested so that they fully understand. In other words, his people have to be involved in the TQM process. They have to be able to contribute and at the same time be guided by their manager. Decisions have to be made, targets set and milestones agreed. Some clear responsibilities and actions must be negotiated. At this stage it is important that these 'requirements' should not be too grand.

Setting achievable requirements

It is easy for everybody to get too enthusiastic about TQM and set unrealistic goals for themselves and their departments. If this happens, and targets are not reached, morale falls and belief in TQM can decline. Change takes a tumble.

Always set realistic goals and objectives at the implementation stage because most people see that they have two lines of responsibility — one is the work for which they are employed and paid while the other is TQM.

Choice: Do I perform my work or promote TQM?

At first there can be a conflict when people have to make decisions about what they get involved in. There is tremendous pressure to do those things for which they are paid. The day-to-day work culture might be orientated towards 'fire-fighting' whereas TQM is preventative. So which work is completed? Where is the majority of time allocated? In reality people do those things and tasks for which they are employed and get involved in TQM action plans at some other time. At first in a TQM drive people see 'work and TQM' as two separate entities. This creates an internal conflict when they have to decide when do they pursue TQM activities in a fire-fighting work culture.

The change from one culture fire-fighting to another is not easy and takes time but gradually TQM and 'the work for which people are paid' become the same thing. There will be many conflicts along the way, when operators and staff at all levels talk to immediate supervisors, often saying, "There seems to be a conflict here. I have to ship the product to the customer but we think there could be a problem with it. If we fail to ship we could lose future business. If we ship and the product fails we could lose any further business. What should I do?"

This is a difficult problem and there is only one solution — that is to be honest. Explaining to a customer, either internal or external to the organisation, the reasons for hold-ups or issues with possibly defective products is the foundation of honesty and trust which is central to TQM. If you lose a sale because of honesty the company still has its integrity and there is always another opportunity with the client. However, if the product is shipped to the customer, inspected at 'Goods Inwards' and rejected, the sale is lost because of poor quality. This is more serious because poor quality has been coupled with deception. The company can never regain its integrity and the word may soon spread to other customers.

Bad news travels fast

If people experience good service, whether on a personal or organisational level, and are delighted with work that has been achieved, research suggests that these 'good feelings' are communicated, on average, to 4 or 5 people. If, however, we experience poor service from our internal and external suppliers, we tend to tell a few more people. Research indicates that on average we tell 24 people of our bad experiences! Bad news travels fast. It isn't long before the stories about others are well and truly passing to everyone and one's reputation is in the balance. This might not appear so serious within the company, but it is. Internal customers might not have a choice still haveing to deal with you, but external customers can choose to vote with their feet.

Informed of progress

Knowing what others have achieved in the drive for TQM is critical. This comes back to communication and the sharing of information. Testing for understanding is one of the most interesting parts of a review of progress. This research activity can help revitalise TQ. The most common method is to specially design a questionnaire to assess progress of TQ. In many cases employees are aware of the progress which has been made within their own areas of work and they may also be aware of the TQM responsibilities which their direct supervisors have undertaken. However, do not assume that this is always the case. It is not. Test for the flow of information by asking simple questions. What do you think your supervisor has done to promote TQM in your immediate work area? You may find that a positive response to the question is low in some work areas and extremely high in others but, by rephrasing the question. What do you think other supervisors, in areas other than your own, have done to promote TQM? The results are interesting.

Quality improvement team

The QIT has the responsibility to implement TQM. It should be composed of most functional heads. As part of the research or progress review, questions about the activities of the QIT can provoke some interesting replies. Pertinent questions include: Are you aware of the current activities of the QIT? What are they? Are you aware of the specific actions taken and commitment given by your representatives on the QIT? If so, what progress has been made? Has a member of the QIT talked with you about TQM and, if so, what did they discuss?

These questions are not designed to catch people out. They are designed to obtain the information which tells us a little about commitment. These questions may not form the 'rigorous' questionnaire for research purposes but the responses to the questions indicate the degree to which TQM is being taken seriously. Responses indicate where an injection of training or enthusiasm is required and can also highlight 'resistance to change'. This is assumed to be negative. Managers and supervisors alike may appear to be resisting change because they have not quite made the transition required (see chapter 5) perhaps due to problems with learning or confidence. Often these fears are groundless but they can be addressed only when information on progress exists.

Information from a stuctured questionnaire administered properly can create the fine tuning to ensure that TQM is taking hold and becoming the dominant culture. Some companies fear that administration of such an instrument would kill morale if the results were widely dispersed. Companies should only fear a fall in morale if they are not committed to take immediate corrective and preventative actions. An attitude of putting right what was wrong is far more constructive than punishing people who did not do as we asked. This 'putting right' orientation is a sure symptom of things changing.

Corrective action teams

If small groups have been set up as part of the implementation phase, such as quality circles or corrective action teams, etc., it is wise to get a feel from the general work of such groups. If the questionnaire and interview techniques are used it can soon be established whether the groups are being taken seriously or not. For instance, if the question, "If you are not already a member of CAT, would you like to become one?" obtains a negative response, then a supplementary question, such as "Why?" will elicit a response which may reflect an attitude. Sometimes people have said, "I was not asked", "They are a waste of time", or "My manager has not encouraged me." Sufficient responses should give an indication of how these groups are viewed.

"Do you believe the progress of CATs has been effective?" with a supplementary question of, "Why not?", if the answer is negative, gives us a feel for the acceptance of CATs, the progress achieved and whether this has been well communicated.

Asking people for specific information is also a key element of review. Too general questions directed to the respondent may give a stereotyped response which is of little value. Specific questions can be more enlightening. "Do you know of someone within your work area who is or has been involved in CATs?" Assessing the progress made and results achieved through supplementary interviewing helps obtain different bearings on the same issue.

Moving away from questioning about quality structures which have been developed, it is then possible to ask in a general capacity about overall involvement. The general response can then be honed down to specifics by a skilled interviewer. "Are you in any capacity involved in promoting TQM?" A supplementary question asks, "What role do you play?" Responses which are general in nature and mean nothing more than a superficial 'psychological commitment' indicate that there may be problems getting TQM to take hold.

Quality improvement proposals

It has been indicated throughout the book that most Japanese companies are committed to total employee involvement. Ideas are forthcoming from all grades of employees in all functions. Toyota proudly boasts that it implements, not just talks about, 5,000 proposals per day. If Toyota's competitors, GM, Ford, etc., are implementing less than 5,000 ideas per day, even if it is 4,500, they are falling behind.

Many quality drives have specific initiatives to promote involvement through processes referred to as error prevention and improvement proposals, etc. (These were highlighted in the previous chapter.) Questions relating to these processes can generate some interesting results and indicate where remedial action should be taken. This will indicate that certain areas in the company are producing 'improvement' while others are not.

Statistics can be compiled and displayed. For instance, a data processing unit and a marketing section in a company had given very few proposals for 'improvement' in relation to all the production areas and administrative functions. Displaying the information prompted the odd quip in jest that 'DP and marketing had no problems.' It also created some interesting issues for discussion: e.g. didn't these two sections create problems for others — their customers? Their response after a fairly short period of time was positive. They gradually came 'on board' and started to become less isolationist or elitist and more self critical. This was a significant shift in 'culture' in both instances.

Asking for a quantifiable measure of involvement can generate interesting statistics for display. How many improvement proposal forms (IPFs) have you generated or been involved in submitting? Although some employees have not submitted ideas, they may have helped others. Some employees may be reticent and not want to get formally involved at first, but feel happy about working with others. This must be respected. People cannot be forced to get involved in a 'paperwork process'. However, we do expect them to become committed to the psychological process of wanting to put things right.

Asking further about the process whereby proposals were submitted is a method of establishing how much 'Leadership Behaviour' is evident in day-to-day management and supervision. Pertinent questions include: If you have been involved in the generation of IPFs, would you like to comment on the help received from your direct supervisor in order to complete the documentation? Do you know of others in your area who have submitted IPFs?

Additional questions can highlight the commitment to action taken in formalising the process of employee improvement. For example, what action has been taken to encourage you in submitting IPFs?

Communication

TQM rests upon effective training, leadership and communication. Assessing the effectiveness of the formalised structure of communication through briefing groups and through the 'process of informal communication' is of value. Do you think finding out about progress of TQM is important? If not, why not? How do you find out about the progress of TQM? Here it is obvious that some optional choice is given, such as direct supervisor, briefing and newsletter, etc.

Examining the factors inhibiting the speedy transmission of progress is critical. Are you aware of progress of TQM? What in your opinion helps or hinders the communication of progress of TQM?

Further checking questions help to give some reliability to other questions. In your opinion, is the communication of progress of TQ adequate or not? Why?

Training

With any training and development activity, there should be some formal appraisal of training workshops. Focus should be on what people have learned — not on whether they enjoyed a session. Often they are not the same experience. We do not have time here to discuss evaluation of training in its most sophisticated form but we would expect a questionnaire at the end of a workshop requesting information on learning outcomes and processes. Most personnel and training departments will have a framework for structuring a form of review but time should be taken to ensure that information required really has been elicited from the group. It may be appropriate to ask further questions. Do you require training to improve your contribution to TQ? If you do require training — in what?

The future

We may also wish to involve people in future progress and at this time if we can elicit a response, implement their idea quickly, recognise and value the contribution from the person, then we are half way to promoting the required cultural change. What suggestions do you have to promote TQM? This can be followed by a more specific question. How could we help you to promote TQ in your immediate work area?

If you are not serious about fixing things do not ask!

It must also be remembered that questionnaires are not designed overnight. What is relevant for one drive may not be so for another. More important than this is the administration of the questionnaire. An open, flexible style, with interviewers trained in interviewing and research is critical. It is probably more likely that an outsider will generate an honest response from interviewees/ respondents — some internal interviewers end up generating information that respondents think they want to hear! The progress questionnaire is an extremely powerful tool for assessment purposes — but if you are not prepared to take action quickly on your findings and conclusions, do not bother going through the exercise at all.

At one company, a review of TQM was undertaken by a member of the personnel function at head office in Europe. Fifteen months later there was no feedback to the plant. The results had not been discussed and no action was taken. Excuses were in abundance but the hopes and aspirations of some of the respondents who had been honest and wanted to change were dashed by a failure to reply. As with all TQM practices, if you are not serious do not do it!

If at first you cannot change the people — change the people!

The results of the survey must be communicated to the QIT, but fed back in a confidential manner. The finger-pointing, reflecting the 'you are not doing your job' attitude, is counter productive. Recognising that often the reason for failure is equally because of poor direction or fear of trying something new, rather than a negative, obstructive attitude, is a good starting point. However, if resistance is evident and not in spirit with the principles of TQM, there is no option but to take necessary action. Removing the chief obstacles may appear harsh but should not be avoided. Far too many senior company officers who are resistant to change are allowed to continue in their positions, slowly killing the company and the spirit, motivation and morale of its people. Remember the phrase, 'if at first you cannot change the people — change the people'.

Selection of trainers and consultants

As with all change strategies, the success of the programme can very much be dependent upon the personal skills of those chosen to implement the changes. The choice from internal resources, of TQM manager has been dealt with in chapter 7, but the choice of external trainers and consultants is also particularly difficult. Obviously, the external people to consider will range from the independent consultant to the national and multi-national consulting agencies. There is no one right way to pursue TQM so a range of people may be appropriate. You may need different people with different skills at different times. You may have to use a variety of agencies.

It is fairly obvious that a potential client will assess previous interventions in which external consultants have been involved but it is surprising how infrequently this is broached. Ideally, before a choice is made, it is important to visit some of the locations and talk with the consultant's other clients about success and failure. This is a true test of the calibre of the consultancy.

Don't be drawn towards the larger consultancies just because they appear to have the reputations. Their names may mean little. It is the person you employ. It is the consultants or trainers you will be allocated which are important — so ask! (Luckily, the practice of major consultancies, using their best resources to obtain a contract and the poorest to implement the programme, has now started to die.)

Small or large: It's the person that's right, smaller consultancies may appear more responsive in changing the way they do things and less inclined to use a standard package, but they have limitations — the relative size can create problems. If they are good at what they do they may have difficulty responding to a special need, i.e. not enough days in the week. However, this can be compensated for by planning and appraising the possibility of problems before they arise.

What is the most important point is whether the consultant can establish rapport with the client and the client group. In other words, with the managers of the organisation, its staff and employees. Social skills, influence and persuasion are, above all, extremely important and employing someone without these attributes is asking for trouble.

Consultants should be 'people' people, it is obvious that we would expect our external resource, man or woman, to have full knowledge of TQM and be a proponent of the behavioural sciences. The major point which this book is projecting is that TQM is behaviourally driven. The requirement to fully understand the people dimension is imperative with people trying to create cultural change. Understanding people is critical but it is not just the understanding achieved through managing people. Understanding through the formalised study of people in organisations is also critical. Understanding and having an appreciation of organisational theory and organisation behaviour is extremely important when trying to bring around significant change. Having experience of the university of life only will give little credence when you had the opportunity to prevent a problem arising through taking the study of organisations seriously.

Managers are not people orientated, there is an incredible lack of 'people knowledge and skills' displayed by many senior managers who attend training workshops. In many cases it is evident that the 'technical competence' to do the job was what had contributed to a manager's present position. In some cases social skills and managerial vision and perception are lacking to such an extent that it is a wonder that managers achieve any results through their people.

When working with one company there were clear signs which identify when managers had difficulty managing and these have been brought to the fore during residential periods of study when a group of managers has engaged in case studies, business exercises and role plays based on a wide variety of business situations.

The poor inter-personal skills demonstrated make one wonder how these managers cope throughout the year. If a manager cannot or does not manage through influence and persuasion then he manages through his authority. If his authority is the only way of getting others to do things it is likely that the style employed is strongly directive and non-participative.

If this case is representative of UK industry, we have a major problem ahead of us. As a nation we are not committed to training our managers to the same degree as our European and American neighbours, yet we expect our managers to achieve the same results. We have to develop a national culture of training and development but this role is too important to leave to government alone. Industry, however, can lead the way.

Training budgets, one training manager said that he spent 0.6% of the wage bill on training in the last financial year. He then pointed to his investment. It was standing outside in the yard. A 'portable cabin' — summing up the problem of training in its entirety. We simply do not recognise the impact that training can make on performance. It is for this reason that, when we appraise the skills of consultants, we should concentrate on their ability to influence, persuade and train — rather than apply a rigid impersonal system.

Employing a consultant who has the knowledge and the skills to influence and who can be perceived as honest, is a major advantage to any organisation. Any consultant can manage through his position and authority but the people with whom he or she comes into contact only accept this on a superficial level. A message which is to be believed has to be projected with passion and honesty. The way to influence people to turn their culture round is not by telling them that they have to do it, but by motivating, persuading and influencing them into wanting to change and take ownership of TQM.

Of course there are other criteria which are important when selecting external consultants. Obviously, the choice will depend upon the experience of the consultant and how it was gained. There is a danger that the client will want such specific experience that he rejects all those without it — with the reason given as, "We are different to every other company in our industry. We need someone who really understands us." This viewpoint is fine, and often voiced, but can create inherent dangers. Employing people who know the company and the culture so well can create problems with objectivity. Likewise employing someone who will fail to challenge management to be self critical is not providing a good service to the client.

There are times when a consultant must stand up and say things which a management team or senior officers would prefer not to hear. It is unpleasant, but necessary. A consultant should be someone who challenges the beliefs of others and who is prepared to be unpopular when the client would really prefer him to pursue the line of least resistance and low success. A good consultant or trainer should challenge the views and prejudices of others and should not be drawn, by future potential business, into saying what is expected and acceptable!

Adopting an incremental approach

To complete the section on implementing change and review it is important to look at the process of managing change, covered in chapters 4 and 5.

There must be a plan or critical path of sequential activities to follow for implementation of TQM which should be owned by all. We would expect all senior members of staff to understand the critical elements of the plan and understand the importance of meeting special milestones. All supervisors should understand the plan so that, if they are asked by their people, they can respond with a good overview at least. Supervisors who are ignorant of the plan and progress do not lend credibility to the drive.

There will be times when the 'Plan' slips two paces back. There will be times when it is no longer realistic because of significant shifts in the organisation environment. There will also be times when moves have to be made to counter a 'negative political climate', in a specific area of the company. These occasions are when managers who are keen to progress changes have to take the responsibility for change on their shoulders.

Living in the real world of organisations, we are aware that the best 'Plan' can often go awry. It is, therefore, the manager or supervisor who may have to temporarily run with TQM who must take responsibility to convert the plan to action. This approach, which some managers use, has been termed 'logical incrementalism'. Quinn in his book 'Strategies for Change' indicates that it is when the formal planning process breaks down, that some managers come into play and run with the ball. They may deal with politics, personal resistance, develop sub-systems previously neglected out of the formal process of planning or develop trust and psychological commitment, etc. These actions are necessary and will only exist in environments where people are allowed to be free in their approaches. Change and progress does not depend on the actions of the 'conformist' but on those of the 'non-conformist', the person who challenges the way things are done. Encouraging this perspective, developing 'transformational managers' (see chapter 6) on whom you can rely later if things go wrong, is critical to the organisation. Every organisation has these heroes. Most are discouraged and held in check. Encouraging the unreasonable for driving initiatives will reap benefits.

It is these managers who can anticipate change and move things forward in an incremental manner who make TQM a living reality. Don't expect progress overnight. Change takes time. The TQ manager might not have achieved a great deal but things are better than they were yesterday. Perhaps that is the best way to sum up TQM! Implementation is based on progress. Do not paint grand visions of the future if you have no way of achieving these visions. Just ensure that things get better in a tangible format every day. Publicise small wins and celebrate with your people. They are the resource you can rely on when things get tough.

This questionnaire was issued to over **40 people** in a 200-person plant. The results were the subject of a separate report. COQ measures were the subject of an additional assessment. The conclusions of this report led to significant changes which created the enthusiasm and results required.

TQ questionnaire: Assessing progress

This structured questionnaire will be read to all interviewees and comments noted. In some cases the answers to 'closed ended questions' carry a supplementary question — this is for further analysis.

The questionnaire is broken down into a number of sections. The responses will be assessed as a percentage of the response from the total interviews. All additional comments will be appended.

Commitment

1. When did you last speak with your supervisor about TQM?

a. Within the last week	21%
b. Last month	30%
c. 3 months ago	38%
d. Never	11%

2. Has your direct supervisor spoken to you about the role you can play in promoting TQ?

a. Yes	50%
b. No	50%

(Two responses were non-applicable)

3. Please specify what you think your supervisor has done to promote TQ

Responses included:
TQ newsletter (1)
Nothing (9)
Above average encouragement (2)
Progressed initiatives (1)
Follows company policy (1)
Regular support (1)
Not a lot (2)
Don't know (3)
Made us aware (1)
Assistance and help, created initiatives and helped complete IPFs (3)
Promoted changes in immediate work area (1)
Started improving things (1)
Suggestions accepted (1)
(a further 7 were not applicable)

Quality improvement team

4. Are you aware of the current activities of the QIT?

a. Yes	32%
b. No	68%

(Three responses were non-applicable)

5. Has a member of the QIT talked with you about TQM?

a. Yes	30%
b. No	70%

(Four responses were non-applicable)

6. If (a) in question 5 above, who was it and what did they discuss?

People named include . . . . . . (a list of senior managers and supervisors). They provided information and encouragement to complete IPFs. Some respondents were not aware of the function and composition of the QIT (2).

CATs

7. Would you like to become a member of a CAT?

a. Yes	40%
b. No	27%
c. Already a CAT member	33%

8. If (b) in question 7 above, why not?

Don't feel that company is committed (1)
Quite happy to contribute, but was never invited! (2)
They don't give you time off (1)
Not seen anything happen (1)
Too many other pressures outside work (1)
Composition of team is wrong — too many outsiders (1)
CAT on XXXXXXXX was a waste of time (1)
ILL (1)
It has to be done in your own time (1)

9. Do you believe the progress of CATs has been effective?

a. Yes	59%
b. No	41%

10. If (b) in question 9 above, why not?

Not involved (2)
Proves more difficult to make things work (1)
No feedback (3)

Don't know (2)
Making progress, slow in coming (1)
Waste of time (1)
Not seen results (1)
Believe some progress but don't have information (1)
No paperwork, not fed back (1)
Started rolling, now stopped (1)
Not progressed enough (1)

Participation

11. Are you, in any capacity, involved in promoting TQM?

a. Yes	52%
b. No	35%
c. Not sure	13%

(Three responses were non-applicable)

12. If (a) in question 11 above, what role do you play?

Most related to working as part of CAT and some said they had integrated the TQM philosophy into their normal work.

13. How many IPFs have you generated or been involved in submitting?
(41 respondents)

 7 completed zero IPFs
10 completed one IPF
 8 completed two IPFs
 5 completed three IPFs
 5 completed four IPFs
 3 completed six IPFs
 3 completed ten–twelve IPFs

14. If you have been involved in the generation of IPFs, would you like to comment on the help received from your direct supervisor in order to complete the IPF?

Most agreed that the help they received was good and that supervisors had been helpful. It appeared that supervisors adapted a reactive role rather than promoting quality initiatives. Many respondents suggested that they had to approach their supervisors — few supervisors adopted the proactive role.

15. Do you know of others in your area who have submitted IPFs?

a. Yes	75%
b. No	25%

16. What action has been taken to encourage you in submitting IPFs? Please specify.

Most agreed that three senior managers were the guiding influences and some suggested that the drive could have had greater support from the management team. A large number also commented on the value of information in the newsletter and on notice boards.

17. Do you know of someone within your work area who is or has been involved in CATs?

a. Yes	74%
b. No	26%

18. Do you think the work of CATs is of value?

a. Yes	88%
b. No	0%
c. Don't know	12%

19. If response was (b) or (c) in question 18 above, why? Please comment.

Nothing has happened — things have stayed as they are! (1)
No visible results (2)
Don't know; no feedback; don't know what they do (2)

Communication

20. Do you think finding out about progress of TQM is important?

a. Yes   100%
b. No   0%

21. If (b) in question 20 above, why not?

No comments.

22. How do you find out about the progress of TQM?

(As a percentage of all employees interviewed)
a. Direct supervisor   20%
b. Briefing sessions   23%
c. Newsletter   67%
d. Other — please specify   32%
e. Not aware of progress   8%

In (d) respondents referred to the following:
Minutes of QIT
Asking for feedback
General unstructured comments from QIT members
Accident
Monthly reports
Informal talks
Boards

23. Are you aware of the IPFs which are submitted by your department and area?

a. Yes   65%
b. No   35%

24. Are you aware of progress of TQM?

a. Yes   47%
b. No   53%

25. In your opinion, is the communication of progress of TQM adequate or not?

a. Adequate   19%
b. Not adequate   71%

26. If (b) in question 25 above, why not?

No feedback on IPFs . . . low priority, too busy with other things (5)
No feedback . . . should be compulsory (3)
Information too general, not specific enough F/B, need to make it 1:1 (1)
No communication since workshop (3)
Could do better (4)
Information from CATs not transferred to other areas (3)
No enthusiasm (1)
No return for investment; no COQ figures (1)
Nothing apart from newsletters (1)
Production demands are greater than quality (1)
No feedback; bulletin is full of exhortations . . . not practical (1)

Training

27. Do you require training to improve your contribution to TQ?

a. Yes   50%
b. No   50%

28. If (a) in question 27 above, please specify

Revision of TQM . . . refresher and update (12)
Meeting management (1)

Personal action planning . . . telling me what I can do (1)
Equipment (job) related training (2)
Everyone needs training . . . it sparks off ideas (1)

The Future

29. How, in your opinion, could we progress TQM?

(Some respondents had multiple suggestions)
More communication and impetus/boost (8)
Briefing meetings . . . don't know what is happening (1)
More job related knowledge (2)
Improve morale . . . interference from headquarters (1)
Better feedback and communication (6)
Promote TQ same as safety (1)
Posters (3)
Need milestones and reports on progress (1)
Not a great deal to do (1)
Start again from the beginning (1)
Complaints board displayed (1)
Senior management take action (1)
Examples of how the system works . . . more successes (1)
Pace of activity (1)
Re-educate managers — they still don't listen! (1)
Don't know how to do it! (1)
Build enthusiasm (1)
Employ people full-time to do TQ rather than adopt a haphazard approach (1)
Spending money is not the answer — everyone should do the job (1)
Change the attitude of staff . . . still 'them and us' (1)
More group work (1)
Develop specific TQ notice board (1)
Reduce management resistance (1)
Enforce meetings in working day (1)
We should get paid for TQ (1)

30. How could we help you to promote TQ in your immediate work area?

Similar responses to those given for question 29 above.

Summary and bullet points

- Do not expect success overnight. However, this is not an excuse for doing nothing. Progress is dependent upon accurate feedback and review.
- Do not hide failure. If one area is not pulling its weight, take action. If the failure to take action is based on personal doubt and incompetence do not take punitive measures.
- If people are openly rejecting the TQM approach you have no choice. If at first you cannot change the people, then change the people!
- Ensure that all criteria for review have been considered before assessing progress and designing questionnaires.
- Ensure that COQ measures are in place, understood, visible and have meaning. Research the service areas first.
- Do not rely only on physical evidence. Ask people if they know what measures relate to their areas!
- TQM can become the common language of a company.
- The response from research on progress requires instant action. If you are not serious about creating change, do not ask for opinions!
- Bad news travels fast. We tend to be attracted to put right what is wrong and not to praise the good things. There will be blockages and hold-ups in

TQM. Bad news travels fast. Ensure that the good news is publicised.

- Share success and information with others. Develop a newsletter and ensure that it is kept up to date. The first time the newsletter fails to be printed, or is two weeks late in distribution, is the indication which the workforce has been looking for to prove that TQM is just another 'fad'.
- Asking staff the likely successes of the QIT is a strong indicator of the QIT's commitment to communication.
- Publicise the success of CATs and quality proposals.
- Select trainers and consultants from outside with care. You can only promote TQM once. Ensure that they can work with rather than for you.
- Ensure the TQM solution matches your problem, not the consultants' package.
- Influence, persuasiveness and enthusiasm are outstanding characteristics critical for projecting TQM. Allowing consultants to rely solely on their status and authority will not convince the more sceptical of shop floor and administrative people.
- Ensure that TQM drives are tailored to your needs and that swift changes can be introduced where necessary.
- Ensure that all internal managers acting as trainers and facilitators are socially skilled. Change in behaviour comes about through dialogue, influence and discussion. Exhortation of slogans and authority can carry little real weight.
- Beware of the consultant with only one package to sell — the one he uses with all clients!
- Ensure that consultants are not just versed in systems but are also students of organisational behaviour. It is impossible to help co-ordinate and drive TQM throughout a company without a high level of understanding of people and their motivations and behaviours. This cannot be learned simply by watching. Experience is important but must be supplemented by genuine understanding, research and study.
- Plans do go wrong on occasion, although they should not do so in a TQM drive. If they do, managers have to take responsibility to run with TQM for a short period of time. This means that the managers have to be the champions of TQM. Have they been prepared for this role?
- Adopt an incremental approach to change. Learn from your mistakes.
- If things are better today than they were yesterday, all is going to plan. This is the vision.

15 WORLD CLASS COMPETITION: HOW DO WE CREATE A TOTAL QUALITY CULTURE?

Just do it!

There is a story told many times about Dr Deming being harassed over break-fast by a journalist. It is believed to be true. The (business) journalist wanted to know the real secrets of quality management and he asked Dr Deming, "What do we have to do in the West to compete and promote total quality?" Apparently Dr Deming looked up from eating, stared the journalist coldly in the eye and told him to tell his readers, "Just do it, that's all, just do it."

It is as simple as those few words. The Japanese and other Western companies who have promoted TQM have adopted the same philosophy. There is no quick fix. There is no secret that can be installed within a structure to move the company from a fix it culture to a preventative, caring and people-centred culture. No 1-day course has yet been developed which can turn a company on its head overnight and produce zero defect products or implement SPC or any other technique. It is a long, tortuous process. It is not a panacea, but is the closest you will get to one. The panacea is not a technique but a commitment to constant innovation and improvement through commitment to be the best, to succeed through people. We can, however, learn from others and implement changes. Some of the guiding principles follow.

Those who have undertaken study tours of Japanese companies, and witnessed first hand their philosophy, cannot be anything but convinced that this is the way.

Many have studied the art of Japanese management and recognised that quality is a major factor which has provided these companies with their competitive edge. Many on such tours are surprised to find that the Japanese have no more knowledge than us or applied techniques unavailable to us in the West.

TQM in the West

TQM goes far beyond the philosophy and practices of quality control and quality assurance. It is a strategy which is concerned with changing the fundamental beliefs, values and culture of a company, harnessing the enthusiasm and participation of everyone, whether manufacturing or service orientated, towards an overall ideal of 'RFT'.

TQM has grown in recent years. Organisations in both the public and private sectors have recognised that quality of product and service is what can differentiate them from their competitors. It can be the most powerful barrier to entry into world markets which organisations can pursue to guarantee a long-term future.

Quality strategy

During a study tour, delegates were to visit and tour manufacturing locations to talk with Japanese senior managements about their strategies for implementing TQM. The companies to be visited included Kawashima Textile (£313m turnover); Sumitomo Electric, based in Itami, a major manufacturer of components to the automotive industry; Daiei, the largest chain of supermarkets throughout Japan (£7bn turnover); Mitsubishi Motors; Kawasaki Steel (£7.2bn turnover); Nippon Denso, a world leader in automotive electronics; Toyota, with domestic production of cars of 30,000 per day; Shiseido Cosmetics; and Hitachi which produces colour display tubes for TVs and LCDs as well as bubble memories and a host of other components.

Each of the visits was instructive and provided a number of lessons which we in the West could adopt to the same effect. All presentations were made by the individuals who implemented TQM.

Eight lessons to learn

Education and training, the commitment to training and education of all managers and operatives is extremely high. The opinion from many of the managers talking with us was that 'managers get the staff they deserve'. In other words, the deeds and achievements of a work group are a direct reflection on the manager. A committed and effective work group meets regularly to discuss and initiate quality improvements. Groups who fail to do so are groups which lack motivation — probably because their managers have not spent sufficient time preparing them for preventing problems arising.

Emphasis is placed on quite sophisticated analysis. At one presentation, at the headquarters of Daiei supermarkets, four young girls, who compose a QC, shared with us their work on quality improvement. They used coefficient of correlation and regression analysis to examine statistical relationships and worked through a thorough approach to problem-solving including fishbone diagrams.

Young women using sophisticated techniques surprised many on the tour. It was a most thorough treatment. They fully understood statistics and their applicability to quality improvement. What was even more surprising was that they were working in the service sector rather than manufacturing industry. There was a great deal of emphasis in other locations where FMEA and Taguchi methods were common techniques used for anticipating and solving problems.

Foolproofing, an approach to designing manufacturing technology in such a way as to produce zero defects, was much in evidence. Walking around Nippon Denso, an original equipment supplier to the automotive industry, one cannot help being surprised by the number of 'foolproofing' devices in the machine shop.

Although robots were not in such evidence, the layout and cleanliness of the work area was superlative. Housekeeping is very much an essential element of preventative action.

Operatives take a few minutes each day to assess the work stations and equipment they will use. They run through a simple check-list and, if they find damaged or worn equipment, will notify the maintenance department immediately. There appeared to be an automatic drive to check and prevent problems arising.

We wonder how many stoppages on the shop floor and waste in down-time could have been anticipated in some of our factories by workers and staff who are aware of problems but insufficiently attentive to take the requisite action.

Quality circles, unfortunately, too many managers in European industry think that QCs are the beginning and end of TQM. In fact, research in the UK suggests that most QC initiatives have been less than successful because of lack of commitment from managerial grades — so why do they work in Japan?

We think the first factor is that quality as an over-riding philosophy has been led from the top — not just in words but actions. Managements have been keen to initiate quality improvements because they trust the experience of operatives and work groups. QCs are successful because the ideas they pursue are actioned, thus reinforcing the behaviour of all circle members.

The evidence which was presented to us regarding QC activity was staggering. Toyota maintain that on average they receive 100–140 ideas per employee each year, of which 97% are actioned. The QC acts as a vehicle to discuss these ideas and suggestions prior to being submitted to management for approval.

Circles seemed to meet outside work time and were paid for their efforts. Methods of payment differed radically. Employees in one factory received a wage of a third their normal rate, because this was perceived as a training rate, not a job rate. Others received no payment but did receive incentives for the ideas implemented. Money did not seem to be a major motivator in itself. What seemed much more powerful was the opportunity to influence events and make work easier.

Perhaps the over-riding thoughts about QCs in Japan and the UK is that, in Japan, circle members can significantly influence events. Actions are agreed by the management team and are put into effect immediately.

What we need to learn is that, if we pursue the QC approach as a tool of TQM, we must ensure that all operatives are thoroughly trained in SPC and other related techniques, that ideas which come from the circle are debated and actioned immediately and that, if ideas are not feasible, this should be communicated immediately back to the circle.

Communication, a major point highlighted by a production engineer was that if quality is to be the factor which links all units and departments then a prerequisite for the TQM culture is an effective means of communication. It was evident that, in Japanese organisations, communication has a high profile. There were constant visual reminders of quality and, in almost every company we visited, we found organisational charts with photographs of managers attached. The operatives were aware of their supervisors and their responsibilities.

QCs in themselves are an effective means of communication, but emphasis seems to be placed more on lateral communication than vertical. Not that the latter was not encouraged or applied — far from it. However, managers seemed to realise that the key to effective communication is the emphasis placed on departmental communication.

For instance, the Japanese pride themselves on being generalists. This is not strictly true. They are specialists in their functions, whether it be production engineering, research and development, management services or whatever. However, they are encouraged, through education and daily interaction, to mix with others. More importantly, they are taught to reject the specialist approach to problem-solving. They look at a problem wearing different hats and tend to appreciate it from different perspectives. What is interesting is that this 'global perspective' reduces the misunderstandings which can be created between departments and functions. Conflict and negative stereotyping between organisational units does not arise.

Unfortunately, we in the West tend to assume that conflict is endemic within structures and take it as normal that the R&D boys fail to work with manufacturing units, that systems departments impose their wills on other units and that sales departments drive production. The Japanese seem to have developed a communication network and commitment to solve these problems. They do it simply by moving people around, particularly at supervisory level, through job rotation, and listening and responding to ideas from all quarters.

Automation, the Japanese have looked at robotics and automation and used them when necessary. 'When necessary' refers to processes where defects are difficult to control due to human error, or where the nature of the work is boring and routine and where the quality standards can drop when the attention of operatives wanders.

This was evident not only in the Toyota and Mitsubishi car plants but also in Kawasaki Steel. On a visit lasting 2 hours, walking through rolling mills and past blast furnaces, there was contact with only 12 people. The process was almost completely automated. Kawasaki Steel is using artificial intelligence to run its steel-making process to great effect. The majority of staff was housed inside moving gantrys, monitoring the process.

Obviously, automation requires a great financial investment, but this is a problem which the Japanese have resolved. Increases in productivity and quality cannot be made without a substantial investment in the future. They ensure that their future is well planned, examined and assessed, then debated again so that the choice to borrow and invest is the end of a natural sequence of events. The decision not to invest is anathema to them.

Measure and display, the Japanese seem to have a passion for displaying their talents, not just in a creative but also in an informative sense. In a Japanese company it is unlikely that you will pass a notice board which does not display current information. These are not the locations for historical data. You cannot travel very far without coming across a board which is proclaiming success in terms of productivity, reduction in defect rates, quality improvements and cost reduction. In comparison take a look at your departmental/company noticeboard!

The Japanese are sure to keep data on all movements within production. If a problem exists they will have been monitoring performance using graphing techniques to illustrate problems.

When being shown around the training headquarters of Daiei, the supermarket leader, posters were seen which had been completed by operatives illustrating the drive towards quality. It was not a multi-colour, professional glossy, but a carefully designed message and hand-painted poster which adorned the wall.

The Japanese put a great deal of effort into illustrating their progress and highlighting areas for concern — but would it catch on in the UK? We are not talking about employees entering poster competitions. Measure and display is a philosophy to encourage employees and managers at all levels to communicate in a visual manner.

Part of this approach is to monitor progress and isolate disturbing trends.

Let's face it, this is the purpose behind SPC. What we require is sufficient discipline to identify an activity which is giving us problems or be so radical as picking a process which has gone out of control.

Once the process has been highlighted we need to measure and display progress in order to understand the causes which create these problems. This illustrative approach is stimulating and creative. Writing and recording progress is the best way yet of keeping the attention of ourselves and others on the problem.

Consider the alternatives of the poor practice in many European plants: posters on safety and quality which have occupied the same spot for the past 3 years, read but not remembered; charts which are not updated; company slogans and exhortations devised in the '70s but still suspended from ceiling lights in the '80s; and notices 3 months out of date.

Keeping and displaying graphs, charting real progress devising a tailored poster campaign with strategic emphasis, never created quality by itself but could not hinder the promotion of a sincere drive for quality. As long as a drive utilising a visual approach has more depth than the thickness of the printed paper, it will play its part in ensuring that quality is always in the mind of whoever is the recipient.

Quality is not just a manufacturing concept, quality is very much rooted in the service as well as the manufacturing functions. Companies in the UK which practice TQM ensure that all aspects of service are 'RFT' including delivery, service contracts and invoicing, etc. This is very much in evidence in Japan, except that the 'JIT' principles exercised by most companies are directly related to JIT payments for services and goods provided — not 60- or 90-day payment terms.

Sumitomo Electric, supplier of braking systems to major car manufacturers, cited an example which is common practice to the company but was a surprise to many people on the tour. If a manufacturer does find an error it reports it directly to the supplier. This does not happen often because the principles behind JIT suggest that a defective component causes a production line to stop. In this rare instance, the operations manager, designer, production engineer, foreman and the operative who made the component, visit the customer immediately and sort out the problem so that the defect never arises again. This a real team effort. This responsiveness is characteristic of the TQM approach throughout Japanese industry and illustrates the level of co-operation and harmony which is generated within and between departments. This team-building approach does much to halt the negative elements of allocating blame in favour of the philosophy of preventative action.

Long-term planning, needless to say, the Japanese could not have created a meaningful TQM philosophy without a devotion to long-term, strategic planning. How else would they have been so successful in the markets where they currently hold a competitive position? The Japanese had targeted the electronics, car, motorcycle, television, video and audio markets years ago. They are actively examining the relaxing of trade barriers in 1992 in Europe and already thinking of ways to increase market share.

Many European companies follow suit but, in all honesty, are not as meticulous as the Japanese. TQM really does play a major part in strategy formulation and this is perhaps the most important lesson we can learn.

The philosophy from which these lessons are learned

Four basic factors can be outlined which all Japanese companies seemed to use to great effect to penetrate new markets and give them a competitive advantage.

Systems, Deming, Juran and others introduced the techniques and tools we now know as SPC, QA and TQC, into Japan many years ago. We are not ignorant of these practices but we never seem to get around to applying the ideas. Some companies still have difficulties adapting to meet the requirements of BS 5750/ISO 9000, much less making the transition to TQM.

Regarding Western practice, as stated above many organisations have the systems but don't seem to apply them. Asking operatives to complete SPC charts is meaningful only if they are aware that some action is taken to resolve the problems they have encountered. If no action is taken, why bother? SPC must have a function and be seen to lead to preventative action.

The Japanese have applied techniques, systems and procedures rigorously to ensure that quality is improved continuously. All operatives are fully conversant with these and the problem-solving tools which give rise to better quality.

The Japanese are also committed to the use of production engineers who are not perceived as an indirect cost. The quote which seemed to tell so much about the priorities the West put on the role of preventative action in manufacturing processes in comparison to the Japanese is as follows: "The USA has twice the population of Japan, sixteen times more lawyers, but only half the number of production engineers."

Leadership and commitment, managers are judged on the performance of others. They would lose face if they failed to consider options which would lead to defect reduction.

'Managers leading by example' seemed to be the underlying theme in Japan. One manufacturing manager from an automotive components supplier said that he would be personally failing his people if he did not instruct them in the techniques and practices of TQC.

Managers are directly rewarded for the efforts they make on cost reduction, productive capability, defect rates and quality. The difference is that the Japanese do not compromise on quality for a short-term fix or cost reduction!

Training and participation, all operatives are trained in techniques geared to quality improvement. Training is a continuous affair and not a 'lick and a promise' compromise. Operatives and staff are encouraged to put forward suggestions which are actioned. On average, most companies stated that they implemented 80% of ideas after investigation.

Commitment to change through people, there are very few companies in Europe which do not state with pride that they are 'people driven'. In reality there are many cases where this is no more than exhortation and PR.

People are the organisation's most valuable resource. Although many manufacturing plants in Japan are highly automated the improvements came from groups of workers who met regularly to discuss improvement. The morale and motivation of workers is increased if their contribution towards zero defects is recognised and praised.

Listening and analysing is something which we are not very good at practising. We tend to be action orientated and rarely allow sufficient time to think through the next 'quick fix'. We need to be more patient and thoughtful in our approach to quality improvement.

Moving towards the philosophy

We need to develop a commitment to a philosophy based on building those things which led to achievement prior to entering into world class competition.

Organisational structure

Too many companies have too many levels of management. The more levels, the greater the communication difficulties and the slower the response time. We have to reject the 'multiple layers' and concentrate upon reducing these levels to 3 or 4. More than this, we have to ensure that people talk to each other.

Horizontal management

We should devote time to increasing lateral communications between functions and departments. We are so worried about increasing our headcounts that we fail to understand that work is achieved through integration, not vertical specialisation.

Move from product lead to customer led strategies

Many of our organisations have developed a skill for leading the market with their products. When demand for the product declines, many feel that the product life cycle is nearing its maturity phase. So they develop a new range, when the problem could, in fact, be to do with quality. We have to think of our customers more and develop products and services which meet their needs best. This is critical in the service sector. We forget the customer and his or her needs. We need to develop a TQ service approach and recognise that this can only come from within the organisation. Advertising and public relations can do so much to project our product but true TQM only comes from meeting the requirements of our internal customers and suppliers. Getting 'close to our customers' comes from being self critical and constantly looking for improvements.

Loving our people

People is what this book is all about. If we manage our people with respect, if we value them and if we treat them with dignity, they can help us achieve the impossible. We have to develop human resource strategies in training and development, recruitment and selection, manpower planning, employee relations, career development, motivation, team building and job design. We have to value people to win their commitment. We have to love them, not think of them merely as a tool or a factor of production.

Cultural change

We need to develop a culture where people can blossom and want to stay with the organisation — where there is a genuine opportunity to contribute and develop. Employees who are not developing are going backwards. We need to develop simple values and live by them.

Quality of working life

Work is a central life interest for many people and in the time of the 'Demographic Timebomb' we have to realise that people have a need to belong. We want people to be proud of their companies and, in non-company time, talk glowingly about the reputation and commitment of the enterprise. Developing a sincere quality of working life comes from the application of human resource policies.

Developing partnerships

Learn to work with customers. Get involved in the design of new products and services. Work with suppliers to reduce errors and ensure that they are aware of your new developments. Work with competitors on joint projects. Look for innovation in the way business is organised not just with competitors but with other industries.

Leadership

Tom Peters tells us that leadership is about emotion. There is little one can add. The people who lead the company have to understand the impact of their presence, actions and behaviour on others. Leading by example must be the guiding principle in everything they do.

Change management

We have to recognise that change is not constant but increasing at an accelerating rate. As well as loving people we need to love change. We must encourage others to want to change and improve everything they do.

TQM: A political philosophy

TQM is a means of achieving a strong competitive position. But it should be seen in wider socio-economic perspective. There is no reason why our school and educational system, our social services and national manpower planning cannot benefit from this approach. Nothing which has been referred to within this book is 'ivory tower stuff'. It is simple and based on fundamental principles of concern for others, a concern for planning and a motivation to succeed, achieve and do even better. That is not more than any human being strives to achieve throughout his or her life.

The future

The future holds many fears and opportunities for individuals, organisations and societies. We have the foresight and the opportunity to mould our future the way we think fit. We should take what we have and find ways to make things better. We need to reject the old view of finding 10 ways to make a good idea fail and find one way to make it work. We should encourage and motivate others to do the same.

The time for excuses has gone. We need to think over some fairly simple words and act upon them:

"Just do it, that's all, just do it"

Summary and bullet points

● There are no special advantages that the Japanese and others have over us.

It is their commitment to doing things right which is the guiding principle to their success. Nothing they use is not available in the West.

- Develop a TQM strategy and relate it to every function.
- Train people in all they need to know and beyond. People who are trained and feel they are valued can achieve anything.
- Commit to improving all aspects of people management.
- Systems and structures have a large part to play in quality improvement. Do not neglect to give your people the best.
- Find as many ways as you can for a process to fail. This is applicable to manufacturing and all service areas.
- Given the opportunity, people will tell you how things can be improved — but only if they feel they have dignity as a treasured resource.
- Effective communication will spread the word of TQM. Ineffective communication will fuel the fears of the doubters.
- Use automation when necessary — in work where there is a high defect rate or where the opportunity for self expression is so low that the job itself creates opportunities for rework.
- Plan, measure and progress results side by side.
- Ensure that quality initiatives start in service as well as manufacturing areas.
- Spend more time planning and preventing problems arising. Devote attention to long-term planning.
- Passion for quality is not enough. Rigorous systems must complement the enthusiasm for TQM.
- Lead by example. Commit to real change.
- Spend as much as you can on training. (It still will not be enough.) Hire the best trainers. Train line managers to train.
- Value your people.
- Reduce the lines of management. Increase horizontal management and promote short-term job rotation practices.
- Move from product led to customer led strategies.
- Change to a responsive, people orientated culture.
- Develop partnerships with others — your competitors and suppliers.
- Learn to love change.
- Live in the future not the past. You have to change now to cope with the environment that will exist in 3–5 years.

INDEX

Chapter 4

Chapter 5

Chapter 7

Chapter 12

Chapter 13